CAPITALISM'S
CRISIS
DEEPENS

Capitalism's Crisis Deepens

Essays on the Global Economic Meltdown 2010–2014

Richard D. Wolff
Edited by Michael L. Palmieri and Dante Dallavalle

Chicago, Illinois
Haymarket Books

© 2016 Richard D. Wolff

Published by
Haymarket Books
P.O. Box 180165
Chicago, IL 60618
773-583-7884
info@haymarketbooks.org
www.haymarketbooks.org

ISBN: 978-1-60846-595-8

Trade distribution:
In the US, through Consortium Book Sales and Distribution, www.cbsd.com
In the UK, Turnaround Publisher Services, www.turnaround-uk.com
In Canada, Publishers Group Canada, www.pgcbooks.ca
All other countries, Publishers Group Worldwide, www.pgw.com

This book was published with the generous support
of the Wallace Action Fund and Lannan Foundation.

Printed in Canada by union labor.

Cover design by Josh On.

Library of Congress CIP Data is available.

10 9 8 7 6 5 4 3 2 1

Contents

Preface

The second worst crash of global capitalism in seventy-five years continues, approaching its tenth year. The so-called recovery since 2009 has bypassed the lower 90 percent of the people and left them further below the top 10 percent. Those who gained the most wealth in the last half-century—the very people most responsible for bringing on the crash—are the only ones now recovered. Those who gained the most wealth in the last half-century—the very people most responsible for bringing on the crash—are the only ones now recovered. The government bailouts they sought and obtained quickly in the dark days of late 2008 benefited mostly them. The weakness, slowness, and partiality of the recovery both reflect and worsen growing economic inequality. To preserve their accumulating wealth, large corporations and those they enrich wield ever more undemocratic power over the political and cultural realms of society. Their goals are self-preservation and self-aggrandizement.

These features of capitalism are all social failures in terms of justice, democracy, equality, liberty, and ecological sanity. Yet mainstream media, politicians, and academics doggedly act and speak as though capitalism were the obviously "optimal" system to be continued, reinforced, and celebrated. By proceeding as though we are not in fact experiencing capitalism's systemic failures, they perform their ideological assignments.

They also proceed as though either no alternative systems exist or the alternatives merit no discussion and debate. What "problems" of capitalism are even admitted are then quickly buried under mountains of commentary on the finer points of this or that fiscal and monetary policy presumed adequate to solving them. Questioning the capitalist system, let alone discussing system change, simply does not occur to mainstream academics and the journalists and politicians they trained. Such discourses are repressed.

The importance of publications like *Capitalism's Crisis Deepens* lies in their reinsertion of repressed discourses into public conversations. The once robust debates over capitalism and alternative economic systems were never settled in the Cold War or by the implosion of the former Soviet Union. They were only temporarily submerged first by anticommunist hysteria and then, after 1989, by delusional capitalist triumphalism. The 2008 crash of global capitalism reopened the space for those debates to resume. Now however, they have to take account of the many changes within capitalism, socialism, and communism—conceptual as well as practical—over the last half century.

The essays gathered here engage those debates on their changed terrain. They include many written after September 2014, when democracy@work published an e-book of my essays, *Capitalism's Crisis Deepens: Essays on the Global Economic Meltdown, 2010–2014*. Interest in alternatives to capitalism grows rapidly now much as popular support for capitalism wanes. The essays in this book both respond to and seek to advance and develop this remarkable shifting of ideas and ideological positions.

Richard D. Wolff
September 2015

Part I: Crisis Capitalism

The ramifications of the global effects of the crisis that began in 2007 continue to unfold. Eight years into the crisis, the social and economic costs keep mounting. Levels of unemployment and poverty remain high, wealth and income inequalities worsen, and the housing market remains depressed—a significant indicator when one considers that for most Americans, their homes are their single largest asset. The only "recovery" since the massive bailout programs has been in the stock market, big corporations' profits, and the portfolios of the top 10 percent of income earners. Recovery has bypassed the vast majority of Americans. The idea that the United States's economic system is "exceptional" has imploded. Fading fast, the American Dream of upward mobility is giving way to an ever-harder struggle just to make ends meet.

In spite of this, business and political leaders continue to defend capitalism and rigidly restrict their debates mostly to modest reforms and the endlessly repeated arguments for more or less government intervention in the economy. Opinion shapers refuse to consider that the causes for today's economic crisis are structural and recurring. Meanwhile, large segments of the public are beginning to understand that capitalism itself has been brought into question because of the depth and duration of the crisis since 2007.

The essays in Part I explore the depths of the crisis and specifically the interaction of economic stresses with political and cultural changes. Together, these essays sketch the contours of the major, long-term changes in capitalism that underlie this crisis and explain why it cuts so deep and has lasted so long.

Capitalist Crisis and the Return to Marx

March 18, 2010

Marxian analyses are now resurfacing in public dialogues about economy and society. A generation of marginalization is fading as a new generation discovers the diverse richness of the Marxian tradition's insights. Just as an economic crisis in 1848 helped provoke and shape Marx's original insights, today's crisis helps renew interest in Marxism.

In the century before the 1970s, the victims of capitalism's recurring crises and its critics increasingly turned toward the work of Marx and other Marxists. The Marxist tradition of social analysis therefore spread widely and deeply across the world. As it interacted with many different cultural, political, and historical contexts, the tradition developed multiple, different—and sometimes sharply contested—interpretations or versions of Marxist social theory. Marxism became the richest available accumulation of critical analyses of capitalism and of critical engagements with the theories that supported capitalism. It gathered the theoretical and practical lessons drawn from successes and failures of political movements more or less inspired by Marxism. Today it is an invaluable resource for theorists of and activists for social change beyond capitalism.

Capitalism's defenders have mostly sought to repress, ignore, or otherwise marginalize Marxism and Marxists. While often successful, their efforts could only slow and punish Marxism's advances in the century before 1975. Unevenly yet relentlessly, the tradition grew. From a handful of theorists and activists, Marxism spread to Marxist labor unions; political parties; newspapers; research institutes; local, regional, and national governing regimes; and internationals. It also generated

internal differences, debates, and conflicts, mostly peaceful but sometimes violent, among its constituent tendencies.

However, the 1970s changed the conditions of the social prospects for Marxism. Capitalism had recovered from much of the damage to its support and reputation caused by the Great Depression of
the 1930s. Post–World War II reconstructions, time, and hope had all
helped weaken memories of that Depression. Economic, political, and
cultural conditions had ripened enough by the 1970s to enable a major,
sustained counterattack against reforms, regulations, and other Depres-
sion-era state interventions imposed upon capitalists. The deepening
internal contradictions of the "actually existing socialist countries" that
officially celebrated Marx and Marxism facilitated the global campaigns
against them by leading capitalist nations. That program targeted those
countries, but also Marx, Marxism, and communism everywhere as syn-
onyms and as the dangerous end point toward which social democratic
state intervention led.

A resurgent capitalism celebrated its renewed strength and the weaknesses of its enemies. In the United States, the New Deal, already compromised from 1945 to 1970, was afterward systematically undermined.
Unions' social influence was greatly reduced. Labor market conditions
shifted to allow a permanent end to the pre-1970s record of rising real
wages for 100 years. The Reagan election of 1980 sealed the change.
Economics, politics, and culture shifted rightward markedly in the Anglo-American spheres but beyond as well. An era of neoliberalism was
promoted that took the form of privatization, deregulated markets, get-
ting-rich-quick schemes, and a pervasive individualism that suspected
and dismissed most collective efforts and values.

In the 1970s, a new world of investment opportunities also opened
up for multinational capitalist enterprises. Technological changes in internal enterprise controls (computers), transportation (jet aviation), and
communication (the Internet) enabled greatly enhanced global coordination within and among capitalist corporations. Producing, install-
ing, maintaining, and improving those technological changes became
extremely profitable investment opportunities as well. Most important
was the global opening up of vast new sources of relatively cheap labor

(especially in and also immigrating from the former "second" and "third" worlds). Just as technological changes drove up the productivity of labor, real wages were prevented from rising. Whenever productivity rises while real wages stagnate, the result is an explosion of the capitalist surplus. In the thirty years before 2008 the United States experienced one of the greatest profit booms in capitalist history.

Capitalism's admirers celebrated, as labor, socialism, and Marxism weakened and shrank, unevenly but nearly everywhere. Capitalism's apologists insisted yet again that capitalism had "overcome its crisis tendencies." Thus Alan Greenspan, former chairman of the US Federal Reserve, said in the late 1990s that we live in a "new economy." Once the former Soviet Union had officially imploded, Marxism's enemies changed their way of marginalizing if not eliminating the tradition. Where before they had portrayed Marxism as an erroneous theory informing a failed and also treasonably dangerous practice, over the last thirty years they treated it more as a fading historic relic that no modern person need consider, let alone study. Capitalism, they repeated, had won the struggle with socialism and emerged as the system to which there is no alternative. The United States was its appropriate superpower champion.

Adjusted rationales were correspondingly developed to continue to exclude Marxist analyses from the mass media and Marxists from academic and political positions. There was no need for them; history had rendered them anachronistic. The world had moved on. Not a few Marxists found it difficult to sustain their beliefs in so changed an environment; they therefore modified their positions or abandoned Marxism altogether.

Once Greenspan's "new economy" had collapsed in 2008 and been exposed as the same old crisis-prone capitalism, Marx and Marxism began to be rediscovered again. People are turning to the Marxian tradition for help in understanding the crisis's causes and finding solutions. They soon encounter the tradition's crisis-focused debate over reform versus revolution: how should the capitalist economy and society be changed in response to the crisis? In this classic form of the debate, some Marxists—reformers—propose diverse sorts of "transitions to socialism" while others—revolutionaries—attack such socialisms in the name of "communism." Still other Marxists criticize both socialism and communism as theorized and actualized over the last century. It turns out that the anticapitalist impulses shared by nearly all Marxists inform multiple, different, and sometimes incompatible theories and arguments. While this yields a rich tradition of critical social analysis, it obliges every writer within the tradition to identify and justify whichever particular kind(s) of Marxian theory inform(s) that writer's analyses.

So let me be clear here. In this essay, I use a particular interpretation of Marxian theory to provide a unique explanation of the current capitalist crisis's multiple causes with emphasis on the United States. I also use that interpretation to criticize both sides in the classic reform versus revolution debate that is resurfacing among Marxists and many others. On the bases of this interpretation and criticism, I offer a Marxian argument for a different sort of revolutionary response to capitalist crises. My intervention, together with those of other Marxists, demonstrates again that Marxism represents capitalism's most persistent, most developed, and most profound self-criticism.

Oscillating Capitalist Forms and Theories

Capitalist economies everywhere display a recurring pattern of oscillation. Periods of relatively limited state regulatory and other interventions in markets and private property repeatedly encounter and manage crises until one arrives that cannot be managed. Then, transition occurs to a period with relatively more state economic interventions. Crises continue to erupt and are managed until a crisis appears that cannot be managed. Then a transition occurs back to a period of relatively less state economic intervention. What remains the same across both periods (in my interpretation of Marxian theory) is the capitalist structure of production. In that particular structure of production, a small group of people—typically a corporate board of directors—appropriates the surplus produced by a large, different group of hired laborers.

We shall use the names "private" and "state" to differentiate these alternating periods or forms of capitalist economy. Thus, for example, the 1929 crisis of a private capitalism in the United States ushered in a state capitalism, Roosevelt's New Deal. Then, in the 1970s, that state capitalism encountered a crisis serious enough to provoke a transition back to private capitalism. When the latter experienced a meltdown in 2008, that crisis produced yet another oscillation back to a form of state capitalism. Comparable oscillations characterize all capitalisms.

Two different and contending mainstream (i.e., non-Marxian) theories have also explained capitalism's repeated crises over the last century. For each crisis, those theories proposed correspondingly different solutions. Today's crisis is no exception. Ideological hegemony has oscillated between those two theories just as capitalism has oscillated between its two forms.

One theory—called, after one of its founders, "Keynesian economics"—claims that unregulated private markets have limits and imperfections that periodically push capitalist economies into inflations, recessions, or even depressions. Without intervention from outside, private capitalism may remain depressed or inflated long enough to threaten capitalism itself. Keynesian economics identifies the key mechanisms that produce crises in private capitalisms and recommends various state interventions (regulations and monetary and fiscal policies) to prevent or offset private capitalist crises.

The other mainstream theory is associated with Adam Smith, the classical "founder of modern economics" who celebrated private capitalism (free markets plus private property) as the economic system that generated the maximum possible wealth. In its evolved form, "neoclassical" economics emphasizes how and why private capitalism yields the best ("optimum") of all possible economic outcomes. For neoclassical economists, if a nonoptimal outcome occurs, the best solution is to let private capitalism heal itself through the internal mechanisms of private property and free markets. They denounce Keynesian-inspired state interventions as inevitably yielding regulators' mistakes; politically manipulated markets; and such resulting inefficiencies as inflation, stagnation, and stagflation. State officials cannot replace, let alone improve upon, the unregulated ("free") market mechanism. Neoclassical economists insist that free markets accommodate the infinity of different demands and supplies and communicate the infinity of information more efficiently that any state could.

As today's global capitalist crisis unfolds, Keynesian state interventions are suddenly on the rise in the United States after hibernating for more than thirty years. Since the 1970s, as part of global campaigns for neoliberalism, neoclassical economists had widely reversed and suppressed Keynesian interventions. They had overthrown the domination of Keynesians and Keynesian macroeconomics that emerged from the Great Depression of the 1930s. Neoclassical economists had always attacked the Keynesian economics associated with Roosevelt's New Deal for seriously distorting and slowing economic growth and promoting social conflict (sometimes dubbed "class war"). They sought to reinstitute the neoclassical utopia: private and competitive markets lifting the incomes of both labor and capital and thereby avoiding class conflicts by means of growth.

After the 1970s, market deregulation and privatization became the official and prevailing principles of business, politics, journalism, and academia. Neoclassical economics became once again, as before the Great Depression, the modern economics. It banished Keynesian economics as a theoretical mistake; only neoclassical economics was "correct." Unrepentant Keynesians found their professional advances blocked and their careers often ended. Such extreme intolerance of differences between neoclassical and Keynesian economics in the realms of theory, academic discipline, and professional careers replicated the ways both of them had jointly suppressed Marxian economics and economists since the late 1940s.

After the 1970s, and in a context of technologically driven rapid productivity gains and stagnant real wages, deregulated markets yielded, at first, the changed incentives, prices, and growth the neoclassicists had promised. As the years passed, however, the economy also exhibited the market swings, uneven income and wealth developments, and eventual economic bubbles in stock markets, real estate, and finance darkly predicted by Keynesian critics. Then the new millennium opened with a stock market crash followed a few years later by a real estate collapse, a liquidity crisis, and now a deep recession threatening to slide into a depression of major proportions. Neoclassical economists are in retreat as Keynesians emerge from ideological exile.

The Keynesian message remains what it always was: the state must save capitalism from itself. It has become, again, today's wisdom. Faced with the current crisis, only a few neoclassical economists still advocate what has become yesterday's wisdom. However, if President Barack Obama's Keynesian program fails or if a state interventionist form of capitalism endures for a while, capitalist crises will recur as they always have. Crises set the stage for yet another oscillation to a private form of capitalism and to the hegemony of neoclassical economic theory.

Both sides share a profound conservatism vis-à-vis capitalism, despite holding radically different views of the need for state intervention. The oscillation between them serves their shared conservatism. It prevents crises in capitalism from becoming crises of capitalism, when the capitalist production system itself is placed in question. Oscillation between the two theories shapes and contains public debates when capitalist crises cause serious social suffering. Is the solution to the crisis more or less regulation, more or less monetary or fiscal policies? Such constricted debate keeps the public from imagining, let alone considering the Marxian alternative solution, namely, transition out of either form of capitalism into a different system.

A Marxian Alternative

The particular Marxian economic theory described in the referenced sources will be used to explain the causes of the current crisis and to offer a new solution.[1] Both the explanation and the solution differ radically from the neoclassical and Keynesian alternatives.

The crisis of US capitalism in 2008 has deep roots in the previous 125 years. From the 1870s to the 1970s, two key trends emerged: the average real wage of workers rose by about 1.3 percent per year while workers' average productivity rose by just under 2 percent per year. For a century, workers enjoyed a rising standard of living with rising real

---

1. Stephen A. Resnick and Richard D. Wolff, *Knowledge and Class: A Marxian Critique of Political Economy* (Chicago: University of Chicago Press, 1987), chapter 3; Stephen A. Resnick and Richard D. Wolff, *New Departures in Marxian Theory* (London: Routledge, 2006).

wages. And capitalist employers enjoyed a rising surplus (because value added to output per worker rose faster than wages paid per worker). The gap between workers and capitalists thus grew but posed no political problem if workers could be satisfied with rising real wages.

The century before the 1970s was a sustained success for US capitalism. Capitalists' steadily rising surpluses were distributed effectively to enhance the conditions for their growth. Their surpluses paid for technical change, for taxes to enable infrastructure development and public education of the labor force, and for mergers and acquisitions to gain economies of scale. Workers became focused on the rising consumption enabled by their rising wages. As they came to identify more as consumers than as workers, consumerism became a powerful ideological and therefore social force. Unions were oriented chiefly toward enabling more consumption through better pay and not toward basic social change. The exceptional "success" of US capitalism reflected and depended on the continued growth of real wages at a rate below that of real productivity.

However, that success had its costs, its "other" side. As surpluses appropriated by capitalists rose faster than wages, the growing economic gap enabled growing political and cultural gaps. Across the century before the 1970s, more or less real, local democratic institutions gave way to the merely formal democracy of money-driven elections and bureaucracies. Likewise deepening cultural divides separated the growing mass of workers from concentrated elite of multinational corporate capitalists and their better-paid dependents.

The dangers of deepening social divisions were avoided by the combination of rising personal consumption and a culture that celebrated rising consumption as the goal of life, the measure of one's personal achievements and worth, the adequate compensation for increasingly demanding work (the "other" side of rising productivity). The birth and remarkable growth of the modern advertising industry both resulted from and reinforced that culture. The widespread social acceptance of consumption as the key standard of personal success and achievement provoked dissenting religious leaders, politicians, writers, and others to react by denouncing mass obsession with material rather than spiritual "values." Their reactions reveal the great social power and influence of consumerism. They failed to stop, let alone reverse, the rise of a mass consumerism that had become a key part of the social glue binding the growing social gaps between workers and capitalists.

Starting in the mid-1970s, the long-running success formula of US capitalism stopped functioning. Real wages in the United States stopped rising while productivity per workers continued to rise (see Figure 1). Capitalist employers' appropriated surpluses exploded, since the workers no longer shared in the rewards of their productivity gains. The social divide between producers and appropriators of the surplus surged as well.

Capitalist employers no longer had to pay rising wages for four major reasons. First, the computer revolution started displacing millions of US workers in the 1970s. Likewise, US corporations responded to growing European and Japanese competitions by shifting production out of the United States to lower-wage production sites. These developments slowed the demand for workers inside the United States. At the same time, the mass movement of women from households into paid labor positions and growing immigration increased the number of job seekers. Thus, the labor market changed and employers no longer had to raise wages.

Most important, the end of rising real wages closed an era. The impact on the United States cannot be overstated. A capitalism that had come to define, celebrate, and defend itself by reference to rising consumption enabled by rising wages could no longer do so. The impact was all the greater because no public debate about the meaning and implications of the change occurred. Workers experienced the change as a personal and individual matter rather than a historic economic and social change.

The post-1970s explosion of surplus value production transformed US capitalism. Wealth poured into capitalists' accounts and financed a stunning expansion of corporate wealth, power, and social influence. Corporate boards of directors distributed most of the exploding surpluses partly to themselves (as fast-rising top managerial salaries, stock options, and bonuses) and partly to lower-level managers (as their remuneration and operating budgets), bankers (interest and fees), and shareowners (dividends). These groups prospered, while the vast mass of workers found life increasingly difficult.

Figure 1. Indexes of Output and Real Wage per Hour, Manufacturing, 1990–2007, Index 1890 = 100

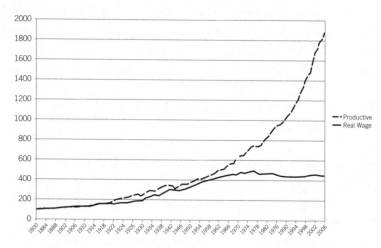

Sources: US Department of Labor, Bureau of Labor Statistics; US Department of Commerce, Bureau of the Census, Historical Statistics of the United States. Jason Ricciuti-Borenstein produced this graph.

The end of rising real wages confronted workers' families with a choice. They could forgo rising consumption since they lacked the rising wages to afford it. They did not do so. Rising consumption was the realization of personal hopes, the sign of social success, and the promise to one's children that had to be kept. When their wages no longer rose, workers responded by finding two other ways to continue raising their consumption.

First, with real hourly wages stagnant, workers' households sent more of their members to do more hours of paid labor. Husbands, teenagers, and retired people did more work, and millions of housewives and mothers entered the labor markets. While these responses helped raise some additional family income, they also increased the supply of job seekers, which further undermined real wages for everyone.

Increased paid labor by more members of workers' households imposed enormous personal and social costs. Women increasingly held two full-time jobs, one outside the household and one inside, since they continued to do most of the housework. The added stress of this double shift altered and strained household relationships. The divorce rate rose as did signs of alienation (e.g., drug dependency, intrafamily abuse). The added costs of added household labor (in women's work clothes, transportation, purchased meals, cleaning expenses, drugs, etc.) largely negated the net contribution it could make to resuming rising consumption. For that purpose, another source of funds had to be found.

That additional source was household debt. The Federal Reserve records a total household debt in 1975 of $734 billion. By 2006, it had risen to $12.817 trillion. This thirty-year debt explosion has no historical precedent. Workers depleted their savings and took on ever-increasing debt levels. By 2007, US workers were exhausted by their long labor hours, emotionally stressed by the disintegration of families and households, and extremely anxious about unprecedented and, for millions of citizens, unsustainable debt levels.

The post-1970s squeezing of the American worker financed unprecedented prosperity for US capitalists. They and their associates enjoyed a new "gilded" age. Extreme personal wealth became the object of media adulation that cultivated mass envy. The United States at the end of the twentieth century was a replica of what Rockefeller and associates had achieved at the end of the previous century. Corporate boards of directors could and did spend lavishly on computerization, research and development, and moving production facilities abroad. They generously lubricated politicians to reinforce the conditions (such as technical change, job exports, immigration) for their exploding surpluses. Exploding wealth concentrated in relatively few hands led to very rapid growth in enterprises specialized in managing such wealth: investment banks, hedge funds, and so on. Wealth management slid seamlessly into speculation fueled by the euphoria of exploding wealth at the top.

Symptomatic of the deepening divisions in US society, one major financial speculation undertaken with corporate surpluses involved lending them at high interest rates to risky working-class families who needed to borrow to sustain their consumption. Called "subprime" loans, they eventually betrayed investors because the workers could not afford to pay them back. They and their families could no longer work more, earn more, borrow more, nor pay back loans. The stagnant real wages that had enabled the capitalists' boom came back to burst the capitalists' investment bubble. Marx would have smiled at the irony.

Contradiction and Crisis

With the end of rising real wages, workers borrowed chiefly because they had no other way to realize the American Dream and secondarily because they were endlessly reassured that borrowing was safe, appropriate, and itself very American. Bankers were flush with the deposits of corporations' exploding surplus revenues. Competition among them drove all to seek newer, more profitable outlets for loans. Accusations that borrowing workers were stupid or irresponsible or that banks and other lenders were particularly devious or greedy substitute moral denunciations for social analysis. In the Marxian idiom, the class conflicts inside each enterprise and competition among capitalists interacted with a changing social context in the 1970s to end a century of rising real wages and thereafter to accumulate all the components of a major capitalist crisis, the second in seventy-five years.

Capitalists could and did exult after the 1970s as the system delivered wealth to them on an unprecedented scale. Although without acknowledging the fact, they had substituted rising loans to their workers in place of the rising real wages their workers had enjoyed for the previous century. This was little short of a capitalist fantasy come true. However, they preferred to believe instead that the entrepreneur-led, efficiency-driven mechanisms of private enterprise and free markets accounted for their good fortune. To them and their ideological supporters, their wealth proved that private, unregulated capitalism was superior to any conceivable alternative system. While the good times for capitalists rolled, the worlds of politics, media, and academia affirmed such beliefs only too eagerly.

Ideas informed by Marxian theory (e.g., that the end of rising real wages was the hard reality underlying a debt-dependent prosperity and that the capitalists' gains were the workers' losses) were fundamentally unacceptable and therefore generally ignored. Only when mass worker exhaustion, stress, and debt drove the system to collapse did that "other side" of capitalist euphoria become visible. The return to Marxian analysis was partly an effect and also a further cause of that visibility.

A Marxian Solution

Stagnating wages alongside rising productivity are perpetual goals of capitalists in their relentless struggle with their productive laborers. If and when conditions permit, capitalist corporations will achieve those goals. When they do, the results have repeatedly been growing inequality of wealth and income, financial speculation, booms, bubbles, and their bursting into crises. The Marxian solution to such repeated crises would be to change out of such a system. Social conditions will always shift and change, but a different, noncapitalist organization of production would respond to changing conditions differently.

A Marxian policy of pursuing a transformation of production sites—enterprises—from capitalist to noncapitalist organizations would sharply distinguish it from today's Keynesian or yesterday's neoclassical policies. Such a Marxian policy would not aim to reform capitalism by either increasing or decreasing state economic intervention, by regulating or deregulating credit and other markets. Instead, it would aim to eliminate capitalism in the precise sense of fundamentally changing the class structure in production with or without more or less state intervention or regulation.

The policy implication of Marx's critique of capitalism would be to put workers inside each enterprise in the collective position of receiving the surpluses they produced in that enterprise. That would, of course, position them as also the distributors of those surpluses. The surplus-producing workers in each enterprise would, in effect, become their own collective board of directors. They would replace traditional corporate boards chosen by and responsible to major shareholders. This would eliminate the capitalist enterprise's confrontation of workers and capitalists. It would thereby change the methods and results of board decisions about what, how, and where to produce and what to do with the surpluses.

Such a change out of capitalism could be a major first step in the democratization of the economy generally. Democracy would require that in each enterprise, productive employees have equal roles in reaching such decisions. Subsequent steps would entail enlarging economic democracy by including those residential communities interdependent with each enterprise. Workers and residents would then share democratic power over the products and the surpluses produced in and distributed by each enterprise.

Changing the class structure in this way will not eliminate contradictions or even crises arising in an economy. But postcapitalist crises will be different, will be understood differently, and will be responded to in different ways. And these differences matter. First of all, crises will less likely emerge, as the current one did, from stagnating real wages. Had US workers also collectively composed their own boards of directors, the conditions of the 1970s would not likely have led them to stop raising their own real wages. What crises did arise would be responded to much more humanely and equitably precisely because of the extension of democracy entailed by eliminating capitalist class structures of production. The costs and pains of crisis response would be equitably shared in principle, since that principle is embedded in and follows directly from the postcapitalist class structure. The grotesque disparities of today—when foreclosure and unemployment stagger millions while others suffer neither, when some collapsing industries receive massive government bailouts and others are left to die, when some municipalities and states continue to provide basic public services and others do not—would less likely occur on the basis of a postcapitalist class structure.

There is another key difference to consider. FDR's New Deal imposed a mass of regulations upon capitalism with the explicit intention of ending the Great Depression and preventing another such depression in the future. New Deal regulations and taxes constrained the ways and means for capitalists to pursue their goals. However, those regulations and taxes never changed the capitalist class structure of production. Capitalist employers always remained in charge of enterprises, appropriating the surpluses and distributing them. Corporate boards of directors had every incentive—given their responsibilities to shareholders and their own self-interests—to evade, weaken, or undo the New Deal regulations. Moreover, as appropriators of the surpluses produced inside each enterprise, they also had the resources to evade, weaken, or undo the New Deal regulations. In fact, capitalists responded to their incentives and utilized their resources to undo the New Deal, especially after the 1970s under the regimes of Ronald Reagan, George H. W. Bush, Bill Clinton, and George W. Bush. In a postcapitalist class structure of the sort sketched above, it would be far less likely for enterprise boards to want or to be able to similarly undermine future anticrisis reforms.

The Myth of "American Exceptionalism" Implodes

January 19, 2011

One aspect of "American exceptionalism" has always been economic. US workers, so the story went, enjoyed a rising level of real wages that afforded their families a rising standard of living. Ever harder work paid off in rising consumption. The rich got richer faster than the middle class and poor, but almost no one got poorer. Nearly all citizens felt "middle class." A profitable US capitalism kept running ahead of labor supply. It kept raising wages to attract waves of immigration and to retain employees, across the nineteenth and twentieth centuries until the 1970s.

Then everything changed. Real wages stopped rising, as US capitalists redirected their investments to produce and employ abroad, while replacing millions of workers in the United States with computers. The US feminist movement moved millions of adult women to seek paid employment. US capitalism no longer faced a shortage of labor.

US employers took advantage of the changed situation: they stopped raising wages. When basic labor scarcity became labor excess, not only real wages but eventually benefits, too, would stop rising. Over the last thirty years, the vast majority of US workers have, in fact, gotten poorer, when you sum up flat real wages, reduced benefits (pensions, medical insurance, etc.), reduced public services, and raised tax burdens. In economic terms, American "exceptionalism" began to die in the 1970s.

The rich, however, have become much richer since the 1970s, as every measure of US income and wealth inequality attests. The explanation is simple: while workers' average real wages stayed flat, their productivity rose (the goods and services that an average hour's labor provided to employers). More and better machines (including computers), better education, and harder and faster labor effort raised productivity since the 1970s. While workers delivered more and more value to employers, those employers did not pay workers more. The employers reaped all the benefits of rising productivity: rising profits, rising salaries and bonuses to managers, rising dividends to shareholders, and rising payments to the professionals who serve employers (e.g., lawyers, architects, consultants).

Since the 1970s, most US workers postponed facing up to what capitalism had come to mean for them. They sent more family members to do more hours of paid labor, and they borrowed huge amounts. By exhausting themselves, stressing family life to the breaking point in many households, and taking on unsustainable levels of debt, the US working class delayed the end of American exceptionalism—until the global crisis hit in 2007. By then, their buying power could no longer grow: rising unemployment kept wages flat, and no more hours of work or more borrowing were possible. Reckoning time had arrived. A US capitalism built on expanding mass consumption lost its foundation.

The richest 10–15 percent—those cashing in on employers' rising surplus from stagnant real wages—helped bring on the crisis by speculating wildly and unsuccessfully in all sorts of new financial instruments (e.g., asset-backed securities, credit default swaps). The richest also contributed to the crisis by using their money to shift US politics to the right, rendering government regulation and oversight inadequate to anticipate or moderate the crisis or even to react properly once it hit.

Indeed, the rich have so far been able to use the crisis to widen still further the gulf separating themselves from the rest, to finally bury American exceptionalism. First, they utilized both parties' dependence on their financial support to make sure there would be no mass federal hiring program for the unemployed (as President Franklin Delano Roosevelt used between 1934 and 1940). The absence of such a program guaranteed that real wages would not rise and, with job benefits, would likely fall—as they indeed have done. Second, the rich made sure that the prime focus of government response to the crisis would benefit banks, large corporations, and the stock markets. These have more or less "recovered."

Third, the current drive for government budget austerity—especially focused on the 50 states and the thousands of municipalities—forces the mass of people to pick up the costs for the government's unjustly imbalanced response to the crisis. The trillions spent to save the banks and selected other corporations (AIG,[2] General Motors, Fannie Mae, Freddie Mac, etc.) were mostly borrowed because the government dared not tax the corporations and the richest citizens to raise the needed rescue funds. Indeed, a good part of what the government borrowed came precisely from those funds left in the hands of corporations and the rich, because they had not been taxed to overcome the crisis. With sharply enlarged debts, all levels of government face the pressure of needing to take too much from current tax revenues to pay interest on debts, leaving too little to sustain public services. So they demand the people pay more taxes and suffer reduced public services, so that government can reduce its debt burden.

For example, Governor Jerry Brown of California proposes to continue for five more years the massive, broad-based tax increases begun during the crisis and also to cut state services for the poor (reduced Medicaid funding) and the middle class (reduced budgets for community colleges, state colleges, and the university system). The governor admits that California's budget faces sky-high interest costs and reduced federal government assistance just when the crisis increases demands for public services. The governor does not admit his fear to tax the state's huge corporate and private individual wealth. So he announces an "austerity program," as if no alternative existed. Indeed, a major support for austerity comes from the large corporations and wealthiest Californians, who hold the state's bonds and want reassurances that the interest on those bonds will be paid.

California's austerity program parallels similar programs in many other states, in thousands of municipalities, and at the federal level (e.g., Social Security). Together, these programs reinforce falling real wages, falling benefits, falling government services, and rising taxes. In the United States, capitalism has stopped "delivering the goods," as it

---

2. Chris Arnande, "The Audacity to 'Fart in the Elevator' and the Lingering Anger over the Bailout," *Guardian*, October 9, 2014.

so long boasted of doing. The reality of ever-deeper economic division clashes with expectations built up when wages rose over the century before the 1970s. US capitalism now brings long-term painful decline for its working class; the end of "American exceptionalism"; and rising social, cultural, and political tensions.

The Revenge of Trickle-Down Economics

February 14, 2011

President Barack Obama's basic budget for fiscal year 2012 is mostly a done deal, supported by the entire political establishment.[3] The hyped choreography of forthcoming battles between Democrats and Republicans is a very secondary sideshow. The battles clothe basic agreement in a disguise of fierce oppositions—perhaps aimed to mollify each party's none-too-discerning militants.

Both sides agree that the US private economy is in such a poor and dangerous condition that it needs massive fiscal stimulus from the federal budget: classic Keynesian policy. Washington thus plans to spend roughly $3.5 trillion, while taking in tax revenues of roughly $2 trillion—a deficit of $1.5 trillion. In the light of such numbers, the debates of Democrats and Republicans over spending cuts likely to be of the order of $40–60 billion are inconsequential. They become yet more inconsequential in light of the fact that the federal budget's projected deficit of $1.5tn will carry an annual interest cost of $40–60 billion. That interest will be an additional budget outlay offsetting the likely cuts arrived at the end of loudly publicized debates over spending reductions.

Both sides agree that government spending will continue to follow the old "trickle-down" theory, despite its failure to date. Massive federal outlays on the largest banks, insurance companies, and selected other large corporations produced a "recovery" for them, but not in the rates of unemployment, home foreclosures, and state and local austerity budgets that

---

3. Dominic Rushe, "Barack Obama to Unveil $1.1tn Cuts in US Budget over Next Decade," *Guardian*, February 13, 2011.

keep crippling the US economy. Federal largesse has yet to trickle down, but both parties proceed on the assumption that it eventually will. Neither party tallies the economic and social costs of massive unemployment, home loss, and state and local austerity budgets. Neither party offers any alternative to "trickle down," as if no alternative exists or is worth debating.

Yet of course, there are alternatives. In the 1930s, capitalism's last major global breakdown, then President Franklin Delano Roosevelt eventually pursued the alternative "bubble up" theory. Between 1934 and 1940, he created and filled 11 million federal jobs with unemployed workers. Their incomes enabled them to maintain mortgage payments and buy goods and services that provided jobs to millions of others and profits to many US businesses. That alternative to trickle-down economics did not suffice to overcome the Great Depression. However, it certainly alleviated more of the economic damage and individual suffering of that breakdown than George W. Bush's and Barack Obama's trickle-down economics have achieved in this one.

Then, too, there is the alternative of taxing corporations and the rich to finance federal stimulus without huge deficits and increasing costly national debts.[4] That alternative is even more taboo in Washington than a bubble-up government employment program. Politically, Roosevelt's bubble-up approach won him the greatest outpouring of electoral support ever achieved by any US president. So it might today for Obama. Why, then, would a politically besieged president hesitate to repeat some variant of Roosevelt's successful strategy?

During the 1930s, the Congress of Industrial Organizations was successfully recruiting millions of workers into unions: a powerful labor movement, combined with socially influential and growing socialist and communist parties, organized pressure from below. Today, those movements are either gone or extremely weakened. Then, the flow of money into US politics from corporations and the rich was relatively less powerful than it has now become, in terms of campaign contributions and legislating lobbying funds dependent on those sources. Republicans

---

4. Richard Wolff, "Ben Bernanke's Silence Speaks Volumes," *Guardian*, February 9, 2011.

and Democrats alike depend on them. No wonder both parties and the president agree on so much and dare not consider or debate alternatives, of which their benefactors might disapprove.

Of course, the groups immediately affected by specific federal budget cuts will suffer. Democrats will posture as their defenders and, by extension, defenders of the environment, or poor people, or pregnant women, that those groups champion. Republicans will posture as the punishers and reducers of an arrogant, outsized, and inefficient state, as well as champions of reduced tax burdens on businesses and people.

No matter what their sideshow yields, however, the basic prognosis for the fiscal 2012 federal budget, combined with the current crisis in state and local budgets, is grim. The social safety net is being further frayed; public employee layoffs will increase and thereby worsen unemployment; ecological concerns will continue to be neglected, and no significant individual tax relief is anywhere on the horizon.

In the United States, the federal government is the tail that definitely does not wag the dog. This capitalist crisis is being "resolved" the way crises usually are. As unemployment deepens and lasts, wages and benefits decline. As businesses close, the costs of secondhand machines, the rents for office and factory space, the fees of business-serving professionals (accountants, lawyers, etc.) drop. Eventually, when those cost declines proceed far enough, capitalists will see enough profit in resuming production to generate a broad and sustainable economic upturn.

In short, just as the crisis was brought on by the profit-seeking investments and speculations of the private sector, so now we wait until the private sector sees a profit in resuming production and thus ending this crisis. The federal government fusses and fumes about it all. It throws public money at the private sector to keep it afloat. It debates details with great fanfare. But all the while, the mass of people tighten their belts, do without, and wait for this economic system to rebound.

The vast social and personal costs of this irrational economic absurdity—tens of millions unemployed, one third of US productive capacity unutilized (rotting and rusting), and vast quantities of needed output forgone and lost—are ignored lest they raise the uncomfortable question: why do we retain a system as dysfunctional as this?

In Economic Crisis, Capitalism Delivers the Bads

July 22, 2011

Throughout its history, capitalism never succeeded in preventing recurring economic crises. However, they were usually contained within the system. Economic crises usually did not become social crises; the system itself was usually not called into question. Transition to a different system was then an idea kept away from public discussion, a project kept from public action. During cyclical downturns, production was reduced, unemployment and bankruptcies rose, deflation often hit and hurt, and mass working-class suffering spread.

Downturns typically drove down wages and the prices of productive inputs. Eventually, those declines provided sufficient profit opportunities for employers to resume production. Then downturns became upturns, the unemployed (or at least some of them) were rehired and prosperity replaced depression until the next cyclical downturn (usually within a few years). Before the 1930s, government interventions to offset or manage downturns were mostly marginal, minor, and sporadic. Mass resignation to endure "hard times" was the norm, although voices for fighting back were also evident.

During and since the 1930s, however, crises in capitalism have provoked significant government economic interventions. This happened chiefly for two reasons. First, the Great Depression of the 1930s cut so deep, lasted so long, and damaged so many that resulting mass dissatisfaction extended, for growing numbers, to the capitalist system itself. Second, when labor unions and anticapitalist political movements (socialists and communists) were strong, they functioned as antidotes to resignation. Periods of mass suffering were no longer accepted quietly or fatalistically. Labor and left organizations blamed capitalists and capitalism, and they mobilized popular responses that often challenged the system and not just its latest crisis. In the 1930s, the combination of a severe crisis with fast-growing industrial unions and anticapitalist political parties forced the Roosevelt administration to undertake massive economic interventions. They aimed to prevent cyclical crises contained within capitalism from becoming social crises of capitalism bringing the system itself into question.

In the 1930s and since, governments' economic crisis interventions usually had two purposes: to save capitalists from the huge losses and possible collapse that the system routinely reproduced and to save the system by shortening and softening mass suffering (thereby blunting the appeal of labor unions and anticapitalists). Roosevelt's New Deal achieved bailouts for banks and corporations, regulations trying to prevent the worst capitalist abuses, and social welfare institutions such as Social Security, unemployment compensation, and direct federal hiring of the unemployed (11 million after 1933).

Governments' services to capitalism were also evident in how they financed such costly interventions. In the United States, Roosevelt got capitalists to accept the new social welfare institutions by carefully not taxing their wealth (either corporate or personal) and limiting tax increases on their incomes. Roosevelt got workers to accept the bailouts of capitalists by not taxing workers to pay for those bailouts. Of course, financing very costly government interventions without taxing corporations, the rich, or the workers enough to pay for them meant that the government had to borrow what it did not raise in taxes. The federal budget had to run big deficits that rapidly increased the national debt.

Roosevelt got corporations and the rich to lend Washington the money that they could not profitably invest during a depression without taking huge risks. Instead, they would earn interest on very low-risk loans to the Treasury. Moreover, Washington would use that borrowed money to speed recovery from depression and offset threats to capitalism. Corporations and the rich could cash in their loans to the government whenever they wanted to use their money for other purposes. Finally, capitalist enterprises and the rich understood that if they did not lend to the government, either the Internal Revenue Service might tax the money from them or capitalism itself might collapse. With mass union, socialist, and communist demonstrations in the streets, Roosevelt's program won the support of the majority of capitalists and the rich. With the streets silent, President Barack Obama does not even conceive of such a program.

Since the 1930s, politicians in capitalist countries have used government deficit financing more and more, not just in cyclical downswings. Corporations and the rich—like the mass of people—always want more from government and less taxes to pay, so politicians accommodate both sides by borrowing (state deficit financing). They remind corporations and the rich that deficit finance is far preferable to their being taxed more. The last seventy-five years have thus yielded repeated government budget deficits and rising national debt levels. So when the 2007 crisis cut back government tax revenues and required costly government interventions, huge additional budgetary deficits were enacted in all capitalist countries, but this time they came after a long period of rising national debts.

The most indebted capitalist economies discovered that corporations and the rich had become wary of a new risk: lending more to countries with already high debt levels meant huge interest and principal repayments that citizens there might refuse. Politicians there might be unable to devote ever more of their citizens' tax payments to pay off creditors rather than provide public services. Countries such as Greece with strong labor and left traditions became flashpoints for a Europe-wide (and indeed, a global) struggle over sacrificing mass living standards (austerity) to satisfy creditors' demands.

Capitalism's new contradiction: It can no longer easily use deficits and rising debt to prevent economic crises from becoming social crises. Yet politicians fear to tax corporations and the rich, whose money now makes or breaks political careers. Hence, governments everywhere impose austerity on their people. Relatively weakened (compared to the 1930s) labor and left organizations cannot stop the process; at best, they slow it. For the mass of people, austerity adds to the burdens that capitalism's crisis already imposes.

Capitalism is not "delivering the goods." It is piling on the bads. These conditions do not prevent an economic crisis from becoming a social crisis. Quite the contrary. Resignation never was the only response of working people to capitalism's dysfunctions. After the initial shock— at an American Dream fast disappearing and lasting economic decline looming—rebuilding old and/or creating new labor and left organizations will resume. The old mole of real class struggles will return to the surface of contemporary politics.

A Tale of Two Lootings

August 3, 2011

The political posturing around the debt ceiling "crisis" was mostly a distraction from the hard issues. The hardest of those—underlying US economic decline—keeps resurfacing to display costs, pains, and injustices that threaten to dissolve society. Its causes—two long-term trends over the last thirty years—also help explain the political failures that now compound the social costs of economic decline.

The first trend is the attack on jobs, wages, and benefits, and the second is the attack on the federal government's budget. The first trend enables the second. A capitalist economy suffering high unemployment with all its costly consequences shapes a bizarre, disconnected politics. The two major parties ignore unemployment and the system that keeps reproducing it. They argue instead over how much to cut social programs for the people while they agree that such cutting is the major way to fix the government's broken budget.

The first trend amounts to looting the US working class (the media softens that to "disappearing middle class"). Since the 1970s, real wages have been flat to declining, while productivity per worker has risen steadily. What employers give workers (wages) has remained the same while what workers produce for their employers (profits) rose. Workers and their families responded by working ever more hours and borrowing ever more money to get or keep the "American Dream." By 2007, they were physically exhausted, and families were emotionally stressed and deeply anxious about the debts that their flat real wages could no longer sustain. When the system crashed, zooming unemployment, further wage and benefit reductions, and home foreclosures made everything still worse for most Americans.

The second trend was looting the government. This happened because exhausted and stressed workers turned away from participation or even from political interests after the 1970s. In contrast, employers used the profits made possible by flat wages and rising productivity to buy politicians, parties, and policies. More than ever before, businesses and top executives grabbed the levers of political power. They made government serve their interests. Starting in the 1980s, Washington lowered business taxes, deregulated businesses, cut taxes on executives' and other high incomes, increased spending on the military-industrial and medical-insurance complexes, provided more opportunities and freedom for financial speculation, and so on. To distract people from recognizing, debating, or opposing this political shift, more was also spent on social programs and supports.

Washington was thus deprived of tax revenues (chiefly on corporations and the richest individuals) while spending more on defense, business supports, and social programs. As this gap between revenues and expenditures rose, Washington kept borrowing ever more. Rising annual budget deficits added to the national debt. When the private capitalist system crashed in 2007, business and the rich made sure the government spent vast sums to bail out banks, insurance companies, and large corporations and to revive the stock market. Accordingly, government deficits and debts zoomed upward.

Business and the rich made trillions from both trends. By keeping workers' wages flat, profits soared as employers alone kept the full fruits of rising worker productivity. Employers and the rich profited further by getting Washington to lower their taxes. They then lent at interest to the government what they no longer needed to pay in taxes. After all, the government needed to borrow precisely because it had stopped taxing corporations and the rich at the rates of the 1940s, 1950s, and 1960s. Business and the rich happily financed a political system that converted their tax obligations into secure, well-rewarded loans to the government instead.

Looting the working class and the state widened the gap between rich and poor in the United States to what it was a century ago. Now the corporations and the rich want the state, whose budget they looted, to cut back social supports and services for the working class whose wages and productivity they also looted.

Republicans yell "class warfare" against advocates of a return to the 1940s tax rates on business profits and the 1950s and 1960s rates on high-income individuals. Both were far higher than they are today. "Class warfare" better describes government policies since the 1970s. Business and the rich made sure those policies shifted the burden of federal taxation from business to individuals and from rich individuals to everyone else.

Despite this double looting of working people and the state, many victims direct their anger at the government instead of those who control the government. Unemployed millions fired by private capitalist employers (or suffering wage and benefits cuts imposed by them) blame the government, not their employers. Millions foreclosed out of their homes by private capitalist banks blame the government. They want the government punished, made smaller and weaker, and they are desperate to avoid further taxes. Republicans promise to do all that. Those who fear that a smaller, tax-starved government will do even less for them hear Democrats promising to cut less than Republicans. This is politics disconnected from economic realities (e.g., high unemployment) and twisted into a contest between more and less government spending cuts imposed on a working class already reeling from economic crisis.

Neither party dares to return taxes on corporations and the rich to what they were. Neither party dares to advocate that government hire the unemployed to rebuild the United States so that they can spend their government-job wages on maintaining their mortgages (reviving the housing industry) and thereby stimulate the whole economy from the bottom up. Above all, neither party dares admit that so long as production remains in the hands of tiny groups of rich shareholders and boards of directors, they will keep looting the system.

Can the United States do better than this capitalist system's performance? We need to debate honestly and decide whether and how we can do better. We should have had the courage to debate that over the last fifty years. The Cold War—and the priorities of corporations and the rich—prevented that. Now it's long overdue. We need new political organizations mobilizing people to demand and engage that debate, theoretically and also in practical, political struggles.

Capitalism and Poverty

October 12, 2011

The US Census Bureau recently reported what most Americans already knew. Poverty is deepening. The gap between rich and poor is growing.

Slippage soon into the ranks of the poor now confronts tens of millions of Americans who long thought of themselves as securely "middle class."

The reality is worse than the Census Bureau reports. Consider that the bureau's poverty line in 2010 for a family of four was $22,314. Families of four making more than that were not counted as poor. That poverty line works out to $15 per day per person for everything: food, clothing, housing, medical care, transportation, education, and so on. If you have more than $15 per day per person in your household to pay for everything each person needs, the bureau does not count you as part of this country's poverty problem.

So the real number of US citizens living in poverty—more reasonably defined—is much larger today than the 46.2 million reported by the Census Bureau. It is thus much higher than the 15.1 percent of our people the bureau sees as poor. Conservatively estimated, about one in four Americans already lives in real poverty.

Another one in four is or should be worried about joining them soon. Long-lasting and high unemployment now drains away income from families and friends of the unemployed who have used up savings as well as unemployment insurance. As city, state, and local governments cut services and supports, people will have to divert money to offset part of those cuts. When Medicare and if Social Security benefits are cut, millions will be spending more to help elderly parents. Finally, poverty looms for those with jobs as (a) wages are cut or fail to keep up with rising prices, and (b) benefits—especially pensions and medical insurance—are reduced.

Deepening poverty has many causes, but the capitalist economic system is major among them. First, capitalism's periodic crises always increase poverty, and the current crisis is no exception. More precisely, how capitalist corporations operate, in or out of crisis, regularly reproduces poverty. At the top of every corporation, its major shareholders (fifteen to twenty or fewer) own controlling blocks of shares. They select a board of directors—usually fifteen to twenty individuals—who run the corporation. These two tiny groups make all the key decisions: what, how, and where to produce and what to do with the profits.

Poverty is one result of this capitalist type of enterprise organization. For example, corporate decisions generally aim to lower the number of workers or their wages or both. They automate, export (outsource) jobs, and replace higher paid workers by recruiting domestic and foreign substitutes willing to work for less. These normal corporate actions generate rising poverty as the other side of rising profits. When poverty and its miseries "remain always with us," workers tend to accept what employers dish out to avoid losing jobs and falling into poverty.

Another major corporate goal is to control politics. Wherever all citizens can vote, workers' interests might prevail over those of directors and shareholders in elections. To prevent that, corporations devote portions of their revenues to finance politicians, parties, mass media, and "think tanks." Their goal is to "shape public opinion" and control what government does. They do not want Washington's crisis-driven budget deficits and national debts to be overcome by big tax increases on corporations and the rich. Instead public discussion and politicians' actions are kept focused chiefly on cutting social programs for the majority.

Corporate goals include providing high and rising salaries, stock options, and bonuses to top executives and rising dividends and share prices to shareholders. The less paid to the workers who actually produce what corporations sell, the more corporate revenue goes to satisfy directors, top managers, and major shareholders.

Corporations also raise profits regularly by increasing prices and/or cutting production costs (often by compromising output quality). Higher priced and poorer quality goods are sold mostly to working people. This too pushes them toward poverty just like lower wages and benefits and government service cuts.

Over the years, government interventions like Social Security, Medicare, minimum wage laws, and regulations never sufficed to eradicate poverty. They often helped the poor, but they never ended poverty. The same applies to charities aiding the poor. Poverty always remained. Now capitalism's crisis worsens it again. Something more than government interventions or charity is required to end poverty.

One solution: production would have to be organized differently, in a noncapitalist way. Instead of enterprise decisions being made by directors and major shareholders, the workers themselves could collectively and democratically make them. Let's call this Democracy at

Work (DAW), since it entails the majority making the key enterprise decisions about what, how, and where to produce and what to do with the profits.

If the workers made those decisions, here are some likely results. Primary goals would no longer be to reduce their own numbers or their wages. If technological changes or reduced demand for their outputs required fewer workers, they would likely maintain the wages of workers and retrain them for other jobs meeting growing demands. Workers would not be fired and thereby pushed into poverty.

Second, workers making democratic decisions would not likely allow today's huge differences between average wages and top managers' salaries and bonuses. By eliminating concentrated income and accumulated wealth at the top, resources would be freed finally to end poverty at the bottom. A DAW system could produce and secure the vast "middle class" that this country has pretended to have but never really has. Workers disposing of their enterprises' profits would no longer distribute a portion to politicians and parties to protect a rich minority against the envy and resentments of the majority. By establishing a far more egalitarian income distribution, a DAW system could also transform a political system now corrupted by the money of corporations and the rich.

Third, a DAW system would be less likely to raise prices or reduce output quality. When workers are both decision-makers at work as well as consumers of their enterprises' outputs, they would more likely pass and sustain laws to outlaw the price gouging and quality deterioration common in capitalism.

A serious commitment to end poverty and its costly social effects requires us to face that capitalism has always reproduced widespread poverty as the other side of profits for a relative few. No wonder such a system has provoked Occupy Wall Street and so many of its signature slogans and demands.

Five Reasons Why the Crisis Persists

August 14, 2012

This crisis is not going away. Officially begun late in 2007, nearly five years later, no end is in sight. Trillions in government-funded bailouts and interventions failed to do the trick. The private sector's hyped resilience disappeared. "Recoveries" proved weak, uneven, and short-lived. The president who rode the crisis into power risks being ridden out by its persistence.

It is difficult to imagine and impossible to count all the costs of this persistence. Consider, just for examples, (a) damaged physical and mental health of the unemployed, (b) rising anxiety about increasingly insecure jobs and benefits, (c) strained and destroyed relationships, (d) interrupted or aborted educations, and (e) lost skills and job connections. Consider, too, the gross inefficiencies (tens of millions of unemployed alongside trillions in unused raw materials, tools, equipment, offices, factories and stores; millions of empty homes and millions of people rendered homeless by the crisis).

Five major reasons shape this crisis's persistence. First is the exhausted purchasing power of the US working class. Capitalist employers have raised profits by replacing workers with computers since the 1970s and by relocating production jobs to lower wages abroad. Later, they likewise exported white-collar and service jobs. The previous century's history of steadily rising real wages ended, thereby threatening the rising consumption, which had created ever more jobs in capitalism's virtuous cycle. Starting in the 1970s, that cycle turned and became vicious instead. Real wages stopped rising as jobs dried up. For a while, rising workers' debts papered over the vicious cycle. But eventually, the combination of rising debts and stagnating wages exhausted the working class's purchasing power. Today, workers' real wages continue to stagnate or fall and they cannot sustain more debt. Since big business, the banks, the Federal Reserve, Republicans, and Democrats have done nothing to deal with the basic real wages problem in the US economy, the crisis persists.

Second, large nonfinancial corporations, in their competitive rush to low-wage investments in China and elsewhere, have created yet again excessive capacity to produce, creating more pressure on already-depressed US workers' real wages. They cannot sell all their automobiles, electronics, and so on. So they reduce hiring—which only worsens their selling problems. They accumulate hoards of cash for which they cannot find profitably productive outlets. They blame politicians—yet they make sure those politicians say and do nothing about the wage problem or the irrationality and social irresponsibility of those corporation's self-defeating capacity-building investments. So the crisis persists.

Third, large financial corporations took bailouts and used them to become even bigger than before 2007, to water down new regulations provoked by the crisis, to lend to over-indebted governments, and to find new speculations. Finance is riding a forty-year wave of growth as debts became the way workers, corporations, and governments do most of their business (from buying groceries with credit cards to borrowing to pay for college to exploding national debts). Financial companies handle all this debt (they issue the credit cards, buy the government debt, etc.) and profit from every step in every loan and loan-based speculation. Financial companies also collect the wealth concentrated in the top 1 percent and invest it for them. They compete for those wealthy clients by promising ever better returns that require them to take rising risks. That helped generate the financial part of the current capitalist crisis. Nothing is being done to deal with the underlying problem of proliferating debt dependence and its vast economic and social costs. Finance remains a major cause for crisis persistence.

Fourth, corruption and dysfunction, impossible to disentangle, afflict US politics more than ever. They preclude any serious economic intervention other than massive bailouts for the well-connected (i.e., well-paying) big business patrons of politics. Thin rationales based on "trickle-down economics" cover those bailouts. Endless "inducements, incentives, jaw-boning," and other appeals to big business (to hire, lend, invest, or otherwise stimulate the economy) sustain the fiction of government activity while business ignores, mocks, or abuses them. The obvious alternatives—President Franklin Delano Roosevelt's creation of Social Security, unemployment compensation, and massive federal hiring systems during the last comparable capitalist crisis—are treated by political leaders as if they never happened. These leaders offer no argument for rejecting an FDR-type alternative now—nor do they admit their policies' failures to end or reverse the crisis. So the crisis persists.

Fifth, no domestic opposition or external alternative model is sufficiently strong to compel or frighten political and business leaders to end or at least significantly reduce the mass burdens imposed by this crisis. In the 1930s, FDR intervened in large part because of domestic pressures exerted by the intertwined forces of the Congress of Industrial Organizations and the socialist and communist parties that had successfully organized millions into labor unions and many thousands into the parties' ranks. The other cause of his interventions was fear concerning the Soviet Union, a concrete alternative that avoided the Great Depression while "taking care" of its people in ways that attracted attention and support among US workers and intellectuals. After World War II, the business community led sustained campaigns to undo exactly those causes of FDR's interventions. Big business mobilized its political allies and subordinates to encircle, intimidate, and undermine the Soviet Union militarily, to use anticommunism against the socialist and communist parties, and to direct endless assaults against the legal protections and ideological supports for labor unions.

The success of those campaigns yields the current situation. No opposition yet exists comparable to what was achieved in the 1930s and early 1940s (although the Occupy movement is a first step). Having first destroyed its working class's defensive organizations, US capitalism now can and does impose on that class the immense social costs of its latest extreme periodic convulsion. Hence, the crisis persists and becomes a central economic and political issue of our time.

Capitalism's Ideological Crutches

September 3, 2012

Capitalism's crises have always threatened the system. True, capitalism's defenders could fairly easily dismiss shallow and short crises with limited suffering for the unemployed, the bankrupt, and their dependents and communities. Some said they were merely "bumps in the capitalist road" to growth and prosperity. Others saw crises as capitalism's way to "clean out inefficient firms" and thus prepare its next upswing. Such interpretations of capitalism—ideologies—have long served to counter criticisms of its instability and recurring cycles and the suffering they impose.

However, such ideologies arouse many more than the usual skeptics when—as in the 1930s and again since 2007—capitalism's downturns cut deep and persist. Then capitalism's stark inefficiencies become too glaring as millions of unemployed workers alongside idled productive capacity yield massive waste and long-lasting social costs. Bailouts of large financial capitalists by the governments they control turn skeptics into critics. The critics then become mobilized into a real political opposition when subsequent government "austerity" policies shift the costs of crisis and bailouts onto the mass of people.

Capitalists and the rich remain determined now not to bear the costs of the bailouts or the crisis. Unlike in the 1930s, they don't see organized, determined, and militant workers' movements to worry about today—nor any Soviet Union positioned as an alternative to modern capitalism. So they push austerity policies for governments everywhere. To sustain governments' austerity policies, capitalists and the rich lean on their ideological crutches to try to thwart political opposition.

The mainstream ideology that works best as capitalism's crutch is to blame the government. This interpretation of modern society insists that the ultimate root and cause of economic problems is the government, not capitalism or capitalists. If you are unemployed, face foreclosure, or are underpaid, the problem is not the capitalist who refuses to employ you, evicts you, or pays you poorly. It is instead partly your own fault, but mostly that of the government: the politicians and the bureaucrats.

Blame-the-government ideology serves capitalists and the rich executives, managers, professionals, and advisers who depend on them. They can boost their profits and wealth by cutting wages, jobs, and benefits; using toxic technologies; relocating businesses overseas; jacking up prices; foreclosing; evicting; and so on. They can provoke global crises and take massive bailouts with public money. To cover all that, business and political leaders, media spokespersons, and academics compose a chorus that endlessly repeats, "blame the government." They seek to transform that idea into "common sense" so victims of capitalists' actions will automatically not blame them, but instead get angry at politicians.

The blame-the-government ideological crutch aims to stop, deflect, and demoralize political coalitions of those hurt and outraged by capitalist crises. Consciously or unconsciously, capitalism's ideologues want to prevent any repeat of what happened in the 1930s. Then, a coalition of workers, farmers, intellectuals, and others forced President Franklin Delano Roosevelt to do the opposite of austerity. He raised taxes on corporations and the rich to pay for creating Social Security, unemployment insurance, and a massive federal jobs program. A similar coalition today could return taxes on corporations and the rich back to those much higher Roosevelt-era rates. That revenue could fund a government jobs program now like Roosevelt's, reducing unemployment without any deficit and thus no additional national debt. It could, of course, go further and question capitalism itself.

Blame-the-government ideology aims to prevent workers' angers and resentments about their deprivations under capitalism from building effective, organized political power. That ideological crutch seeks to assure that what capitalism does to the people economically will not be undone by the people politically.

Blame-the-government ideology supports capitalism in another way. By portraying government as wasteful, incompetent, corrupt, power mad, and oppressive, it strives to establish another "commonsense" idea. Government should be kept economically weak: Keep its spending down, its budget balanced, or else in debt to capitalists and the rich (main government creditors). Limit the taxes it can levy, the regulations it can impose, and so on. Hobble the government while painting it as a negative social force, not to be trusted. Corrupt the politicians with the resources only corporations and the rich have and spend for such purposes, and then denounce that corruption as the government's fault. Turn workers away from engagement in, respect for, or even interest in politics. Disgusted and alienated, many workers withdraw, leaving the political arena to the capitalists and the rich to buy and shape. US mainstream politics thus serves and never challenges capitalism.

Blame the government, like all ideologies, has contradictions and blind spots. When war is on the agenda, politicians get quick makeovers from "crooks" into "commander in chief" and "national leaders." When workers strike and otherwise resist employers, capitalism's ideologues want to unleash government on those workers. In such conditions, ideology waffles from blame and reduce to celebrate and strengthen government. Similarly, when politicians get caught working for and being paid by capitalists and the rich, a troubling question invades public discussion. Who really is to blame: the politicians who serve, the capitalists who pay and get served, or the system they built and maintain together?

Mainstream blame-the-government ideology is a fig leaf that hides (and thereby protects and supports) how capitalism works. In crisis times, it intensifies (e.g., Sarah Palin, Paul Ryan, and Rush Limbaugh) to shift public attention away from capitalism's breakdown and gross injustice. Its ideologues then urgently ratchet up blame on the government for taxing us; allegedly limiting guns and attacking marriage, religion, and heterosexuality; mandating health insurance; and imposing regulations. Their mission: redirect mass hurt, fear, anxiety, and resentment about the effects of capitalist crisis into rituals of resisting the evil politicians and bureaucrats who want to control us.

Capitalism's ideological crutches do not necessarily or always stress blaming the government. In Germany (1930s) and Italy (1920s), for example, deep crises saw capitalists embrace instead fascist ideologies and political parties that exalted extremely powerful government. Hitler and Mussolini merged powerful government with major capitalist enterprises. They used state power directly to subordinate labor to capital and to destroy capitalism's major critics: labor unions and socialist and communist parties.

Increasingly since 1945, capitalists in the United States have preferred a blame-the-government ideology that best reflects their thinking and advances their interests. They used it to help eradicate the socialist and communist parties that had been crucial to the powerful union-based workers' coalition of the 1930s. It helped likewise weaken decisively the main labor movement (American Federation of Labor–Congress of Industrial Organizations, AFL-CIO) across the last half century. Workers persuaded that it is "common sense" to blame their economic conditions on government rather than their employers undermine union solidarity and militancy. Finally, blame-the-government ideology helped roll back the New Deal as workers were invited to identify with corporations fighting against an evil government seeking to control them. Thus, corporations could, for example, win public support for cuts in taxes on their profits even when those cuts threatened government programs that workers wanted.

To expose and challenge capitalism's blame-the-government ideological crutch does not mean reversing its one-sidedness. We need not and should not celebrate governments and their policies just because capitalism's ideologues blame them. Governments are creatures of their societies. In capitalist societies, corporations and the rich use their resources and power to shape government to their advantages. They also lean on ideological crutches to win enough public support to keep control of the government and society. Workers have been and will continue to be victimized by capitalist controls of economy and politics. To change government policies they need to see through capitalism's ideological crutches. More than that, they will have to organize politically as they did briefly in the 1930s. Yet that, too, was not enough. The New Deal struck by Roosevelt, the CIO, and the socialists and communists in the 1930s was a change in government policy, but one that did not change the underlying capitalist economic system. It left the tiny minority of capitalists (major shareholders and boards of directors) in charge of the corporations, and they used that position over the last half-century to negate and reverse what happened in the 1930s. A different economic system would have prevented that outcome. A different economic system would shape and sustain altogether different government policies.

A different economic system from the ground up means reorganizing enterprises to put democratic majorities (of employees and of residents of communities that interact with the enterprise) in charge of all the basic decisions: what, how, and where to produce and what to do with the profits. With the people in charge of enterprises—instead of tiny groups of capitalists—the economic resources they send to the government (e.g., taxes) will require it finally to serve the people in return. Just as capitalist enterprises always made sure to shape government to work primarily for them, so a social transition to workers' self-directed cooperative enterprises would make sure that government, for the first time, genuinely works for the majority.

Capitalism Efficient? We Can Do So Much Better
March 16, 2013

What's efficiency got to do with capitalism? The short answer is: little or nothing. Economic and social collapses in Detroit, Cleveland, and many other US cities did not happen because production was inefficient there. Efficiency problems did not cause the longer-term economic declines troubling the United States and Western Europe.

Capitalist corporations decided to relocate production: first, away from such cities, and now, away from those regions. It has done so to serve the priorities of their major shareholders and boards of directors. Higher profits, business growth, and market share drive those decisions. As I say, efficiency has little or nothing to do with it.

Many goods and services once made in the United States and Western Europe for those markets are now produced elsewhere and transported back to them. That wastes resources spent on the costly relocation and consequent return transportation. The pollution (of air, sea, and soil) associated with vast transportation networks—and the eventual cleaning up of that pollution—only enlarges that waste.

The factories, offices, and stores abandoned by departing capitalist corporations increase the waste of resources and workers' lives. In the surrounding communities, tax bases eroded by capitalists' departures mean reduced social services, public spaces, and qualities of life for all but the richest. Those vast wastes of resources and damages to lives offset whatever small efficiency gains corporate relocations only sometimes achieve.

Corporations rarely count, let alone compensate for, the resources and lives wasted because of their relocation decisions. They only count the benefits to their profits, growth, and market share from moving. Moving is advantageous for them; they neither worry about nor count whether moving is efficient for the economy or society at large.

They simply calculate that they will do better elsewhere than in the United States and Western Europe. Wages elsewhere are far lower. Levels of pollution are allowed that save corporations the environment-protection costs required in Europe and the United States. Bribes or political "contributions" cost less and/or buy more favors, tax breaks, and subsidies there than back home. Efficiency for the economy or society has nothing to do with it: advantage for them is all that matters to them. That is how the system works.

Capitalism's last 250 years in Europe and the United States repeatedly devastated the natural environment and imposed horrific conditions on working people. Multinational corporations are now reproducing that history elsewhere around the globe. China displays some of the most polluted industrial cities on the planet, alongside another "gilded age" of new millionaires. India and Russia display equally stunning inequalities. And so on.

We can and should do better than this kind of global "economic development."

Throughout capitalism's history, major decisions were justified by claims and promises that capitalism failed to realize. When new machinery automated production—saved on labor costs—the gains went chiefly to profits, while the workers, their families, and their communities suffered "technological" unemployment. When capitalists settled into communities "bringing jobs," there followed years of threatening those communities that they would leave if not given incentives such as tax breaks, subsidies, and loans—no matter their costs to the local population. When capitalists dumped toxic wastes into the air, water, and soil—often for generations—massive cleanup costs later were socialized, made everyone's responsibility, while the profits from dumping stayed largely in private hands.

Efficiency was often claimed as the cause or result of capitalist decisions. We heard that greater "efficiency" would mean less labor for the mass of workers. Yet today, US workers do more hours of paid labor per year than the workers of any other country. Their average real wages have declined over the last thirty-five years. Their average standard of living stopped rising since 2007 and rose during the generation before that only because of rising household debt.

Efficiency did not and does not deliver what its supporters claim. That is because efficiency was not and is not what drives capitalists' decisions. The structure of a capitalist economy—exclusive power in the hands of major shareholders and boards of directors; competitions; tensions; and unequal resources among enterprises, shareholders, directors, managers, and workers—drives the decisions made by shareholders and directors. Those decisions primarily advance capitalists' interests in greater profits, growth, and market shares.

A chief defense of capitalists' decisions—that they "bring economic development" to poor countries and regions—is easily rebutted. First, the economic underdevelopment in the former third world was and is partly the result of the colonialism and neocolonialism practiced by capitalists and their governments in Europe, the United States, and Japan. Second, the kind of development now being installed in the former third world replicates the colossal wastes, inequalities, and inhumanities that attended capitalist development in Europe, the United States, and Japan.

Third, a far better approach would be to reorganize Western economies so that they yield far lower inequalities of wealth and income and far less waste of resources than are associated with capitalism. The resulting huge savings could support a different kind of economic development in poorer regions of the world—with, likewise, far lower inequalities of wealth and income, far less waste of resources, and far less inhumanity.

Less inequality among and within societies and increased efficiency that benefits everyone with less work and more or different output: these goals require confronting the capitalist system. The particular capitalist way of organizing how goods and services get produced and distributed and who makes the key decisions is the problem.

What, how, and where to produce and how to use the profits are those key decisions. To serve most people, those decisions must be made by most people. To do that requires converting capitalist enterprises into cooperative enterprises where workers become their own collective board of directors. Workers' self-directed enterprises would be far less likely to relocate production, far less likely to distribute profits among workers in extremely unequal ways, and far less likely to install technologies with negative impacts on the environment in which they, their families, and their communities live.

Democratizing the economy in this way can yield the kinds of economic and social results that capitalism has long promised—but increasingly fails to deliver.

From Detroit to China to Bangladesh: Capitalism's Costs, Capitalists' Freedom

April 2, 2013

Over recent decades, profits and competition drove automobile capitalists to abandon Detroit and move to China. Tears, pain, and costly social suffering have never stopped afflicting Detroit. China thought it could harness capitalism to its needs. Now China is worrying that it, too, will face Detroit-type costs. Therein lies a lesson about capitalism's costs, freedoms, and its "efficiency."

Bloomberg News recently reported that in Wuhan, the capital of China's Hubei Province, the auto factories of Nissan and Honda pay a basic wage of $333 per month. Even lower-tier auto workers in Detroit get $560 per week. No wonder capitalists saw profit gains from moving. But Chinese wages have been rising over recent years because of workers' demands and strikes and because the number of young Chinese workers is shrinking with urbanization and industrialization.

Meanwhile, wages in other Asian locations have not—yet—risen comparably. Average monthly factory wages are $111 in Hanoi, Vietnam; $82 in Phnom Penh, Cambodia; and $78 in Dhaka, Bangladesh. Hong Kong–based bra maker Top Form International closed its Shenzhen, China, factory last year and is expanding production in Phnom Penh. The logic of capitalism has long driven employers to leave the United States, Western Europe, and Japan for the lowest-wage countries elsewhere. It now also impels capitalists in China to do likewise.

Of course, moving from Chicago or Hamburg or Tokyo to Shanghai raised some production costs for capitalists. Products had to be shipped immense distances, loaded and off-loaded, insured and inspected at each point, and so on. Vast energy resources were expended on that transportation, and its attendant pollution and global warming consequences. Far less of those resources were needed when production occurred much closer to final consumption. Only because the extra costs of producing in China were less than their gains from paying low Chinese wages did capitalists move there. Nor did laws compel US capitalists to spend any of those extra profits to help US workers, their families, or their communities devastated by those capitalists' relocation decisions.

Any rational calculation of capitalism's efficiency would have to count not only the profit gains of capitalists but also the livelihood, household, physical and mental health, and myriad other losses resulting from their relocation decisions. Jobs gained in China would be one part of the calculation, but so would jobs lost elsewhere. Modern capitalism allows capitalists to capture the profit gains of relocation decisions; it does not make them compensate for the losses. How nice for the capitalists.

For the last twenty-five years, China—and especially its capitalists—gained a massive inflow of capital and capitalists. It achieved a spectacular industrialization and urbanization in a historically very short time span. Of course, undeveloped and underdeveloped regions of China remain, as they do in the United States and Europe. Where before, capitalism's uneven development hurt Detroit and benefited China, it may soon hurt China, too.

Over the past eight years, the total gap between manufacturing costs in the United States and China has been reduced by half, and it continues to fall. Wages rising much faster in China than in the United States, plus rising transportation and associated costs, explain this. Cheaper wage nations are therefore drawing US, European, and Japanese—but now also Chinese—capitalists away from China. Serious difficulties may confront China in the near future.

After all, China moved hundreds of millions of people from agriculture to industry, from interior to the coast and from countryside to city during the past twenty-five years. They developed new needs, desires, and expectations. What enabled that was a sustained capitalist growth spurt (with immense costs for other parts of the world). Yet that growth spurt changed its own conditions and thereby undermined its future. When profits drive capitalist enterprises out of China, it will discover the other, uncounted side of "capitalist efficiency."

Some defend capitalists' "freedom" to move at will without covering the costs to others of that freedom. They say that when capitalists moved production, as from Detroit to China, consumers got lower prices. The facts are these: (1) lower prices sometimes happened, but often did not, and (2) even when they happened, lower prices rarely lasted very long. The reason for this is clear. Capitalists did not relocate to China primarily to reduce their prices but rather to increase their profits by reducing their costs. While small and often temporary price cuts may accompany relocation, profit considerations sooner or later reassert their primacy. The last twenty-five years of capitalists moving to China have been years of stunning profits for them. The gap between the rich and everyone else in the United States rose dramatically—in part because of capitalists' relocation profits.

With or without price cuts, capitalist relocations occur because they make money for capitalists while their disruptive costs get shifted onto others (the people and communities left behind). The latter might well be better off to prevent relocations or else make capitalists pay the costs of their decisions' collateral damages. But the capitalists would be better off keeping their "freedom" to make relocation decisions and their "freedom" not to cover collateral damages.

So far in the history of capitalism, with important exceptions, capitalist preferences have governed what politicians do. So capitalists leave Detroit for China and then China for Bangladesh. Capitalists' relocation decisions were never about "efficiency." No one ever could or did count all of the social costs and benefits associated with those decisions. No one knows or could know whether the benefits outweigh the costs. Efficiency claims are fiction used to disguise the victory of some social interests over others as if society as a whole had gained. The Detroits of the world—past, present, and future—stand as powerful wake-up calls about the costs of capitalist freedoms and the injustice governing who bears them.

Economic Development in Rana Plaza

May 16, 2013

The official death toll from the April 2013 collapse of the Rana Plaza building in Dhaka, Bangladesh, which housed clothing factories, has passed 1,100. How exactly will the staggering costs of that overwhelming tragedy be figured? Will they count as part of capitalism's contribution to economic development across Asia, Africa, and Latin America?

In capitalism's earlier history, steadily replacing feudalism across Europe from the seventeenth century onward, capitalism became colonialist on a global scale. Most of Asia, Latin America, and Africa were carved into colonial territories whose economies were radically reorganized to serve their European capitalist masters. These reorganizations involved slavery and the slave trade, massive population relocations, destruction of existing industries and their replacement with others, massive loss of life, and so on. Colonies became dependent on a few agricultural or mining exports to their European masters and also often became protected markets for them. The results amounted to the development of underdevelopment. Colonial economies were systematically subordinated to the needs of their colonizers' capitalism. The costs of that subordination, then and since, have been mostly imposed on the subordinated.

Of course, the Europeans who operated colonial capitalism mostly understood it differently. For some of them, colonialism had chiefly to do with missionary work, bringing Christianity to people not yet blessed with its benefits. For others more secularly inclined, Europe was bringing all (or at least most of) the achievements of advanced cultures to backward civilizations. Colonial subjects, they assured themselves, were better off than they had been before European conquerors had arrived.

For over a century now, a massive critical literature interacting with historic movements against colonialism have countered that self-serving image of colonialism's effects. Former colonies and semi-colonial territories (e.g., China) have mostly achieved political independence as the formal empires were overthrown. However, economic underdevelopment of the former colonial territories continued, although changed by new conditions associated with political independence. Bangladesh's tragedy illustrates the process.

After World War II, struggles for independence ended formal colonialism. In subsequent decades, capitalist development in Europe, the United States, and Japan organized a new kind of (independent, postcolonial) underdevelopment in most of Asia, Africa, and Latin America. Alongside continuing exports of raw materials and foods, first manufacturing and later service industries were started or massively expanded in the latter. Mostly these took a capitalist form from the beginning. Where they did not, they eventually shifted over to capitalist forms (mostly private, but sometimes state capitalist enterprises).

The mechanisms and pressures of capitalist competition in what had become a world economy governed the relocation of much capitalist industry to the former colonial countries. One cause was the relatively high level of wages won by the struggles of the working classes in Europe, the United States, and Japan. Capitalists therefore saw increasing competitive advantages to be gained by relocating to the much lower wage levels that colonialism had established in the former colonies. Simultaneously, smaller capitalists in those former colonies competed ferociously for contracts or partnership deals with the larger capitalists arriving from the former colonizing countries.

Globalized capitalist competition destroyed the clothing industries of the former colonizing countries, for example, and relocated them in the former colonies and semi-colonial territories. Thereby, the kind of primitive capitalist industrialization exposed by Charles Dickens in England exploded in Bangladesh, among many other parallel locations. Such awful conditions are often punctuated by catastrophic tragedies such as occurred at Rana Plaza. Meanwhile, the former colonies remain dependent not only on exports to the former colonizing countries but now also on the latter's capital markets, distribution networks, and so on.

Once again, supporters of capitalism everywhere will portray all this otherwise. They will extol the gains brought by capitalist industrialization in former colonies. We will be assured that workers, however poorly paid, housed, and educated, are better off than they would have been without that industrialization. In other words, so terrible was the earlier capitalist colonialism that primitive capitalist industrialization since independence represents progress. US, European, and Japanese consumers will be directed to think about the benefit of lower prices they pay rather than the costs of lost jobs when capitalists relocate to low-wage former colonies and semi-colonial territories.

Twenty-first-century global capitalism thus rests on nineteenth-century conditions for more and more of its core proletariat. The other sides of relocating production to former colonies are the declines of jobs, working conditions, and crises, as well as the austerity policies imposed on working classes in Europe, North America, and Japan. Everywhere, this uneven capitalist development displays growing inequalities of wealth, income, political power, and cultural access. Everyone moves closer to explosive social tensions and conflicts—in China and India as in the United States and Europe.

The issue in global economic development today is not whether former colonies and semicolonial territories have legitimate claims to "help" in their passage from poverty to well-being. Of course they do. The issue is how those claims are to be satisfied. The current method stresses capitalism's competitive investments in the former colonies. A radically changed economic system in the former colonizing countries would enable a different way of satisfying those claims. Suppose a genuine socialist commitment to full employment become policy in the United States and Europe. Suppose further that governments provided capital for workers' cooperatives to be the prevailing organization of state and private enterprises securing that full employment. A good portion of the resulting output could facilitate much better economic development in the former colonies, including support for workers cooperatives there as enterprise organizations.

In the United States, the Federal Reserve reports that 20 percent of productive capacity lies idle. The Bureau of Labor Statistics reports roughly the same percentage of the available labor force as idle. Since the remaining 80 percent produced over $15 trillion in GDP last year, what full employment here could produce and share with the former colonies is huge. Apropos of capitalist "economic development" after Rana Plaza, the appropriate response is TIAA: there is another alternative.

Capitalism, Democracy, and Elections

June 21, 2013

Capitalism and real democracy never had much to do with one another. In contrast, formal voting in elections has worked nicely for capitalism. After all, elections have rarely posed, let alone decided, the question of capitalism: whether voters prefer it or an alternative economic system. Capitalists have successfully kept elections focused elsewhere, on non-systemic questions and choices. That success enabled them first to equate democracy with elections and then to celebrate elections in capitalist countries as proof of their democracy. Of course, even elections were and are allowed only outside capitalist enterprises. Democratic elections inside them—where employees are the majority—never happen.

Real democracy means that important decisions affecting people's lives are made genuinely and equally by the affected people. The capitalist organization of enterprises thus directly contradicts real democracy. Inside the corporations that dominate modern capitalism, a tiny minority—major shareholders and the boards of directors they elect—make key decisions affecting those below them in the corporate hierarchy, the employees. That tiny minority decides what products the corporation will produce, what technologies will be used, where production will occur, and how the corporation's net revenues will be distributed. The majority is affected, often profoundly, by all those decisions, but it does not participate in making them.

Inside typical modern capitalist corporations, real (as well as electoral) democracy is excluded. Societies that celebrate commitment to democracy and justify government policies (including wars) as promoting democracy also exclude democracy from their workplaces. That stark contradiction raises serious problems. Consciously or unconsciously, workers there sense, feel, and express dissatisfactions reflecting that contradiction.

For example, workers sense disrespect descending from corporations' commanding heights. They often feel that their capacities and creativities are unrecognized, unused, and/or devalued. Expressions of such feelings include absenteeism, interpersonal tensions, and job-related dysfunctions (e.g., alcoholism, insubordination, pilfering). The exclusion of democracy from workplaces often provokes workers' resentments and resistances that reduce productivity and profits. Corporations have long responded by hiring multiple layers of costly workplace supervisors and providing big budgets for them. Those corporate expenditures are among the wasteful costs of capitalism: sums deflected from investment, economic growth, technical progress, and other preferable social uses.

Elections outside the workplace stand in an ambivalent relation to capitalism's exclusion of real democracy inside. On the one hand, elections distract people from their conscious and unconscious upsets with working conditions. Elections focus instead on political candidates, parties, and alternative policies around issues other than capitalism versus alternative economic systems and other than their respective working conditions. That is why supporters of capitalism appreciate elections. Well-controlled elections do not question, let alone threaten, capitalism. On the other hand, they always carry a risk, the potential to make big problems for capitalism.

Workers denied democracy on the job may conclude that such crucial problems as inadequate wages, job security, and benefits flow from and are sustained by that denial. Given capitalism's celebratory equation of democracy with elections, workers may then turn toward elections as a way to respond to democracy's absence from the workplace. Knowing they compose the voting majority, workers may see elections as the way to change their economic conditions. Electoral politics may become their route to undo the consequences of a capitalist economic system. The majority could make the issue of choosing between capitalist and democratic workplace organizations a ballot decision. Workers could use elections outside enterprises to finally bring elections and real democracy inside them. Conventional electoral politics leaves that possibility open, a perpetual risk to worry capitalists.

Among solutions found for this problem, capitalists fund candidates and parties in and between election campaigns. In return, elected officials support their funders' desires, especially concerning what is and what is not presented for voters to decide. Capitalist enterprises also fund think tanks, academic programs, mass media, and public relations campaigns that shape public opinion to favor capitalism. In the last half-century, another solution has emerged: keeping the state on the defensive not only ideologically but also financially by means of budget deficits and debts.

For example (and thanks to Doug Korty for this point), the total deficits of the federal government from 1950 to 2009 were $6.6 trillion. During those years, three Republican presidents (Ronald Reagan, George H. W. Bush, and George W. Bush) accounted for the vast majority of those deficits. All the other presidents (Harry Truman, Dwight Eisenhower, John F. Kennedy, Lyndon Johnson, Richard Nixon, Gerald Ford, Jimmy Carter, and Bill Clinton) combined accounted for a small fraction only. The three deficit-happy Republican presidents were the most conservative and sub-servient to major capitalist interests. They all increased spending (chiefly for military and countercrisis purposes) while cutting taxes (especially for corporations and the richest individuals). Such policies forced huge federal deficits and rapid national debt hikes. The Obama administration ran very large deficits and boosted the national debt through huge stimulus outlays and costly wars without offsetting tax increases

The predictable ideological storms followed: (a) federal deficits and debts were defined as the urgent problems, and (b) austerity programs to cut government spending were the appropriate solution. Republicans and Democrats played their predictable roles arguing over the pace, size, and targets of austerity. All their arguments kept the issue of capitalism off the agenda for popular and political debate despite that system's crisis.

When conventional solutions fail and ever more people begin to question, challenge, and oppose capitalism, capitalists generally support police and military repression. In extreme situations, they end electoral democracy by means of military coup, dictatorship, or otherwise. How-ever, ending electoral democracy usually provokes anxiety even among the capitalists who support it. They worry that ending electoral democ-racy provokes social criticism and systemic opposition that can expand to include an undemocratic production system. They do not wish to lose a key benefit of properly controlled elections: distracting workers away from the issue of capitalism per se. Such elections are the cheapest and least dangerous way to secure the distance that capitalism keeps between itself and real democracy.

"Pure" Capitalism Is Pure Fantasy

July 1, 2013

As the global economic meltdown drags most of us through its sixth year, one kind of explanation is heard often and from several sides, including the libertarian right. The crisis since 2007, we are told, is not capitalism's fault or flaw. That is because capitalism is not the system we now have; it is not the systemic problem the world now faces. If only we could "get back to" something like "pure" capitalism, our economic woes would disappear. (Proponents envision "pure" or "real" capitalism as a world of perfect competition among enterprises who are all market price takers [none has the power or size to shape markets], where no advertising enables producers to shape the desires of consumers, where all workers bargain individually for their wages, and so on. It is the capitalism of the introductory economics textbook, the one that seamlessly delivers efficiency, prosperity, and optimal growth.)

Policy prescriptions flow smoothly from this explanation. We must end the bad economic system we now have. "Crony," "gangster," "casino," and "monopoly" are among the adjectives designating today's actually existing—impure—capitalism. It fails to achieve all the progress and prosperity that a pure capitalism would deliver. Those who reason in this way then denounce one or another of the demons they believe to have rendered capitalism impure. Those demons—external and antithetical to pure capitalism—include big government, monopolies, the Federal Reserve, welfare, taxation, and labor unions. Their intrusions interfere with pure capitalism and block its intrinsic efficiency. They prevent economic justice: how pure capitalism would allocate incomes according to each person's and each enterprise's contributions to economic output. Those demonic outside institutions distort economic rewards to favor "special interests." And so the economy and society suffer.

By celebrating pure capitalism, such arguments can criticize the economic crisis without sounding anticapitalist. They reaffirm their loyalty to capitalism in the abstract even as they attack its concrete here and now. The trick is to identify the present system and its enduring, deep crisis as anything but capitalist.

This is fantasy. Impure capitalism is the only kind we have ever had. For example, government always accompanied capitalism. Government often served a rising capitalist class to undermine, defeat, and destroy other classes. In the French Revolution, the rising class of merchants, bankers, and small capitalists captured state power and used it to undermine French feudalism. American revolutionaries took over government from Britain and used it to facilitate the growth of capitalism in the United States in countless ways. Those include the wars on native people and the taking of their land, the enabling and often building of crucial infrastructure (harbors, canals, railways, roadways, and airports), the Civil War and its aftermath, the postal system, the judicial system (police and courts to adjudicate disputes), modern public education, and so on. Capitalism without government is a fantasy.

Likewise, monopolies have always been with capitalism. Each enterprise constantly fears and seeks to block or undermine monopolies within industries from which it must buy inputs. Each enterprise likewise seeks opportunities to organize monopolies for what it sells. The profit motive prompts both behaviors. Competition thus leads to monopoly and vice versa. Capitalism always displays monopolies being erected (competition eroded) and monopolies being dissolved (competition strengthened). A pure capitalism without any monopolies is another fantasy.

The Federal Reserve replaced alternative monetary institutions when and because the latter proved unacceptable for capitalists (among others). Money and credit and their roles within capitalism evolved together with institutions to control or manage them. Every modern capitalist economy has developed a central bank with functions comparable to those of the Federal Reserve. All such central banks serve as well as depend on the larger capitalist economy. Developed or modern capitalism without a central monetary authority is a fantasy.

Capitalism's profit-driven automation and its recurrent business cycles often yielded more workers than there were available jobs. Especially when prolonged and large, unemployment generated suffering, anger, and eventually rebellion. Capitalism's automation and instability, separately or combined, always risked provoking threats to its survival. To limit such threats by easing the suffering, capitalism developed various modes of charity and welfare for the unemployed. Welfare systems are not external intrusions on but rather self-protective outgrowths of and within capitalism's actual functioning. Full employment has been extremely rare in capitalism's history; unemployment was and is the norm. Debates over how much and whose wealth will be diverted to support the unemployed through welfare systems have always agitated capitalism. However, to imagine a pure capitalism without one or another kind of welfare is a delusion.

Finally, capitalism's recurring tendencies toward greater inequality of income and wealth have always and everywhere led to social mechanisms of redistribution. Taxation has been such a mechanism because it almost always functions as more than a means to raise money for government activities. Shifting between more progressive and more regressive tax structures and their enforcement redistributes income and/or wealth as social conditions shift and political tensions permit. Incomes and wealth get redistributed among capitalists and between them and the rest of the population. A pure capitalism without a tax system that redistributes income and wealth is imaginary.

Labor unions, too, are products of capitalism. Workers' problems in capitalist economies have almost universally provoked them to try to form unions. They are not some external institution intruding upon some pure capitalism. Capitalists have always struggled to prevent, destroy, or weaken them. They have never fully succeeded. A pure capitalism without unions is wishful thinking.

Yet such fantasies, delusions, and imaginary scenarios serve ideologically. Beliefs in the possibility and desirability of a "return to pure capitalism" divert people from considering or supporting social change going forward beyond capitalism. Instead, they work to reduce or destroy government, monopolies, the Federal Reserve, tax systems (and agencies like the Internal Revenue Service), the welfare system, and unions. Even when libertarians and others partially achieved such goals, they never thereby solved capitalism's problems. The capitalism that generated those institutions always responded to their partial destruction by regenerating them or variations of them.

The economic crisis and decline most of us are now living through will not be overcome by fantasies of return to some golden age of pure capitalism. We need to push forward, to do better than actually existing capitalism. For the first time in a long time, we can ally with the fast-growing number of people reaching that same conclusion.

How Capitalism's Great Relocation Pauperized America's Middle Class

July 9, 2013

Detroit's struggle with bankruptcy might find some relief, or at least distraction, by presenting its desperate economic and social conditions as a tourist attraction. "Visit Detroit," today's advertisement might begin, "see your region's future here and now: the streets, neighborhoods, abandoned buildings, and the desolation. Scary, yes, but more gripping than any imaginary ghost story."

Detroit, Cleveland, Camden, and many other cities display what capitalism left behind after it became profitable for capitalists to relocate and make their investments elsewhere. Capitalism and its driving profit motive first developed in England before spreading to Western Europe, North America, and then Japan. Over the last two centuries, those areas experienced the mix of horrific working conditions, urban slums, environmental degradation, and cyclical instability that accompanies the rise of capitalism. Capitalism also brought economic growth, wealth for a minority, labor unions, and other workers' organizations. Writers like Charles Dickens, Émile Zola, John Steinbeck, and Maxim Gorky saw capitalism's workings clearly, while those like Karl Marx, John Stuart Mill, and Mikhail Bakunin understood it critically.

Workers' struggles eventually forced capitalists to pay rising wages, enabling higher living standards for large sections of the working classes (so-called middle classes). Capitalists and their economist spokespersons later rewrote that history to suggest instead that rising wages were blessings intrinsic to the capitalist system. How wrong that was, as I describe below.

Capitalists eventually had to reach beyond their original bases in Europe, North America, and Japan to the rest of the world. Capitalism's growth required enlarging its hinterland from the agricultural regions near the industrial centers where modern capitalism began. That initial hinterland had provided food, raw materials, and markets for the commodities flowing increasingly from the growing urban capitalist centers. The hinterland also sent refugees fleeing from declining job opportunities there to work in and crowd those centers.

As capitalist growth accelerated across the eighteenth and nineteenth centuries, more hinterland was required. The response included formal and informal colonialisms that encompassed much of the planet outside its capitalist centers. Capitalism thereby reorganized the whole world's economy to serve as provider of raw materials, food, labor supplies, and markets.

Starting especially in the 1970s, several historical trends coalesced to provoke a massive, historic relocation of capitalists and of capitalism's growth. One trend grew out of a US growth spurt after the war ended in 1945. That spurt renewed capitalists' self-confidence and determination to roll back the New Deal and secure better control of government. They systematically destroyed the social forces (unions, socialists, and communists) that had produced the New Deal and the greatest wave of criticism of capitalism in US history.

Meanwhile, competition among major capitalist countries renewed as Germany and Japan recovered from the war. Capitalists everywhere redoubled efforts to cut costs. Postwar technical revolutions in jet air travel and telecommunications offered competitive advantages to those relocating from older, high-cost production sites to newer, distant, low-cost sites.

At the same time, former formal and informal colonies—recently become relatively more independent nations—also lured capitalists to relocate and invest by offering low wages, tax holidays, subsidies, and other supports. Formerly colonized people were pressing their leaders for significant, sustained increases in mass standards of living. Those leaders' early efforts to use development-oriented government intervention, guided by Keynesian economics, to achieve rapid economic growth had not satisfied those mass pressures.

Across the 1970s, many of those leaders shifted to the neoliberal focus on private capitalist development. This not only represented a strategic change of course but also pandered to the neoliberalism that swept the old capitalist centers at that time.

Different from the earlier colonialism, after the 1970s the private capital that flowed in from capitalist centers in Europe, North America, and Japan did not aim primarily at producing raw materials and food for export. Instead, it increasingly financed the relocation of capitalists and capitalist growth away from the former centers of world capitalism.

Manufacturing moved first, but within two decades, service capitalism joined the exodus. Capital first abandoned the Detroits, Clevelands, and Camdens of the United States. Now, it abandons the country more generally. Similar moves afflict the more developed countries in Europe and Japan as well, although in ways that reflect their different histories, including the greater strengths of their working-class organizations. Even Germany, despite its special price, legal, and other advantages within the European Union, confronts growing pressures from German capitalists relocating to places with lower wages, benefits, and government social services.

Capitalism is now reconfiguring centers and their hinterlands on a truly global scale. The United States increasingly approaches the formerly "third world" pattern of a few centers surrounded by vast layers of more or less desperate hinterland dwellers. In the language of US politics, its "middle class" disappears.

Capitalism's great relocation places a remarkable political question on history's agenda today: can the system survive its relocation?

Capitalism grew successfully in its old centers despite working-class oppositions, expressed by labor unions, socialist and communist parties, anticapitalist intellectuals and artists, and the resistances of its colonized subordinates. Part of that success—a basis of its 200-year global hegemony—was the ability of its working classes to wrest rising wages and/or standards of living.

In sharp contrast, capitalism's great relocation now under way both presses and enables capitalists to cease raising wages and standards of living in its former, old centers (Europe, North America, and Japan). Indeed, it is lowering them.

Competition requires capitalists to raise wages instead in the newer, growing centers, where new sections of better-paid workers arise.

Will capitalism in its old centers of North America, Europe, and Japan be able to hold the grudging support of their working classes, as it now delivers long-term declines of wages, working conditions, and living standards? Can capitalism achieve the social acceptance in the new centers that its first 200 years found in the old centers?

Even if it can, the working classes in the old centers may soon withdraw their traditional acceptance. If they do, we can expect monumental social struggles pitting supporters against opponents of capitalism.

US Political Dysfunction and Capitalism's Withdrawal

October 27, 2013

After 200 years of concentrating its centers in Western Europe, North America, and Japan, capitalism is moving most of its centers elsewhere and especially to China, India, Brazil, and so on. This movement poses immense problems of transition at both poles. The classic problems of early, rapid capitalist industrialization are obvious daily in the new centers. What we learn about early capitalism when we read Charles Dickens, Émile Zola, Maxim Gorky, and Jack London, we see again in the new centers.

The October 2013 shutdown of the US government teaches us new lessons about what is happening to the increasingly abandoned old centers of capitalism. Similar lessons flow from the long, painful economic crises now besetting Western Europe and Japan. In the simplest terms, these old centers of capitalism are suffering the effects of capitalism's withdrawal.

The causes of withdrawal are well known. In the century before 1970, it became quite clear that the long history of class struggles inside the old centers of capitalism had produced a basic compromise. Capitalists retained their nearly total control over enterprise decisions: what to produce, how to produce, where to produce, and what to do with the profits. Employees, in exchange for ceding that control, obtained rising real wages. Over the same period, capitalists reorganized the world economy (through formal and informal colonialisms) to serve as the "hinterland" for the capitalist centers in Western Europe, North America, and Japan.

That hinterland provided the food, raw materials, migrant laborers, and part of the market for those old capitalist centers. Real wages in that hinterland stagnated or fell.

In the 1970s, the gap between real wages in the old capitalist centers and those in the hinterland had become enormous. At the same time, the development of jet engines and modern telecommunications opened new opportunities for capitalists in the old centers. Their response is transforming the world. Those capitalists realized that they could manage production and distribution facilities almost anywhere in the world as easily as before they had managed facilities within their town, cities, and countries. The more competitive among them moved quickly to take advantage of the much lower real wages in the hinterland by moving old facilities or establishing new facilities there. The laggards are quickly following to avoid competitive destruction.

Capitalism is establishing new centers and withdrawing from many of the old. Indeed, "withdrawal" does not capture the extent of the movement. For example, Detroit, Michigan, was the center of the US automobile industry in 1960 with a population of just under 2 million. Today it is a bankrupt city with a population of under 700,000. Its decline since the 1970s mirrors that of Cleveland, Ohio; Camden, New Jersey; and many other formerly thriving capitalist centers where "withdrawal" needs to be replaced by "abandoned."

Among the social effects of capitalism's withdrawal from many old capitalist centers in the United States are rapidly widening wealth and income inequalities there. These in turn provoke rising tensions within and between the two major political parties and a growing disaffection of the population with political leadership in general. The US government shutdown in October 2013 and the acrimony afflicting US politics reflect capitalism's withdrawal and its social effects.

The consequence of political dysfunction (on top of the crises that punctuate capitalism's withdrawal) is to reinforce that withdrawal. The October shutdown and the ongoing stalemate over the national debt ceiling and federal budgets are events that force corporations, wealthy individuals, and central banks to rethink the proportions of their portfolios held in US-based assets. Comparable rethinking affects the proportions allocated to Western Europe and Japan. The last half-century's net flows of wealth into the old capitalist centers—that supported their economies—are being and likely will continue to be cut back or reversed.

Those old centers simply can no longer function as the safest havens for the world's wealth. However problematic the new capitalist centers, diversifying risk prompts the continuing withdrawal of capitalism from the old centers. Economic conditions in those old centers will suffer.

Beyond the economic consequences of continuing withdrawal, the political effects will likely be more pronounced and visible. The old political compromise will no longer be honored. Capitalists withdrawing from the old centers need not and will not pay rising real wages there. Indeed, they have not done so for several decades. For a while, household and government debt increases postponed the effects of those stagnant or falling real wages. Because the credit bubble built on that debt burst in 2007, North America, Western Europe, and Japan now face the full force of a withdrawing capitalism without the debt cushion. That means fewer and/or poorer jobs at shrinking pay levels with fewer benefits and reduced government-provided services. Will workers accept a capitalism that preserves all the power and income ceded to capitalists while ending the workers' compensation of rising real wages?

Europe has had more general strikes in the last three years than at any time since the Great Depression. The Occupy movement grew very quickly and commanded majority mass support. Its activists are learning the lessons of their movement and will respond to conditions that are mostly worse now than when Occupy began in September 2011.

The withdrawal from so many of its old centers and establishing so many new centers—on a global scale—is a new experience for the capitalist system. It homogenizes the conditions for workers across countries even as it sharply deepens inequalities in both the old and new capitalist centers. It differs from such experiences when they happened within countries or regions. It is an open question whether and how the system can manage the process. New contradictions are emerging that promise new crises, political as well as economic.

Capitalism and Unemployment

November 15, 2013

Capitalism as a system seems incapable of solving its unemployment problem. It keeps generating long-term joblessness, punctuated by spikes of recurring short-term extreme joblessness. The system's leaders cannot solve or overcome the problem. Before the latest capitalist crisis hit in 2007, the unemployment rate was near 5 percent. In 2013, it is near 7.5 percent. That is 50 percent higher despite the last six years of policies claiming to address unemployment.

Capitalism makes employment depend chiefly on capitalists' decisions to undertake production, and those decisions depend on profits. If capitalists expect profits high enough to satisfy them, they hire. If capitalists don't, the result is unemployment. Capitalism requires the unemployed, their families, and their communities to live with firing decisions made by capitalists even though they are excluded from participating in those decisions. The United States revolted against Britain partly because it rejected being victimized by tax decisions from which it was excluded. Yet employment decisions are at least as important as tax decisions.

Unemployment has three dimensions that often escape public discussion, perhaps because they raise such fundamental questions about the capitalist system. The first dimension concerns the immense losses for society from the kind of unemployment that capitalism reproduces and that we experience today. According to the Bureau of Labor Statistics, the sum of unemployed people, "marginal" workers (those who stopped looking for work), and involuntarily part-time workers (the "underemployed") is roughly 14 percent of the labor force. That is 20 million of our fellow citizens. Alongside that statistic, the Federal Reserve reports that 20 percent of our "industrial capacity" (tools, equipment, raw materials, floor space in factories, offices, and stores, etc.) is sitting idle, wasted, not being used to produce goods and services. Capitalists make the decisions to not hire those millions of workers and to not buy, lease, or use all that industrial capacity.

Capitalists make those decisions based on what is privately profitable for them, not on what is lost to society. And that loss is huge. A simple calculation based on the numbers above proves the point. We as a nation forgo about 15 percent of extra output of goods and services because of unemployed people and idled tools, equipment, and so on. That comes to roughly $2 trillion per year. Yes, you read that correctly. We could produce an annual extra output far greater than the government's budget deficit ever was. We could use that extra to reduce global poverty by more than what has been done by all advanced industrial nations for decades. In short, we have taken staggering losses for our planet because we are trapped within an economic system that permits employment decisions to be held hostage to capitalists' profit calculations.

The second dimension of unemployment is the actual costs it imposes on society, costs not borne entirely, or even chiefly, by the capitalists whose decisions determine unemployment. A partial list of such costs includes additional government expenditures for unemployment compensation, food stamps, welfare supports, and stimulus programs. Since the current capitalist crisis began in 2007, these costs are already in the trillions of dollars. It is also well known and documented that rising unemployment is positively correlated with rising physical and mental health problems, alcoholism, family disintegration, urban decline, and so on. Public and private resources are expended to cope with these problems aggravated by unemployment. These resources come from the public much more than from the capitalists whose private decisions produced most of the unemployment. Capitalism socializes unemployment's immense costs.

The third dimension of unemployment concerns how capitalism distributes unemployment among workers. In the United States, when capitalists decide to reduce employment because that is the most profitable decision for their individual, private enterprises, the question is: How will that unemployment be managed? The answer we see most often is that individual capitalists choose which individual employees they will fire. Thus in today's United States, capitalists have selected most of the 7.5 percent of our people who are unemployed or underemployed. These they have condemned to full-time unemployment or reduced to unwanted part-time work.

An alternative option would manage unemployment by reducing everyone's work week by 7.5 percent, or roughly three hours out of a week's forty hours. Every worker would then have three hours of extra leisure for which no pay would be received. Instead, the saved money would be used to hire the 7.5 percent of workers who no longer need to be fired. Their work would substitute for the three hours lost from every other worker's week. In this way, unemployment would be shared by everyone and not imposed on a minority selected by capitalists.

Of course, capitalists oppose this alternative option. It costs them the benefits that have to be provided to all workers—more than if they could withhold benefits from fired workers (the usual practice). More important, if unemployment were shared, the injustice and waste of it would be driven home personally to every worker by his/her reduced hours and reduced pay. Right-wing ideologies would then find it harder to blame the unemployed for their joblessness. It would also make it easier to persuade and mobilize all workers to fight unemployment as their common enemy. Finally, it could help spark the long-overdue debate over the social benefits and costs of more work and output versus more leisure and less pressure on our natural resources and environment.

Capitalists defend their "right" to hire and fire as an "entitlement" that cannot be questioned. Yet it surely should be challenged on grounds of its undemocratic nature and its perverse social results. Employing people in socially useful work (however a democratic society might define that) is more humane to the individuals, families, and communities involved and more productive and less costly than rendering them unemployed. Yet a private profit-driven capitalist system yields the endless unemployment, spiking repeatedly, that society does not want. Except, of course, capitalists—they want it because it keeps them at the top of capitalist society.

Capitalism and Democracy: Year-End Lessons

December 18, 2013

The year 2013 drove home a basic lesson: US capitalism's economic leaders and their politicians now regularly ignore majority opinions and preferences. For example, polls showed overwhelming popular support for higher taxes on the rich with lower taxes on the rest of us and for reversing the nation's deepening economic inequalities. Yet Republicans and Democrats, including President Obama, raised payroll taxes sharply on January 1, 2013. Those taxes are regressive; they take a smaller percentage of your income the higher your income is above $113,700 per year. Raising the payroll tax increased economic inequality across 2013.

For another example, many US cities and towns want to use eminent domain laws to help residents keep their homes and avoid foreclosure. Eminent domain is a hallmark democratic right as well as US law. It enables municipal governments to buy individual properties (at market prices) when doing so benefits the community as a whole. Using eminent domain, local leaders want to compel lenders (e.g., banks) to sell them homes whose market prices have fallen below the mortgage debts of their occupants. They would then resell those homes at their market prices to their occupants. With their mortgages thus reduced to their homes' actual prices, occupants could stay in them. They still suffer their homes' fallen values but avoid homelessness. Communities benefit because decreased homelessness reduces the fall of other property values, the number of abandoned homes (and thus risks of fire, crime, etc.), and the number of customers lost to local stores; and it sustains property tax flows to local governments and so on.

Used this way, eminent domain forces lenders—chiefly banks—to share more of the pains produced by capitalism's crisis. Most Americans support that, believing it will help reverse income and wealth inequalities and also that banks bear major responsibility for the economic crisis.

Yet the country's biggest banks are using "their" money and laws (that they often wrote) to block municipalities' use of eminent domain. "Their" money includes the massive bailouts Washington provided to them since 2007. Big bank directors and major shareholders—a tiny minority—fund the politicians, parties, and think tanks that oppose municipalities' use of eminent domain. In these ways, capitalism systematically undermines democratic decision making about economic affairs.

For yet another example, bankruptcy court decisions about Detroit allow the city to cut retired city workers' pensions. Those workers bargained and signed contracts with Detroit's leaders over many years. They accepted less in wages and benefits in exchange for their pensions as parts of their agreed compensation for work performed. Now that an economic crisis and the unemployment it generated have cut Detroit's tax revenues, this system's "solution" includes cutting retired workers' pensions. Other cities are expected to adopt this solution. Inequality worsens as the costs of this economic crisis shift from lenders to cities (usually rich) to retired city-worker pensioners (never rich).

In these and other ways, 2013 taught millions of Americans that capitalism repeatedly contradicts the democratic idea that majority decisions should govern society as a whole. The system's tendency toward deepening inequalities of income and wealth operated across 2013 in direct contradiction to the will of substantial American majorities.

The same happened in the decades before the Great Depression of the 1930s. However, in that Depression, a mass movement from below (organized by the Congress of Industrial Organizations [CIO] and socialist and communist parties) successfully reversed capitalism's tendencies toward inequality. Supported by majorities of Americans, it was strong enough to obtain Social Security, unemployment compensation, and millions of federal jobs for the people whom private capitalists could not or would not employ. Those programs helped average people rather than bailing out banks and other large corporations. That movement also got the government to pay for those programs by taxing corporations and the rich at far higher rates than exist now. Capitalism's deepening inequality was partly reversed by and because of a massive democratic movement.

However, that movement stopped short of ending capitalism. Thus, it only temporarily reversed capitalism's tendencies toward inequality. After World War II, business, the rich, and conservatives mobilized a return to "capitalism as usual." They organized a massive government repression of the coalition (CIO, socialists, and communists) that led the 1930s movement from below. Key moments of that repression were the 1947 Taft-Hartley Act that prohibited Communist Party members from being union officers and the broad anticommunist crusades epitomized by Senator Joseph McCarthy that lasted well into the 1950s. By such means, capitalism resumed its development of ever-greater economic inequalities, especially after 1970. In the great recession since 2007, the absence of a sustained movement from below has allowed inequality to worsen as our examples above illustrate.

The lessons of recent history include this: To secure democratic decision making and the kind of society most Americans want requires moving beyond capitalism. Capitalism's difficulties (including its crises and inequalities) and its control of government responses to those difficulties keep teaching that lesson. The widening gap between democratic needs and impulses and the imperatives of capitalism is becoming clear to millions in the United States but also in other countries.

For example, the Rajoy government in Spain imposed new levels of repression on the strengthening protests against its austerity policies. Spain's unemployment rate today exceeds the US rate in the worst year of the Depression. Rajoy wants fines of up to $40,000 for offenses such as burning the national flag, insulting the state, or causing serious disturbances outside Parliament. Indeed, some fines go up to $800,000 for demonstrations that "interfere" in electoral processes.

Contradictions between democratic rights and demands and the processes of capitalism are accelerating into clashes in legislatures and the streets. Informed by history's lessons about capitalism and democracy, today's movements more likely will recognize the need to confront and supersede capitalism to secure real democracies. Policies that achieve only temporary reversals of capitalist inequalities no longer suffice. The system's imperatives to profit, compete, and grow are now so costly to so many that its critics and opponents are multiplying fast. Once they confront and solve the problem of politically organizing themselves, social change will happen fast, too.

Political Corruption and Capitalism

February 2, 2014

Nearly daily, mass media report political corruption across the world. Government bureaucrats, from local to national to international, are exposed for having abused their offices for personal gain. That gain is usually financial but can involve career advancement. Much of that corruption is driven and financed by capitalist enterprises. In that kind of corruption, officials enable tax avoidance, provide subsidies, make purchases and sometimes sales, and decide many other "public" matters (e.g., locating roads, zoning cities, constructing state facilities, repressing strikes, investigating corruption, negotiating international agreements).

Official decisions are corrupt when they aim (in exchange for personal gain) exclusively or chiefly to benefit individual firms or groups of enterprises rather than any broad social or public purpose. Corruption can be illegal (when prohibitive laws apply) or legal if such laws were repealed or never passed. Political corruption, when not hidden or secret, occurs under a protective cover (or disguise) as if done for public purposes or benefits.

What chiefly drives this sort of political corruption today is capitalism's structure. For many capitalist enterprises, competitive and other pressures exist to increase profits, growth rates, and/or market share. Their boards and top managers seek to find cheaper produced inputs and cheaper labor power, to extract more output from their workers, to sell their outputs at the highest possible prices, and to find more profitable technologies. The structure provides them with every incentive of financial gain and/or career security and advancement to behave in those ways. Thus, boards and top managers seek the maximum obtainable assistance of government officials in all these areas and also try to pay the least possible portion of their net revenues as taxes. Boards of directors tap their corporations' profits to corrupt mostly the top echelons of the government bureaucracy, those needed to make advantageous official decisions.

Individual capitalists act to corrupt government officials to serve their enterprise's needs. Grouped into associations, they do likewise for their industries. When organized as a whole (e.g., in "chambers of commerce" or "manufacturer alliances"), they corrupt to secure their class interests. When such corruption is not secret, capitalists articulate their demands to corrupted officials as "good for the economy or society as a whole." Such phrases constitute the "appropriate language" that enables officials publicly to disguise and hopefully legitimate their corrupt acts.

Strict moral codes, regulations, and laws have been imposed to prevent individual or grouped capitalists from corrupting government officials. Evidence suggests, however, that neither civic-minded ethics, nor regulations, nor laws have come close to ending capitalists' corruption. Countless government courts and commissions have hardly ended official complicities in that corruption. Mainstream economics mostly proceeds in its analyses and policy prescriptions as if rampant corruption did not exist. Mass media tend to treat capitalist corruption (at least in their home countries) as exceptional and government efforts to stop it as serious. These, too, are further examples of that "appropriate language" with which modern capitalist societies mask systemic corruption.

To reduce corruption from its current high levels requires something more than, and different from, additional laws, commissions, invocations of morality, regulations, and so on. It requires basic, structural economic change. Earlier reforms achieved little success because they ignored the very idea or possibility of such change. They left untouched capitalism's basic incentive structure and capitalists' power to use enterprise profits for corrupt purposes. Capitalists have continued to face all the benefits and gains that corrupted officials can yield (plus the risks and costs of failing to corrupt them). Capitalists have likewise continued to amass ever-larger profits and thus the funds with which to corrupt.

One structural way to reduce corruption would be to democratize enterprises, to reorganize them such that the workers collectively direct the enterprises. Such an economic democratization would render all aspects of the relationship between enterprise and government transparent to all enterprise employees and thereby to a larger public. Hiding and disguising corruption would be much more difficult. Compliance with regulations and laws prohibiting the corruption of officials would likely find at least some support among democratized enterprises' decision makers. Those enterprises would require open discussion and majority decision making. Minorities could more easily acquire the knowledge needed to criticize and influence decisions and thus prevent or reduce using enterprises' net revenues to corrupt government officials.

Ending the capitalist organization of enterprises still leaves the problem of incentives for workers—even in workers' self-directed enterprises—to seek to corrupt government officials. The appropriate step to solve that problem would involve making the democratized enterprises and a genuinely democratized politics (of residence-based government at all levels) interdependent. Governmental decisions would need to be ratified by the democratized enterprises affected by those government decisions. Likewise, democratized enterprise decisions would need to be ratified by the affected democratized governmental institutions.

Then any effort by one or a group of workers' self-directed enterprises to obtain corrupt decisions from officials would activate other workers' self-directed enterprises—hurt or disadvantaged by those decisions—to object. And their objections would have effective teeth given the power-sharing relationship between enterprises and government. This is a way to interrupt the social irrationality of corruption—whereby one or a group of enterprises gains a corrupt advantage at the expense of others, who are thereby provoked to do likewise, thereby generating systemic corruption. The end result is—as capitalism's history shows—an economy that best serves those who can most effectively corrupt and be corrupted.

In effect, legislatures would be reconstructed as bicameral—but in a new sense. One chamber would be enterprise-based, while the other would be residence-based. The key checks and balances of such a system could reasonably be expected to reduce political corruption relative to anything so far attempted. Such a structural change could well outperform the long list of anticorruption reforms that were so often smokescreens to avoid the basic economic changes needed.

The Wages of Global Capitalism

December 8, 2014

Wage growth in the world slowed to an average of 2 percent in 2013. That was less than in 2012 and far less than the precrisis rate of 3 percent. Starker still were the differences between wage growth in the "developed world" (chiefly Western Europe, North America, and Japan) and wage growth in the major "emerging growth" countries, chiefly China.

In the "developed world" wage growth in 2012 was 0.1 percent, and in 2013 it was 0.2 percent. Far from portending any economic "recovery," that level of wage "growth" is called "wage stagnation." In stunning contrast, wage growth in the major emerging growth economies (e.g., China, India, and Brazil) was much better: 6.7 percent in 2012 and 5.9 percent in 2013.

These remarkable statistics come from the "Global Wage Report 2014/15," released on December 5, 2014, by the International Labour Organization (ILO). This report clearly exposes the immense costs of a globalizing capitalism for the wage-earning majorities in Western Europe, North America, and Japan. Allowing their leading capitalists to maximize profits by relocating production out of those regions is deeply and increasingly destructive to them.

Figure 2 summarizes the key wage results of the last decade's capitalism. Economic growth, rising real wages, and rising standards of living are realities in China and other emerging growth countries. Economic crisis, stagnant wages, and declining working and living standards are the realities for Western Europe, the United States, and Japan.

Capitalist enterprises keep moving their operations (first manufacturing, now also many services) from high- to low-wage regions of the world to raise their profits. Departing capitalists leave their former host communities with unemployment and all its social costs. Such conditions force desperate competition for jobs that drives down wages and guts job benefits. Public services decline as government budgets suffer. Capitalism no longer delivers a rising standard of living in the regions where it began and developed first: Western Europe, North America, and Japan. Instead of goods, capitalism delivers the bads.

A second key insight emerges from another chart (Figure 3) in the ILO report. In the developed countries, while real wages stagnated throughout the crisis since 2007, the productivity of workers continued to rise. That explains the deepening inequalities of income and wealth in those countries.

Productivity measures the quantity of goods and services that workers' labor provides to their bosses. The chart shows how labor productivity has kept rising (because of computers, more equipment, better training, speed-up of work, etc.). The chart also shows how much less wages have risen. Wages are what capitalists pay workers for their labor.

Figure 2. Annual Average Global Real Wage Growth, 2006–2013

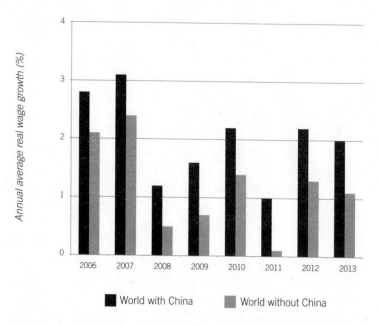

Note: Global wage growth is calculated as a weighted average of year-on-year growth in average monthly real wages in 130 countries, covering 95.8 percent of all employees in the world. Source: International Labour Organization, "Global Wage Report 2014/15: Wages and Income Inequality" (Geneva: Author, 2015), Figure 2, p. 5; available at http://bit.ly/1yv1DaM.

There is thus a growing gap between what workers give capitalists (productivity) and what capitalists give workers (wages). That gap measures profits. They have grown the fastest of all. Major capitalist corporations gather those exploding profits into their hands. They pay their top executives huge salaries and bonuses, pay rich dividends, and deliver huge capital gains to their shareholders. Those top executives and major shareholders are most of the super-rich who have taken so much of the nation's wealth.

Figure 3. Trends in Growth in Average Wages and Labor Productivity in Developed Economies (Index: 1999 = 100)

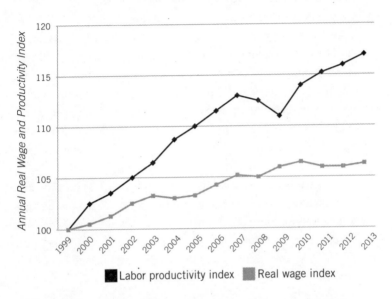

Labor productivity index   Real wage index

Note: Wage growth is calculated as a weighted average of year-on-year growth in average monthly real wages in 36 economies. Index is based to 1999 because of data availability. Data are from International Labour Organization (ILO), Global Wage Database; www.ilo.org/gwr-figures; ILO *Trends Econometric Models*, April 2014. Source: International Labour Organization, "Global Wage Report 2014/15: Wages and Income Inequality" (Geneva: Author, 2015), Figure 7, p. 8; available at http://bit.ly/1yv1DaM.

European, US, and Japanese politicians, controlled by their major capitalists, do little to stop the relocation of production that generates the results seen in the figures above. Labor and anticapitalist movements are still too weak, too divided, or too poorly informed to stop the long-term decline under way.

The real question of the day underscored by the ILO report is this: Will Western European, North American, and Japanese working people consent to the further undermining of their well-being that follows as capitalists leave for higher profits? That is the question even though mainstream politicians, media, and academics cannot see it or refuse to discuss it.

The answer to that question can still be "no." The labor, anticapitalist, and social movements can understand this situation. They could ally politically to stop paying the horrendous costs of globalizing capitalism while a tiny minority grabs its ballooning profits.

A final note: Real wages are still three times higher in developed countries than in economically emerging regions. Thus, capitalists keep getting the higher profits that motivate their relocation out of Western Europe, North America, and Japan. They share some of those higher profits (through mergers, acquisitions, bribes, etc.) with major local capitalist corporations inside the regions to which they relocate. Relocating capitalists offer such payoffs to facilitate their success in these new centers of capitalism's growth.

Those payoffs help explain the gross inequalities of income and wealth deepening in the emerging economies, too. Globalizing capitalism thus imposes on most countries the worsening inequalities that bring ever closer the validity of that old slogan (premature when first articulated): "Workers of the world unite; you have nothing to lose but your chains."

Part II: Crisis Economics

*Capitalist crises always shake and worry the system's defenders. Massive un-
employment, failing businesses, and shrinking job security and benefits are
crisis realities experienced or observed by everyone but the richest few (and
their apologists) who can insulate themselves. Among the system's defenders
are the mainstream economists, mostly products of academic training in economics departments or business schools.*

*Much of the work of such economists strives to show that the crisis is not
systemic. Rather, it has one or another particular cause (too big a financial
sector, Federal Reserve policies, lax regulation, globalization, neoliberalism,
and so on) that can be identified and dealt with. Such economists then offer
solutions to correct those defects of the system. Other economists stress that
the crisis is merely a hiccup on an otherwise healthy trajectory of economic
growth. Still others work to show that blame for the crisis lies entirely with
government actions. They insist that the capitalist economy would work better and avoid crises if only government intervention in economic affairs
would shrink or even disappear.*

*Another group of economists is willing to acknowledge many of the costs
and victims of the crisis. This group even points a critical finger at the big
banks, large corporations, and inadequate government regulators as joint causes of the speculative bubble that burst in 2007 and took the whole economy
down. They then argue that new reforms enacted into laws and regulations
provide a way to exit this crisis and prevent future crises.*

*The appropriate economic policies to be applied by government to the
crisis has everywhere been a major focus of economists. Terms like "stimulus"*

73

and "austerity," central to public discussion, are prime examples. The positions most economists take on those policies emerge from their places in the mainstream profession's broad effort (explicit or implicit, conscious or not) to keep discussions of the crisis from moving to question and challenge capitalism as an economic system.

The essays in Part II explore this range of antisystemic positions taken by mainstream economics. Taken together, the essays represent a sustained critique of what might be called "mainstream crisis economics." They offer an alternative that focuses precisely on how and why the deepening crisis is rooted in the basic structures and mechanisms of capitalism and in the historical shifts it is currently undergoing.

AUSTERITY

US Tax Deal Brings Austerity Closer

December 17, 2010

Once again, the two old wings of the political establishment do business as usual in Washington. In the tax deal passed today between President Obama and the Republicans—passed with the help of a majority of Democrats—cut taxes, especially on the rich, and extended unemployment benefits. In short, the government keeps spending mountains of money to subsidize a deeply recessional private capitalist economy, to prevent it from spiraling down into depression. The result is a further expansion of the deficit that so recently was a pretend concern for so many candidates.

The establishment pandered to corporations and the rich with lower taxes. To win the necessary broader support, it also pandered more modestly to everyone else with tax cuts. Therefore, even more of government spending will now have to be borrowed. Big businesses and the rich will oblige by lending the US government much of the money the government has decided not to take from them in taxes. So will enterprises, rich people, and governments in other countries. All Americans will need to pay yet more billions in taxes in the years ahead to pay interest to all those lenders. That is, all Americans will pay more taxes to service the small minority of Americans rich enough to lend to an ever-more debt-dependent Uncle Sam.

Soon enough, the political establishment will come under pressure from all those who do not want to pay those rising taxes. Then the cry will go up that "we" cannot afford the public services the government provides. So pressure will mount to cut Social Security, Medicare, college student loan supports, and so on. The mass of Americans will be told they must choose between higher taxes or fewer services. It will be neatly repressed or forgotten that today's tax cuts coupled with massive crisis-caused government spending bear much of the blame for the government's costs in servicing its debt explosion.

Maybe then the establishment will yet again evade the political costs of facing that choice and postpone it by another round of borrowing. This can continue until lenders will no longer risk further loans without much higher interest costs. They will then demand an "austerity" program to free up and earmark the money that must be paid to lenders. That's exactly what those lenders have been doing to Greece and Ireland and are threatening for many other countries. Austerity arrives when the mass of people is taxed more and served less by a government that instead pays out ever more of its scarce resources to the richest enterprises and citizens among them. What is conveniently forgotten is that those enterprises and wealthiest citizens became the government's creditors each and every time the government chose not to tax them instead.

With its huge and rapidly growing debts—made worse by President Obama's tax deal with Republicans—the United States moves quickly toward austerity while the political establishment and the media mostly pretend all is well. That was the same path followed by Greece, Ireland, and so many others.

Main Street Moves against Wall Street

March 28, 2011

When the current economic crisis hit, the Obama campaign blew away George W. Bush and John McCain by promising hope, change, and a solution that would overcome this crisis and prevent future crises. Likewise, some governments in Europe came to power based on public fear reacting to the global meltdown. Ongoing crisis, mass economic pain, and deepening public anger keep shifting political winds.

Within six months of Barack Obama's election, those winds had changed again. His liberal campaign rhetoric had hit a wall. What humbled Obama was the determination of business interests to shift onto others the costs of the crisis and of the government's response, namely, its hugely expensive bailout of major corporations, especially in finance. We watched and learned who was really in charge of how this economic crisis would be "managed."

There would not be a 2011 rise in the federal income tax rate from 35 to 39 percent for the richest Americans (even though it had been 91 percent in the 1960s). There would be no legal or other requirement that corporate beneficiaries use their bailout billions in economically and socially useful ways (rather than only for their private profits). There would be no federal employment program, no matter how high the US unemployment rate went, nor how long workers remained unemployed. There would be no real program to lift wages or otherwise offset millions of homeowners' inability to make mortgage payments even if that omission meant that the housing market would tank again. The double dip downward in that crucial industry is now under way.

US governments at all levels (city, state, and federal) dared not raise taxes on businesses or the rich—even as their general tax revenues fell because of unemployment and consequent reductions in incomes and consumers' expenditures. The federal government also slowed its borrowing. Reduced taxes plus reduced borrowings cut the funds all governments had to spend. Political leaders mostly responded by curtailing employees (worsening unemployment) and social services. Federal officials justified no more borrowing by pointing to the trillions added to the national debt since 2007 to finance Washington's "crisis response" program. State and local officials just restated the usual homilies about "living within our means"—as if doing so would alleviate the problems caused by the economic crisis.

The truth is that business interests prefer cuts in social programs over further government borrowing. They fear public resentment over paying higher taxes in order to allow governments to pay more interest to the owners of government bonds. Resentment can grow into active political resistance. After all, the public wants its taxes to fund programs that help people rather than flow to government creditors. And there's the problem. Uncle Sam's creditors include US businesses and the richest US citizens who used the money they did not pay in taxes to lend to the government instead.

So the US economy continues to impose crisis conditions on the mass of citizens. The "recovery" is limited to banks, larger corporations, and those with significant holdings of stocks and bonds. The latter recovered as banks and larger corporations parked their bailout moneys in stock markets (rather than investing them in production, since mass purchasing power in the United States remained hobbled and looks likely to remain so indefinitely). Rage at continued economic suffering (high unemployment, home foreclosures, etc.), mass exclusion from "recovery," and the spectacle of the richest US citizens continuing to draw huge salaries and bonuses brought public anger to the boiling point. Its target was especially whoever was in office: President Obama, associated Democrats, and many incumbent politicians who suffered the consequences in the 2010 elections.

In Europe, the costs of capitalism's crisis and corporate bailouts by governments have also been shifted onto the general population, where they too have "austerity" now. Just as business demands for that shift bent President Obama to their will here, they bent prime ministers there, including ostensibly socialist politicians such as Papandreou in Greece and Socrates in Portugal. It seemed everywhere that business and the rich would be able to achieve stunning results. Their thirty-year profit binge (1977–2007) and mixtures of tax cuts, low taxes, and state subsidies for corporations and the rich would remain unquestioned and untapped. Their disastrous speculations with those profits, the gross irresponsibility in how banks invested depositors' money, and the widening gaps between the very rich and everyone else would fade from public awareness and from most politicians' concerns.

But as the economic crisis continues for majorities in the United States and Europe, current office-holders are held accountable for government layoffs and service reductions.[5] As those austerity policies further damage standards of living and fail to overcome economic suffering, public anger refocuses upon the current incumbents. Political leaders executing the business strategy of socializing the costs of the crisis find themselves in trouble. Governor Scott Walker in Wisconsin faces a far stronger opposition than anyone foresaw. Ohio conservative Republican state senator Bill Seitz mobilizes fellow Republicans to shrink the state's austerity program, fearing "voter backlash."

Portugal's socialist government collapsed last week. All other political parties refused to support its latest installment of the austerity program imposed on the Portuguese people. Recent massive protests against austerity and strikes for higher wages made their points. Continued association with business's austerity strategy is becoming too costly for more and more politicians. They must find new faces, forms, or excuses to continue austerity; otherwise, they will suffer or be forced to defect as public opinion swings behind very different anticrisis policies.

Such policies could shift the burden and costs of overcoming the economic crisis onto the larger corporations and the richest citizens. Indeed, such policies might well go further and change the system that keeps bringing us these crises and breaking its defenders' promises to prevent more crises. To the extent that they significantly alleviate the burdens of austerity, such policies might win the time and political space to achieve those larger goals.

Why Capitalism Is Choosing Plan B

August 22, 2011

Last week, Democratic governors in New York and Connecticut repeated the austerity politics of Prime Minister George Papandreou of Greece and former Prime Minister José Socrates of Portugal. In doing so, they

---

5. Caroline Davies and Polly Curtis, "Anti-Cuts Protest: Police Arrest More Than 200 after Outbreaks of Violence," *Guardian*, March 27, 2011.

likewise imitated the austerity politics of their Republican and Democratic counterparts across virtually all fifty states.

Austerity for labor and the public is capitalism's Plan B. Even capitalists now see that capitalism's Plan A failed.

You will recall that Plan A entailed a crisis-response program of bailing out the banks, insurance companies, large corporations, and stock markets to achieve "recovery." The theory behind Plan A—what used to be called "trickle-down economics"—was that recovery would spread from financial markets and financiers to everyone else. It never did. So now the same servants of capitalism who imposed Plan A are dishing out Plan B.

Governors Andrew Cuomo in New York and Dannel Malloy in Connecticut had very similar Plan Bs. They threatened the public employee unions and the people of their states in nearly identical ways. Either the unions accept new contracts with wage freezes and raised contributions to their health insurance plans (and other declines in their basic remuneration)—or the governors would fire tens of thousands of unionized state workers. In Connecticut, the state workers first voted to reject and then revoted to accept that contract. In New York, the state workers accepted on the first vote.

Let's be really clear on what the two governors were doing. They were forcing a very painful choice onto the mass of people who elected them. Each governor said: I will either fire many thousands of state workers and thereby impose drastic cuts in public services on the entire citizenry, or I will subject tens of thousands of state employees to significant cuts in their wages and benefits.

Each governor spoke and acted as if those were the only two choices—even though that is blatantly untrue. Each governor refused to even consider an obvious alternative Plan C: increasing taxes on corporations and the rich enough to avoid either public service cuts or wage cuts. Instead, each governor thumbed his nose at the public by forcing unions to choose between two awful options.

The public employees' unions voted to accept serious cuts in pay and benefits. That was in the face of the latest government figures showing US consumer price inflation now running at 3.5–4 percent per year. The contracts that state employees accepted in New York and Connecticut give them 0 percent wage increases in the first two years and less than 2 percent per year increases in the last years of their contracts. In addition, New York workers accepted unpaid furlough days, while both states' contracts involved higher health insurance premiums and co-pays to be charged to state workers. These are serious reductions in state workers' standards of living. They will thus reduce their expenditures, thereby hurting communities, businesses, and other workers.

The states will thus learn the same lessons learned in Greece and Portugal and wherever austerities are governments' Plan Bs. Austerities make difficult, painful, and unjust capitalist crises more so.

Corporations and the rich bankroll the parties and governors who design and impose Plans A and B while avoiding Plan C. And so matters will remain unless and until corporations' profits are no longer available to their boards of directors to enrich themselves and major shareholders and buy politicians' servitude. The best response to capitalism's crisis, to its failed Plan A, its unjust Plan B, and the beneficial but narrow Plan C, would be a Plan D: change how we organize productive enterprises in our society. Profits should be distributed by the democratic decision making of all those who produce and depend on them: the workers and affected communities.

The twists and turns of this global capitalism system, painful as they are to endure, nonetheless also move it toward a confrontation with the alternative Plan D. The real question is whether the advocates and supporters of Plan D can be organized, mobilized, and focused on achieving their goals in that confrontation.

The Truth about Profits and Austerity

March 31, 2013

The truth about profits in the United States is simple. Ed Dolan's recent piece in *Seeking Alpha* contains a graph that makes it all too clear.

First, it's clear that profits as a percentage of total US GDP have recovered from the crash of 2008. Unemployment may still be over 50 percent higher than it was in 2007, and real wages may be below what they were then, and the benefits and security of jobs may have fallen, but profits have come back and with them the stock markets. Hence the upbeat talk about "recovery" yet again.

Figure 4. US Corporate Profits, Share of GDP

Source: Ed Dolan, "Latest U.S. GDP Data Show Economy Weak at Year's End But Corporate Profits Near Record High," *Seeking Alpha*, March 31, 2013. Data are from BEA.

Second, it's clear that profits have risen dramatically over the last thirty years. Before-tax profits rose from under 8 percent to well over 12 percent of GDP: a 50 percent real increase. After-tax profits did better still, rising from over 4 to 10 percent, more than doubling in real terms. Businesses made more profits while taxes took less of them. How nice for capitalists.

How nice, too, that both parties agree that those profits should not be tapped now for any revenues needed to offset the crisis since 2007. Both parties collaborate to impose an austerity that does not touch profits—an austerity that is "neutral" toward them as it offsets any closing of business tax loopholes by cutting the profit tax rate. Neutralism toward profits rising for thirty years is thus coupled with raising payroll taxes (as of January 1) and sequestering government social spending (as of March 1).

This is not a government policy to solve economic problems. It is a policy to save the minority of long-privileged economic players no matter what the economic and social costs.

The Great Austerity Shell Game
November 4, 2013

Center-right governments in Britain and Germany do it. So do the center-left governments in France and Italy. President Barack Obama and the Republicans do it, too. They all impose "austerity" programs on their economies as necessary to exit the crisis afflicting their countries since 2007. Politicians and economists impose austerity now much as doctors once stuck mustard plasters on the skins of the sick.

Austerity policies presume that the chief economic problems today are government budget deficits that increase national debts. Austerity policies solve those problems mainly by cutting government spending, and secondarily by limited tax increases.

National debts grow less or drop depending on how much each government's expenditures decrease and its taxes increase. President Obama's austerity policies during 2013 started January 1, when he raised payroll taxes on everyone's annual incomes up to $113,700. Then, on March 1, the "sequester" lowered federal expenditures. Thus, the 2013 US deficit will drop sharply from that of 2012.

President Obama will likely impose more austerity: cutting Social Security and Medicare benefits to compromise with Republicans. Similarly, European governments maintain their "austerity" programs. Even France's government, officially "anti-austerity" and "socialist," has produced budgets that include austerity-type cuts in social expenditures.

The accumulated evidence shows that austerity programs usually make economic downturns worse. Why, then, do they remain the preferred policy for most capitalist governments?

When capitalist economies crash, most capitalists request—and governments provide—credit market bailouts and economic stimuli. However, corporations and the rich oppose new taxes on them to pay for stimulus and bailout programs. They insist, instead, that governments should borrow the necessary funds. Since 2007, capitalist governments everywhere borrowed massively for those costly programs. They thus ran large budget deficits, and their national debts soared.

Heavy borrowing was thus capitalists' preferred first policy to deal with their system's latest crisis. It served them well.

Borrowing paid for government rescues of banks, other financial companies, and selected other major corporations. Borrowing enabled stimulus expenditures that revived demand for goods and services. Borrowing enabled government outlays on unemployment compensation, food stamps, and other offsets to crisis-induced suffering.

In these ways, borrowing helped reduce the criticism, resentment, anger, and antisystem tendencies among those fired from jobs, evicted from homes, and deprived of job security and benefits. Government borrowing had these positive results for capitalists—while saving them from paying taxes to get those results.

That is not all. Corporations and the rich used the money they saved by keeping governments from taxing them to provide the huge loans governments therefore needed. Middle- and lower-income people could lend little if anything to their governments. Corporations and the rich, in effect, substituted loans to the government instead of paying more in taxes. For those loans, governments must pay interest and eventually repay them.

Government borrowing rewards corporations and the rich quite nicely. It amounts to a very sweet deal for capitalists. Yet that sweet deal raises a new problem. Where will governments find funds, first, to pay interest on all the borrowing, and second, to pay back the lenders? Corporations and the rich worry that they might still be taxed to provide those funds. They are determined to avoid such taxes—just as they avoided being taxed to pay for stimulus and bailout programs in the first place.

Austerity is thus capitalists' preferred second policy, a second way to avoid higher taxes as governments struggle with economic crises. Corporations and the rich promote austerity by loudly insisting that today's key economic problems are not unemployment, lost job security and benefits, home foreclosures, and record-breaking inequalities of income and wealth. Rather, the key problems are government deficits and rising national debt. They must be cut.

To do that, taxes should be raised modestly or not at all (to avoid "hurting" the economy). The key solution is thus to cut government outlays on jobs, social benefits, and social services. Money saved by those cuts should be used instead to pay interest on the national debt and reduce it.

Capitalism's way of dealing with its recurring crises is thus a remarkable two-step hustle. In step one, massive borrowing funds stimulus and bailout programs. In step two, austerity pays for the borrowing. This hustle shifts most of the costs of capitalist crises onto the backs of middle- and lower-income people. The shift occurs through the higher unemployment, lower wages, and reduced government services achieved by austerity programs. It occurs as well in the sustained minimization of tax increases—especially on corporations and the rich.

With few exceptions, major political parties everywhere have imposed capitalism's two-step hustle. Only when mass opposition from middle- and lower-income people is sufficiently organized to possibly threaten capitalism itself do capitalists waver and split over borrowing and austerity. Some capitalists then collaborate with that opposition to support "New Deals" instead of austerity.

Even then, when the immediate crisis is over, capitalists revert to their preferred policies of borrowing and austerity. US history from 1929 to the present teaches that lesson well.

Capitalists know their system is unstable. They have never yet prevented recurring crises. They rely instead on policies to "manage" them. The two-step hustle—borrowing for stimulus and bailouts and then austerity—usually does the job. Keynesians promote the borrowing and then seem surprised, even outraged, when austerity follows.

Corporations and the rich should not have escaped taxation in the first place because they helped cause the crisis, they enriched themselves the most in the decades before the crisis, and they can best afford to pay to overcome the crisis. Had they been taxed to pay for stimulus and bailout, there would be no need for borrowing or austerity.

Taxing corporations and the rich would have consequences, too, but they would generate far fewer social costs and fall mostly on those best able to cope with them. But any organized opposition strong enough to make corporations and the rich pay for capitalism's crises would likely also question capitalism itself. Emerging from nearly six years of crisis, the question "can't we do better than capitalism?" pushes forward, demanding discussion, debate, and democratic decision.

Austerity, US Style, Exposed

February 7, 2013

Austerity policies include various combinations primarily of government spending cuts and secondarily of general tax increases. Republicans and Democrats have endorsed austerity since 2010. Austerity was the result of their deal on taxes on December 31, 2012: increasing the payroll tax on wages and salaries from 4.2 to 6.2 percent. Austerity is what they are negotiating now in regard to federal spending cuts.

After 2010, with "recovery" under way for them (following bailouts for them), large private capitalist interests focused on three key interests. First, they wanted to ensure that the bailouts' costs were not paid for by higher taxes on corporations and the rich. By stressing government spending cuts and broad-based tax increases, austerity policies serve that interest. Second, they worried about crisis-heightened government economic intervention and power and wanted to reduce them back to precrisis levels. Austerity's focus on reduced government spending lessens the government's economic footprint. Third, because big banks and other large capitalists are among the major creditors of the US government, they wanted signs that their crisis-increased holdings of US debt were safe investments for them. Austerity policies provide just those signs, as we shall show.

Austerity in the United States, unlike in Europe, is renamed and packaged for the public as "deficit reduction programs" or "fiscal responsibility." Distractions such as "fiscal cliffs" and "debt ceilings" focus public attention on mere secondary details of austerity. Politicians, media, and academics use such distractions to wrangle over whose taxes will go up how much and which recipients of government spending will suffer what size cuts. They do not debate austerity itself; that is, they do not debate the very idea of raising mass taxes and cutting spending in a deep and long economic downturn. They do not explore the interests served and undermined by an austerity policy. So we will.

Austerity promoters repeatedly insist that the dominant economic problem today is government budget deficits. They ignore why those deficits occurred (the crisis plus bailouts). They demand that both parties and the media endorse austerity, because cuts in government spending and increased taxes will reduce deficits. They hype austerity as the solution all must embrace. Otherwise, they fear, a different and dangerous logic might win popular support. In that logic, since capitalism regularly causes crises that cause deficits, another solution for deficits would be changing from capitalism to another economic system not beset by regular crises.

Austerity policies, we are told, will reduce deficits and thereby meet what "the credit market" demands. In other words, those who have lent to the US government (by buying its debt securities) want guarantees of interest and repayment. By cutting government spending and raising taxes, austerity policies redirect government funds to the government's creditors, thereby reassuring them.

Distracting references to an anonymous "market" avoid identifying the government's creditors. However, major creditors holding US public debt are easy to list: large banks, insurance companies, large corporations, wealthy individuals, and central banks around the world. Austerity justified as satisfying "the market" in fact serves those US creditors first and foremost.

Austerity is thus the policy preferred by the private capitalist interests that (1) brought on the crisis, (2) secured the government bailouts almost exclusively for themselves, and (3) are that government's chief creditors. Led by major banks, those interests now threaten the government (that just bailed them out) with higher interest rates or no more credit unless it imposes higher taxes (mostly on others) and reduced spending (mostly on others) to lower its deficits. Distracting struggles over "fiscal cliffs" and "debt ceilings" serve nicely to disguise the reality that both parties' austerity policies represent and illustrate gross government subservience to large capitalists.

Austerity, US style, has its Keynesian economist critics. They point out that the United States has been able to borrow trillions at historically low interest rates through this crisis. US deficits have not worried "the market" at all. Policies should therefore not be driven by deficits. Keynesians insist that raising mass taxes and cutting spending during an economic downturn will reduce outlays on goods and services by taxpayers and government, thereby worsening unemployment. They thus ridicule the argument that austerity, by cutting deficits, will stimulate investment by capitalists.

For Keynesians, austerity is thus unneeded and counterproductive. They prefer to exit the crisis by more stimulus (lower taxes and higher government spending) funded by higher deficits. The resulting economic growth, they believe, will automatically lower government budgetary imbalance. The government can then later, if and when needed, impose tax increases and reduce government spending to shrink deficits. In a growing economy, austerity policies avoid the devastating effects they have in depressed economies (as shown by the recent histories of Greece, Portugal, and the United Kingdom).

Setting aside the question of the validity of Keynesian arguments, they miss key purposes of austerity policies. Those policies do not primarily seek to overcome crisis or resume economic growth. Rather, as argued above, they aim chiefly to (1) shift the burden of paying for crisis and bailouts onto the total population, (2) reduce the economic footprint of the government, and (3) reduce creditors' concerns about rising US debt levels. If austerity policies achieve these objectives, their failure to end the crisis quickly is a price that corporations and the rich are more than happy to pay (or rather, have others pay).

That Republicans and Democrats concur on austerity and differ only on its secondary details testifies to what they share. Both depend financially on capitalist corporations and their top executives. Both serve and never question capitalism. For all the victims of capitalism today—the unemployed, those foreclosed out of their homes, those with reduced job benefits and job security, students with unsustainable schooling debts and poor job prospects, millions without medical insurance—supporting those parties perpetuates their victimization.

Austerity: Another "Policy Mistake"

March 8, 2013

Shoddy political theater distracts people with vague demons called "debt ceiling," "fiscal cliff," and now "sequester." Party leaders posture for major donors, media boosters, and the faithful. They claim to save us from the demons. Meanwhile, backstage they all agree on austerity as the "necessary" response to "our major problem," namely, federal budget "imbalance." "We" are spending "beyond our means," accumulating "government debts." So "we" must raise taxes and cut spending—impose austerity—to regain balance.

On January 1, payroll taxes rose (from 4.2 to 6.2 percent) for 150 million Americans. Their checks shrank as that regressive tax became more so. Obama's hyped "tax increase for the rich" was comparatively trivial. It affected only the very few Americans earning over $450,000, raising their top tax rate from 35 percent to 39.6 percent. Our leaders hope we forgot the 1950s and 1960s, when the top tax rate was 91 percent. On March 1, the sequester hit, unleashing federal spending cuts.

Higher payroll taxes leave less wage and salary income available for spending on goods and services. That worsens unemployment, correspondingly reduces income and sales taxes, and thus also worsens Washington's budget imbalance. By cutting federal spending on goods and services, the sequester also worsens unemployment, reduces tax revenues, and increases unemployment compensation outlays. No wonder critics scream that austerity now is crazy and counterproductive. Europe's three-year austerity program pushed its unemployment rate in February 2013 to 11.9 percent.

Why do "our leaders" agree on austerity (and disagree only on its details)? Why ignore that austerity not only undercuts the economy, but risks the government's budget, too? Why ignore alternatives to austerity? For example, tax the largest corporations and richest 3 percent to fund a bottom-up stimulus program. That could help balance the federal budget, directly aid most people, and likely outperform the failed top-down (trickle-down) policies of Presidents George W. Bush and Barack Obama. President Franklin Delano Roosevelt's policies in the 1930s provide one example to start from.

One reason for austerity: Those who lent to Washington demand assurances that the US government will honor its debts 100 percent. One key assurance is a return to budget balance after the government's costly bailouts of major financial and other corporations. Lenders include chiefly banks, insurance companies, large corporations, rich individuals—the beneficiaries of those bailouts—pension funds, and foreign governments. Those lenders' political contributions and broad social powers usually prevail in Washington.

Another reason for austerity is embarrassment. The financial industry was a crucial cause of the crisis, starting in 2007. It benefited most from the massive bailouts in late 2008 and 2009. Those bailouts caused the budget deficits, now suddenly declared to be "our major problem." The financial industry has been subsidized ever since. For example, it borrows from the Federal Reserve at much lower interest rates than it gets by relending the money to the US Treasury. If public discussion recognized that capitalism, crisis, and the finance industry are systemic roots of our economic troubles today, including the federal budget imbalance, criticism and demands for change might focus there. The system's supporters much prefer to narrow public attention to just the budget imbalance, to "fix" it without attention to its systemic root causes.

Another reason for austerity: It is a kind of "policy mistake" often generated in and by capitalism. Two examples can make this clear. Banks and other moneylenders often encounter borrowers unable to repay their debts. In anger, lenders demand punishment for defaulting borrowers (in poorhouses, workhouses, debtors prisons, etc.) only to discover that imprisoned borrowers are even less able and likely ever to repay debts. Punishing those borrowers, however briefly satisfying to lenders, can hurt lenders, too. So bankruptcy laws and other means emerged for lenders and borrowers to work out less damaging compromises. Periodically, lenders forget, overdo punishment, and rediscover again—after much wasteful suffering and pain—the self-destruction of that approach.

The second example concerns a contradiction at the core of the capitalist system. Capitalists always try to reduce the number and pay of their employees. Saving labor costs is standard business strategy. However capitalists eventually discover that that strategy can boomerang. Reducing workers' incomes—hiring fewer or paying them less—usually means that capitalists sell less. Reduced sales can undermine capitalists' profits as much or more than lower labor costs raise them. Capitalist crises can, and often have, resulted from insufficient demand from workers as consumers. Nonetheless, capitalism's competitive structure imposes the need to cut labor costs, undermining demand and generating crises. The syndrome repeats periodically, notwithstanding its massive social suffering and costs and the denunciation of its critics.

Austerity policies are just like policies of imprisoning defaulting debtors and endlessly cutting payrolls. They are shortsighted: capitalists are deluded into imagining that mass economic suffering will not hurt them, too. Corporations, major shareholders, and top executives are now determined to (1) evade paying the taxes that could balance the federal budget, (2) secure their holdings of government debt, and (3) keep public discussion and politics away from their responsibilities for crisis and keep bailouts exclusively for themselves. They push austerity policies to achieve those goals and imagine no blowback from a deteriorating economy. When Americans catch up with the Europeans, who now increasingly confront exactly that blowback, they too will rediscover and debate alternatives.

Punishing debtors, cutting payrolls, and imposing austerity keep happening. The capitalist system drives its people and enterprises to return to those policies even though their huge social costs and ultimate dangers for capitalists are rediscovered repeatedly. Usually, what forces that rediscovery and suspends those policies are mass resistance and opposition from below, from victims of the system's dysfunction. The critical question remains: When will people realize that the needed solutions are not primarily about debtors' prisons, relentless labor cost-cutting, or austerity policies? The solutions, rather, converge into one basic issue: It is time to face and change the system that relentlessly reimposes these costly "policy mistakes" on us all.

TAXES

Corporations to Government: Give Us More, Tax Us Less

February 21, 2011

Nothing better shows corporate control over the government than Washington's basic response to the current economic crisis. First we had "the rescue" and then "the recovery." Trillions in public money flowed to the biggest US banks and insurance companies. That "bailed" them out (suggestion of criminality?) while we waited for benefits to "trickle down" to the rest of us. As usual, the trickle-down part has not happened. Large corporations and their investors kept the government's money for themselves; their profits and stock market "recovered" nicely. We get unemployment, home foreclosures, job benefit cuts, and growing job insecurity. As the crisis hits states and cities, politicians avoid raising corporate taxes in favor of cutting government services and jobs.

Might government bias favoring corporations be deserved, a reward for taxes they pay? No: corporations—especially the larger ones—have avoided taxes as effectively as they have controlled government expenditures to benefit them.

Compare income taxes received by the federal government from individuals and from corporations (their profits are treated as their income). The table below (in millions of dollars) is based on statistics from the Office of Management and the Budget in the White House.

Table 1. Annual Federal Receipts:
Individual and Corporate Income Taxes, 1943–2008

Year	Total Individual Income Taxes	Total Corporate Income Taxes
1943	6,505	9,557
1948	19,319	9,678
1968	68,726	28,665
1988	401,181	94,508
2008	1,145,747	304,346

Source: The White House, Office of Management and Budget, "Historical Tables," Table 2.1, available at https://www.whitehouse.gov/omb/budget/Historicals/.

The overall picture is unmistakable; the trend is clear. During the Great Depression federal income tax receipts from individuals and corporations were roughly equal. During World War II, *income tax receipts from corporations were 50 percent greater than from individuals*. The national crises of depression and war produced successful popular demands for corporations to contribute significant portions of federal tax revenues.

US corporations resented that arrangement, and after the war, they changed it. Corporate profits financed politicians' campaigns and lobbies to make sure that income tax receipts from individuals rose faster than those from corporations and that tax cuts were larger for corporations than for individuals. By the 1980s, individual income taxes regularly yielded four times more than taxes on corporations' profits.

Since World War II, corporations have shifted much of the federal tax burden from themselves to the public, especially onto the middle-income members of the public.[6] No wonder a tax "revolt" developed. Yet the "revolt" did not push to stop, let alone reverse, that shift.

Corporations had focused public anger against government expenditures as "wasteful" and against public employees as "inefficient." Organizations such as Chambers of Commerce and corporations' academic and political allies together shaped the public debate. They did not want

6. For a detailed study of the changing burden of the US individual income tax on different income groups, see Thomas Piketty and Emmanuel Saez, "How Progressive Is the U.S. Federal Tax System? A Historical and International Perspective," *Journal of Economic Perspectives,* Vol. 21, No. 1 (Winter 2007), 3–24.

it to be about who does and does not pay the taxes. Instead, they steered the "tax revolt" against taxes in general—on businesses and all individuals alike. The corporations' efforts saved them far more in reduced taxes than the costs of their political contributions, lobbyists, and public relations campaigns.

At the same time, corporations also lobbied successfully for many loopholes in the tax laws. The official federal tax rate on profits is now around 35 percent for large corporations who theoretically have to pay additional state taxes on their profits and local taxes on their property (e.g., land, buildings, business inventories). Those official and theoretical tax obligations have been used to support conservatives' claims that corporations pay half or more of their profits to federal, state, and local levels of government combined. However, because of loopholes, the truth is very different. Corporations'—and especially large corporations'—actual tax payments are far lower than their official, theoretical obligations.

The most comprehensive recent study of what larger corporations actually pay by three academic accountants—professors at Duke, MIT, and the University of North Carolina—gets at that truth. It examined a large sample of corporations. Their average turned out to be a rate of total taxation (federal, state, and local combined) below 30 percent. The study concluded: "We find a significant fraction of firms that appear to be able to successfully avoid large portions of the corporate income tax over sustained periods of time. Using a ten-year measure of tax avoidance, 546 firms, comprising 26.3 percent of our sample, are able to maintain a cash effective tax rate of 20 percent or less. The mean firm has a ten-year cash effective tax rate of approximately 29.6 percent."[7]

General Electric (GE) deserves special mention. The *New York Times* reported (February 1, 2011) that GE's total tax payment amounted to 14.3 percent over the last five years. Citizens for Tax Justice promptly (February 4) corrected it: the profits tax it paid in the United States, (as opposed to its worldwide taxes on its worldwide profits) is only 3.4 percent. Thus, GE paid a far lower tax rate on its income than most

---

7. Scott D. Dyreng, Michelle Hanlon, and Edward L. Maydew, "Long-run Corporate Tax Avoidance," *Accounting Review*, Vol. 83, No. 1 (January 2007), 61–82. Available at ssrn.com/abstract=1017610.

Americans paid on theirs. In 2009, GE received a $140 billion bailout guarantee of its debt from Washington.[8] By choosing GE's chief executive, Jeffrey R. Immelt, to head his Economic Advisory Panel, President Obama effectively rewarded the corporate program: give us more and tax us less.

The Brookings Institute pie chart below summarizes the dramatic success achieved by corporations' tax avoidance strategies.

Figure 5. Federal Revenues by Source, Fiscal Year 2009

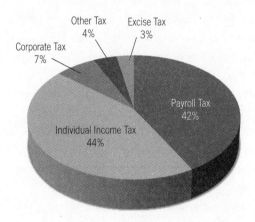

Source: The White House, Office of Management and Budget, "Historical Tables," Table 2.1, available at https://www.whitehouse.gov/omb/budget/Historicals/.

Corporations repeated at the state and local levels what they accomplished federally. According to the US Census Bureau, corporations paid taxes on their profits to states and localities totaling $24.7 billion in 1988 while individuals then paid income taxes of $90.0 billion. However, by 2009, while corporate tax payments had roughly doubled (to $49.1 billion), individual income taxes had more than tripled (to $290.0 billion).[9]

---

8. See Jeff Gerth and Brady Dennis, "How a Loophole Benefits GE in Bank Rescue," *Washington Post*, June 29, 2009.
9. See US Census Bureau, "Table 1. National Totals of State and Local Tax Revenue, by Type of Tax," available at www2.census.gov/govs/qtax/2010/q3t1.pdf.

If corporations paid taxes proportionate to the benefits they get from government and/or to what individuals pay, most US citizens would finally get the tax relief they so desperately seek.

How the Rich Soaked the Rest of Us

March 1, 2011

Over the last half century, the richest Americans have shifted the burden of the federal individual income tax off themselves and onto everybody else. From the end of World War II until the early 1960s, the highest income earners paid a tax rate over 90 percent for many years. Today, the top earners pay a rate of only 35 percent. The gap between the rates paid by the richest and the poorest has narrowed. If we take into account the many loopholes the rich can and do use far more than the poor, the gap narrows even more.

One conclusion is clear and obvious: the richest Americans have dramatically lowered their income tax burden since 1945, both absolutely and relative to the tax burdens of the middle income groups and the poor.

Consider two further points. First, if the highest income earners today were required to pay the *same* rate that they paid for many years after 1945, the federal government would need far lower deficits to support the private economy through its current crisis; and second, those tax-the-rich years after 1945 experienced far lower unemployment and far faster economic growth than we have had for years.

The lower taxes the rich got for themselves are one reason they have become so much richer over the last half century. Just as their tax rates started to come down from their 1960s heights, so their shares of the total national income began their rise. We have now returned to the extreme inequality of income that characterized the United States a century ago.

From 1979 to 2005 (adjusted for inflation), the bottom fifth of poorest citizens saw their after-tax household income barely rise at all. The middle fifth of income earners saw their after-tax household income rise by less than 25 percent. Meanwhile, the top 1 percent of households saw their after-tax household incomes rise by 175 percent.

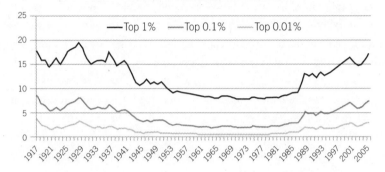

In the simplest terms, the richest Americans have done by far the best over the last thirty years, they are more able to pay taxes today than they have been in many decades, and they are more able to pay than other Americans by a far wider margin. At a time of national economic crisis, especially, they can and should contribute far more in taxes.

Instead, a rather vicious cycle has been at work for years. Reduced taxes on the rich leave them with more money to influence politicians and politics. Their influence wins them further tax reductions, which gives them still more money to put to political use. When the loss of tax revenue from the rich worsens already strained government budgets, the rich press politicians to cut public services and government jobs and not even debate a return to the higher taxes the rich used to pay. So it goes—from Washington, to Wisconsin, to New York City.

How do the rich justify and excuse this record? They claim that they can invest the money they save from taxes and thereby create jobs. But do they? In fact, cutting rich people's taxes is often very bad for the rest of us (beyond the worsening inequality and hobbled government it produces).

Several examples show this. First, a good part of the money the rich save from taxes is then lent by them to the government (in the form of buying US Treasury securities for their personal investment portfolios). It would obviously be better for the government to tax the rich to maintain its expenditures, and thereby avoid deficits and debts. Then the government would not need to tax the rest of us to pay interest on those debts to the rich.

Second, the richest Americans take the money they save from taxes and invest big parts of it in China, India, and elsewhere. That often produces more jobs over there, fewer jobs here, and more imports of goods produced abroad. US dollars flow out to pay for those imports and so accumulate in the hands of foreign banks and foreign governments. They, in turn, lend from that wealth to the US government because it does not tax our rich, and so we get taxed to pay for the interest Washington has to give those foreign banks and governments. The largest single recipient of such interest payments today is the People's Republic of China.

Third, the richest Americans take the money they don't pay in taxes and invest it in hedge funds and with stockbrokers to make profitable investments. These days, that often means speculating in oil and food, which drives up their prices, undermines economic recovery for the mass of Americans, and produces acute suffering around the globe. Those hedge funds and brokers likewise use part of the money rich people save from taxes to speculate in the US stock markets. That has recently driven stock prices higher: hence, the stock market recovery. And that mostly helps—you guessed it—the richest Americans who own most of the stocks.

The one kind of significant wealth average Americans own, if they own any, is their individual home. And home values remain deeply depressed: no recovery there.

Cutting the taxes on the rich in no way guarantees social benefits from what they may choose to do with their money. Indeed, their choices can worsen economic conditions for the mass of people. These days, that is exactly what they are doing.

Who *Really* Pays Taxes

January 30, 2012

As US capitalism suffers from a crisis now in its fifth year with no end in sight, the Republican presidential candidates and President Barack Obama endlessly repeat cheerleading for the system as if it were, as usual, beyond question or criticism. The president's State of the Union address at least found campaign fodder in referring to income inequality.

He tried to make political use of what the Occupy movement inserted onto the mass public consciousness so powerfully last autumn.

President Obama even suggested a 30 percent minimum tax on those earning $1 million or more annually. The details of that suggestion remain murky with little chance that the kinds of Congresses recently elected would pass it. In any case, Obama's suggested 30 percent minimum tax would still remain far, far below the much higher individual income tax rates that the richest Americans had to pay in the 1940s, 1950s, 1960s, and 1970s.

Immediately after the speech, right-wing economists, journalists, and other spokespeople for the 1 percent swung into action to attack. They clearly want to keep the public's awareness and public discussion away from the income and tax issues that the Occupy movement made so important and urgent. They resent the president for even raising issues of fairness and taxation, however modestly.

That usually happens when taxes and justice get discussed in the same public conversation. Stretching the truth gives way to more or less gross lying, and never more so than during election campaigns.

A minimal fact check on federal taxes in the United States might help folks avoid being easily misled. The table summarizes the last seventy-five years to show what happened to the three most important tax revenues collected by Washington (accounting for over 90 percent of total tax revenues now).

Table 2. Federal Government Tax Receipts (in Billions of Dollars), 1943–2010

Year	Corporate Income	Individual Income	Social Security/Medicare
1943	9.5	6.5	3.0
1960	21.5	40.7	14.7
1980	65	244	158
1994	140	543	462
2010	191	899	865

Source: Budget of the United States.

Here are some key truths revealed by these statistics gathered and published by the US government.

After the Great Depression and during World War II, the US government collected relatively much more from corporations than from individuals. Then, too, we were also closely allied with the former Soviet Union. How times change! To think that Washington placed heavier taxes on corporations than on individuals! Clearly, corporations would prefer we forget or never encounter that past reality lest it suggest something for consideration now.

After the war, corporations went to work to change the federal tax system. Not only did they succeed in shifting the tax burden from corporations to individuals already by 1960, but that shifting has gone on steadily to the present.

Consider this basic federal tax fact. Individual income taxes are progressive: the higher your income, the greater the percentage of that income you pay in taxes. In contrast, payroll taxes (for Social Security and Medicare) are regressive: for most people the payroll tax rate is the same (flat) as a share of income while for the richest it declines steadily below that flat rate. Since 1980, the regressive payroll tax has become larger relative to both the individual income tax and the corporate income tax.

The table above also helps show the falseness of arguments frequently made by right-wing economists, politicians, and media representatives. One such argument runs roughly as follows: "Half of Americans pay no income taxes, while the richest 5 percent of taxpayers pay over half of Washington's income taxes." First of all, the vast majority of those Americans who do not pay income taxes do pay Social Security and Medicare taxes. The *Washington Post* made clear (September 23, 2011) using data for 2011: Of the 46 percent of US households that will not be paying federal income tax for 2011, the vast majority will be paying Social Security and Medicare taxes. The truth is that only 18 percent of US households will pay neither income tax nor Social Security and Medicare taxes. The vast majority (99 percent) of those who pay no taxes to Washington are either elderly or else have household incomes under $20,000.

Another such argument runs roughly as follows: "The richest 5 percent of income receivers in the United States pay over half of all of Washington's income tax receipts." First, those same people pay a tiny percentage of Washington's Social Security and Medicare receipts. That is simply because the richest Americans earn the largest portion of their income from sources other than wages and salaries—such as interest, rents, dividends, and capital gains. Incomes from such other sources do not have to pay Social Security or Medicare taxes. Since Washington's Social Security and Medicare tax receipts are now as large or larger than its individual income tax receipts, any honest assessment of what the richest Americans pay cannot exclude counting Social Security and Medicare taxes paid disproportionately by the bottom 99 percent—just what most of the right-wing analyses routinely do.

One way to cut through the misinformation around taxes created by the right is to see what happened to the distribution of incomes among Americans over recent years. Did the US federal tax system hurt the top 1 percent and help the remaining 99 percent; does it operate "unfairly" as they claim? An answer emerges from the best professional statistical work yet done on the US income distribution: that of Professors Piketty and Saez (widely available on the Internet).[10] Their work covers 1993 to 2007 (before the current crisis hit). They found that the average annual growth in US real incomes over those years was 2.2 percent. In contrast, the real annual income growth of the incomes of the richest 1 percent was 5.9 percent. The real annual income growth of the other 99 percent of the United States was 1.3 percent.

The US federal tax system that right wingers portray as unfair and burdensome to the richest Americans allowed them for the last two decades to gather still greater income than everyone else. The US federal tax system enabled greater inequality. And the same results apply to the US distribution of wealth. No wonder the right resents, opposes, and seeks to silence those who suggest even modest changes in a tax system so convenient for the richest.

---

10. See the World Wealth and Income Database, available at http://www.wid.world.

PUBLIC SECTOR

Going Beyond Private versus Public

December 13, 2014

The new, more Republican Congress may "privatize" the US Postal Service: dismantle the public enterprise and turn mail services over to private enterprises. Such a privatization would mimic what the US military has done with part of its activities and what many states and cities did with utilities, transport systems, and schools. Privatizers always assert that private enterprises function more efficiently and will thus cost society less than public enterprises.

Evidence for such assertions ranges from slim to none. For example, the pendulum often swings the other way (e.g., during the Great Depression of the 1930s, after World Wars I and II, and in the 2008 crisis). Then, private enterprises were transformed into public enterprises. Officials always assured us that those public enterprises would get us out of crises sooner and better than private enterprises could or would; in short, the public enterprise was the more efficient way to go.

Recently, debates, conflicts, and even street battles for and against privatization have revived. From the 1970s to 2008, neoliberal politicians, media, and academics celebrated privatization with endless repetitions of the efficiency rationale. Many liberals, leftists, and socialists responded by demonizing privatization as merely means to raise profits at workers' and citizens' expenses. Yet they discovered, especially after 2007, that government takeovers are often bailouts of capitalists also at workers' and citizens' expenses. The US takeover of de facto ownership of General Motors was a clear example. So too were the de facto US takeovers of the private Federal National Mortgage Association, the federal Home Loan Mortgage Corporation, AIG Corporation, and many major banks.

Battles over privatization should not distract anyone from the more basic and ultimately more socially consequential struggles emerging now. These turn on (a) democratic versus capitalistically organized enterprises, (b) egalitarian versus extremely unequal distributions of wealth and income, and (c) capitalism versus new socialist visions. Struggles over these issues should take precedence over battles for or against privatization.

When the Nazis took power in 1933, they quickly turned public banks and other state enterprises into private enterprises no longer owned or operated by state officials. Their actions aimed to solidify support among major German capitalists. Nazis called this "reprivatization" to reinforce the idea (factually incorrect) that state enterprises had always originally been private. Actually, governments were crucially involved in the births of many enterprises in all capitalist countries.

Modern Russian history records the massive shift of private into public industrial enterprises after 1917 and into public agricultural enterprises (state farms) after 1930, yet over subsequent decades, Stalin had to reverse direction and convert parts of state farm enterprises into private individual farms that became important components of Soviet agriculture. Then a reverse shift from public to private industrial enterprises unfolded in Russia after 1989. Similar developments characterized other eastern European economies between 1945 and the 1990s. In the United Kingdom during the 1980s, Thatcher turned many enterprises that her predecessors had made public back into private enterprises. In many countries, utilities, airlines, rail systems, and other industries have oscillated between public and private forms of enterprise.

In short, public enterprises have been important parts of capitalist economies as have private enterprises in socialist economies. Shifts between public and private were practical solutions found for those economies' problems. Those shifts did not change the basic structures; in fact, they were undertaken to reinforce those structures.

Thus, private capitalist enterprises often welcomed public enterprises. For example, private enterprises wanted international air connections, but launching an airline was too expensive and risky for any private enterprise. One frequent solution was a public airline enterprise. Public post offices around the world furnish similar examples. Monopolizing capitalists can raise prices to other capitalists (say, on machines, tools, raw materials, etc.), reducing the latters' profits. One solution is to suppress the monopolist and substitute a public enterprise legally obliged to charge low prices. When burst financial bubbles threaten general economic meltdown, many private capitalists will support the temporary shift from private to public banks and insurance companies as a way to revive the economy.

Under different conditions, private capitalists see public enterprises as threats, competitors with unfair advantages, or profitable targets for purchase if bargain prices can be arranged. Politicians can then curry corporate favor and donations by selling public enterprises to private enterprises. Such privatization also attracts politicians because it brings funds to government coffers without added taxes or deficits.

Strategic oscillations between private and public enterprises are sometimes hampered by economic fundamentalism. Right-wing fundamentalist ideologues insist that private is necessarily, inherently better than public enterprise. As part of its demonization of government (other than police, judiciary, and military), such economic fundamentalism helps keep taxes low and the government unable to redistribute income. Periodic campaigns for privatization (whatever their real goal) can be spun as thwarting bad government. Demonizing government always served nicely to depict the former Soviet Union (and socialism and communism) as the ultimates in public enterprise systems and thus "evil empires."

When private enterprises collapsed and begged for government bailouts, demonizing government and promoting privatization were temporarily suspended. When the crisis passed, they resumed. For example, deficits incurred to bail out capitalists in 2008–2009 were recast in 2009–2010 as wasteful government spending on public services and employees instead. Conservatives insisted that "overfunded" services and "overpaid" employees (rather than costly capitalist bailouts) had somehow and suddenly caused public budget deficits. Their conclusion was to demand corrective "austerity" budgets. Conservatives' resumed demonization of government provided the ideological cover for resumed privatization to reverse (undo) the crisis-driven, private-to-public enterprise shifts.

Leftists understandably oppose privatization campaigns as thinly veneered attacks on working-class interests. Yet those campaigns and the right-wing economic fundamentalism that justified them should not obscure a central fact about capitalism. Privatizations and their opposites have mostly been pragmatic ways for capitalist economies to solve their problems. No great principle was at stake, notwithstanding fundamentalist hyperventilation. Wall Street in 2008 begged for government money and effective takeover of many key private enterprises to secure the survival of capitalism.

Critics of capitalism need not embrace some left-wing counterfundamentalism that public was and is always better than private. Government enterprises (usually with officials in the position of de facto owners and operators) typically exploit their employees. Their behavior usually replicates that of private shareowners and private boards of directors. The reality of most public enterprises to date has been state capitalism. It is different from private capitalism, but both are forms of capitalism. Both have typically kept the workers themselves from operating and directing their enterprises. And state capitalism has often concentrated far too much power in the state.[11]

Critics of capitalism need to go beyond battles over public versus private enterprises, private versus state forms of capitalism. The point is to criticize both in the interest of moving beyond them. That is why we advocate the internal transformation of enterprises so that neither private individuals nor state officials occupy the position of capitalist, of receiver of the surplus or profits produced by the workers.[12] Workers' self-directed enterprises are the institutional form—the social base—of movement beyond either private or state capitalism. Socialized ownership of means of production and socialized economic planning may be necessary, but they are certainly not sufficient conditions for a genuine transition beyond capitalism. Economic democracy inside all enterprises has been a key missing element in socialism's appeal as well as a missing component of the conditions for successful transition beyond capi-

---

11. For a full analysis of state capitalism, see Stephen A. Resnick and Richard D. Wolff, *Class Theory and History: Capitalism and Communism in the USSR* (New York: Routledge, 2002).
12. See Richard D. Wolff, *Democracy at Work: A Cure for Capitalism* (Chicago: Haymarket, 2012).

talism. That is our era's issue, not secondary disputes over the division of production between private and state enterprises.

There are historical parallels to this criticism/displacement of the private versus public debate. Critics of colonialism eventually recognized that after colonies won independence, they still confronted capitalism. Replacing foreign with domestic capitalists may have been necessary, but it proved far from sufficient to achieve the society they sought. Similarly, those who curbed monopolizing capitalists still confronted a competitive capitalism. In the US Civil War, the defeat of the slave kind of exploitation led the ex-slaves into capitalist exploitation. Marx drove the point home with his term "wage slave" for capitalist employees.

Today's choices are not limited to forms of capitalism: monopolist versus competitive, crony versus meritocratic, Anglo-American versus social democratic, national versus international, Christian versus Islamic versus secular, and so on. Nor are we trapped in a choice between public versus private enterprises or state versus private capitalism. The alternative that Thatcher, Reagan, and neoliberals could neither imagine nor understand—nor banish—is to move beyond all forms of capitalism. That requires transforming the internal organization of all forms of enterprise so that the workers become the democratic collective that directs the enterprise. On that basis, we can finally and genuinely democratize the economy and society.

The Hidden Money

April 19, 2013

Recent revelations of hidden money by the International Consortium of Investigative Journalists (ICIJ; available at http://www.icij.org/offshore) have embarrassed governments, large and small, and exposed many rich businesses and individuals. They used places like Liechtenstein, the British Virgin Islands, the Cayman Islands, Switzerland, and, of course, Cyprus. Those countries' private banks wanted the money much as their governments wanted the revenue benefits of hidden money inflows. The rich around the world took advantage of those banks' services to launder money with some illegality attached to it, to evade or avoid taxes, to hide business deals from government scrutiny, and so on.

Reasonable estimates, based on ICIJ and other reports, suggest that many trillions of dollars sit in such hidden money accounts. It follows that debates in most countries about rates of taxation are missing the point. Many among the rich long ago found ways to avoid taxes, whatever the rates. They just needed and used that one "loophole" in the tax law that allows them to hide their money (or "offshore" it) in either personal or corporate accounts or both.

By these means—eagerly abetted by banks competing for their lucrative business—many of the rich avoid whatever taxes the people in their countries of origin tried to impose. How progressive can a tax system actually be when the upper echelons can and do hide so much money from tax authorities? Moreover, so many competing countries and banks and so many easy ways to hide money provide incentives for illegal money-making. Laundering money to cover up its illegal origins has long been so very easy to do.

ICIJ's recent exposés have also shown that not only little countries and their local banks launder tainted money and facilitate tax avoidance schemes. Major money-center banks have recently paid huge fines when caught doing such things. Many of the corporations chartered to do financial business in places like the Cayman Islands turn out to be local subsidiaries of money center banks seeking to service high net worth clients with "special needs."

Hidden money represents the old problem of private financial behavior that deprives societies of tax revenues they need while encouraging and abetting illegality. We could try some new laws and impose some new regulations. That was done often in the past when similar revelations provoked action. Yet we know the inevitable result. The rich seeking to escape taxation and the rich criminals seeking to skirt legality will pay well for the best minds (lawyers, accountants, financial advisors, etc.) to devise ways around new laws and regulations. They have done so repeatedly, successfully, and often quickly.

One logical solution would be to change any economic system that confers on the top 1–5 percent such inordinate wealth and income that they can easily afford the expensive professionals usually required to "legally" evade the taxes everyone else pays. With a far less unequal distribution of wealth and income, we would not depend upon or even need the absurd, repetitive theater in which governmental regulation is established, then evaded; new regulation is imposed, then circumvented—and so on. Moreover, consider the huge deficit-reducing potential: With significantly less income and wealth inequality, tax evasion schemes would be less affordable and attractive to more people, resulting in higher tax revenues, while regulation and enforcement costs for the Internal Revenue Service would correspondingly drop.

Another logical solution would be to socialize banking—or at least the biggest, money-center banks. Given the already highly developed internationalization of those banks, this would be an international socialization. It would parallel the international efforts to confront another set of problems confronting the world, namely, environmental degradation. Major private money-center big banks would become owned and operated by agents directly responsible to political leaders. Their activities would have to become publicly transparent. As state institutions, such socialized banks would have no interest in (and be strictly prohibited from) practices that deprived the state of its proper tax revenues. Because European and US money-center banks are so large, if socialized they could easily "persuade" big banks elsewhere to join for fear of otherwise being boycotted by the socialized combination of dominant European and US banks. Such a solution would win the support, now, of clear majorities of people in many parts of the world. They blame the financial industry—and big banks in particular—for much of the crisis as well as the subsequent bailouts (for the banks) and governments' austerity policies (for the people).

Hiding money in foreign accounts to escape detection and/or taxation has become a routine "financial strategy" for many of the richest people and businesses in the world. Partly protected by special legislation and partly by the refusal of compromised officials to investigate or prosecute, the hiding of money has deprived most countries of huge amounts of desperately needed tax revenues that could have helped their economies grow while lowering their national debts. The heads of the world's major banks—those who demanded and got trillion-dollar bailouts and who now demand austerity programs to balance government budgets—preside over institutions that make money helping the rich escape taxation.

Hiding money in the ways and amounts lately revealed by the ICIJ is a deep kind of social corruption. It goes beyond questions of legality to the heart of modern political economy. Capitalism is a system that fosters deepening economic inequality inside most nations across the world today—unless and until popular revulsion and countermovements stop or undo that deepening. After a certain point, the inequality provokes and enables the super-rich to further expand—in a Midas-like frenzy—their already prodigious wealth. Laws become mere obstacles they have the money to evade, rather than binding social agreements. Then deep corruption sets in. The ICIJ report and documents make us all see the gory details of the vast holdings of hidden money. The real question is whether the people hurt by this behavior will change the system that promotes and rewards it.

Social Security's Explosive Injustices
May 7, 2013

People over age 65 (a growing share of the US population) are suffering a crisis-ridden capitalist system. High unemployment reduced private pensions, fewer job benefits, less job security, high personal debt levels, and falling real wages make Social Security payments more important than ever. Yet President Obama and Congress recently agreed to bargain over how much to reduce Social Security payments from current levels. That would not only hurt seniors but also the children who help them.

Consider these statistics covering 2010, presented in the *New York Times* (April 20, 2013, pp. B1 and B4). Married and single people over 65 earning $32,600 or less per year relied on Social Security for between 66 percent and 84 percent of their total annual income. That is the majority—60 percent—of all US citizens over age 65. Cutting Social Security payments seriously damages their lives. An additional 20 percent of the over-65 population, earning between $32,600 and $57,960, count on Social Security for 44 percent of their annual income. Cutting Social

Security benefits is a cruel "thank you" for a lifetime's work, a default on the payroll taxes they paid into the Social Security system.

Cutting Social Security is an outrageous injustice that may provoke historic shifts and splits in the political landscape. A new left political movement may emerge driven less by students and the young than by their parents and even grandparents. Planned Social Security payment cuts would force many in the older generation to ask the younger for more help just when crisis capitalism distresses them both. Politically explosive pressures are building.

Since its 1935 beginning, the Social Security system has collected trillions in payroll taxes, half paid by employees and half by employers. But employers lowered wages and salaries because of what they paid to Social Security. For that reason, Social Security's whole inflow came ultimately from workers' wages and salaries. Other forms of income—interest, rent, dividends, and capital gains, received mostly by the rich—were exempted from the payroll tax. Also, the payroll tax hits high and low wage and salary earners with the same tax rate. It is not progressive like the federal income tax that imposes higher rates on higher earners. Worse, it is regressive because it applies only to the first $113,000 of income earned in 2013. Individuals whose wages or salaries are above $113,000 pay no payroll tax. Thus, the higher your income over $113,000, the smaller the share of your total income that goes to payroll taxes.

Worse still: Wage and salary earners had to pay excess payroll taxes for the last several decades. Washington taxed more than was needed to pay benefits to eligible Social Security recipients. Excess payroll tax collections were deposited into Social Security "trust funds"—now almost $3 trillion in size. The trust funds lent the excess to the US Treasury; they get interest on those loans. Social Security thus has two income sources: payroll taxes plus that interest. The US Treasury spent all its loans from Social Security on Washington's usual expenditures. By 2021, Social Security payments to the growing over-65 population will likely exceed the system's inflow of payroll taxes plus interest. Then the US Treasury will have to pay back to Social Security the trillions it borrowed.

Setting regressive payroll taxes to yield an excess then lent to the US Treasury was an unnecessary injustice. Part of that money should have come instead from the existing progressive personal income tax. The other part should have come from higher corporate income (profits) taxes. Those least able to pay—middle income and poor—contributed $3 trillion in excess payroll taxes, in addition to the personal income taxes and legitimate payroll taxes they paid, to support Washington's budget. Yet now, because that budget has large deficit problems, the rich and big business favor cutting Social Security payouts. Millions who paid more than was needed into Social Security for years are now to be given less than was promised to them. What kind of system works like that?

Yet another outrage emerges when we remember why the federal budget has the bigger deficits now used to justify cutting Social Security payments. Deficits shot up because of the capitalist meltdown beginning in 2007. Washington suddenly spent much more to bail out/rescue the biggest banks and some major corporations and to "stimulate" the crisis-wracked economy. Washington feared to raise taxes to pay for that extra spending. Federal budget deficits zoomed because more spending was not matched by more taxes. No sudden increase in Social Security payouts happened to cause fast-rising deficits. Rather, capitalist crisis and bailouts did that.

Indeed, the capitalist crisis hurt Social Security finances in multiple ways. High unemployment meant that millions fewer paid payroll taxes. Likewise, payroll tax revenues fell as the crisis replaced lost high-paying jobs with lower-paying jobs. Meanwhile, the crisis did not reduce the number of eligible Social Security recipients. So Social Security's inflow fell, but not its outflow.

To cut Social Security payments now punishes the people already most afflicted by the capitalist crisis that they did not cause. The richest Americans and the large financial and other corporations are the least affected by cutting Social Security, yet they push the hardest for those cuts. The rich and the corporations gained the most over the last thirty years, bear much responsibility for the crisis, and got big bailouts exclusively for themselves. The rich and the corporations saved billions as working people overfunded Social Security with their excess payroll taxes over decades.

The abuse of Social Security, already decades old, reaches a new level of injustice with the impending cuts in payouts to eligible beneficiaries. Alongside unemployment, home foreclosures, reduced job benefits and security, falling real wages, and rising indebtedness, the assault on Social Security further squeezes the mass of Americans for the benefit of the few at the top. This reality trumps words of concern for "the middle class" pouring from Republicans and Democrats, House Speaker John Boehner, and President Obama. Politically, pressures keep building. Social Security may prove to be an explosive spark.

BANKING

Lehman Brothers: Financially and Morally Bankrupt

December 12, 2011

The *Wall Street Journal* reported (December 7, 2011) that federal court Judge James M. Peck approved the final phase of the Lehman Brothers bankruptcy, which began with the investment bank's collapse on September 15, 2008. That bankruptcy, the largest in US history, precipitated the credit markets' disintegration that cascaded into the global economic meltdown that has deepened ever since. With roughly $450 billion still owed by the bank, Judge Peck approved that Lehman Brothers has only $65 billion left to settle creditors' claims. The latter must thus accept just over 14 cents for every dollar Lehman Brothers owed them. "Thieves," they are probably muttering.

Lehman Brothers' bankruptcy has revealed multiple layers of ramifying corruption and theft among global banks in the United States and elsewhere, as well. Many juicy details are covered in the nine-volume court examiner's report of March 11, 2010.[13] It documents the bank ex-

---

13. Anton Valukas, "Lehman Brother's Examiner Report," Vol. 1, March 11, 2010, available at http://bit.ly/1HX8GAJ.

ecutives' mammoth misjudgments in their investment decisions, including their repeated violations of the basic banking principle not to borrow short-term and lend the proceeds long-term. The bank examiner shows misleading statements made about their activities and how they disguised Lehman's financial health and credit-worthiness. It appears that various legal and semilegal mechanisms were used to manipulate their accounts and otherwise violate the spirit and letter of laws and regulations.

Lehman Brothers' top bank executives rewarded themselves stupendously while directing the company into collapse. In October 2008, the chief executive officer of Lehman Brothers, Richard S. Fuld, argued over pay with Congressman Henry Waxman during public hearings on the bankruptcy. Fuld insisted he had taken "only" $310 million in compensation during the seven years before 2008, whereas Waxman's figure was $485 million. "Thieves," one can imagine Waxman muttering.

Lehman Brothers failed partly because of massive investments in subprime mortgage–backed securities notoriously misrated as "secure" by rating companies like Moody's, Standard and Poor's, and Fitch. The *New York Times* reported (April 12, 2010) that Lehman had secretly manipulated its balance sheets by using a small "alter ego" company it owned, Hudson Castle. Later in 2010, New York Attorney General Andrew Cuomo filed suit against Ernst and Whitney, Lehman Brothers' accountants, accusing them for having "substantially assisted ... a massive accounting fraud."

The bankruptcy of Lehman Brothers opened a window on strategies and tactics of many large private banks around the world. The hows and whys of their catastrophic mishandling of their "fiduciary duties"—basically, to be fundamentally prudent and trustworthy in how they manage other people's money—stand revealed. They no longer deserve public trust. Yet to date, the weak new rules and laws passed in the wake of the global crisis have changed little.

Lehman Brothers' collapse and its aftermath threatened global capitalism and not merely other big global banks. "Too big to fail" thus became those banks' slogan in demanding and obtaining the dominant influence over governments. After Lehman's collapse, governments bailed out those banks, no matter the cost. By borrowing vast sums to fund those bailouts, governments raised national debts to reduce the big banks' private debts. Hence today's European sovereign debt crisis.

Consider the irony: governments today impose austerity on the rest of us because "the markets" demand no less to keep credit flowing to those governments. Behind this dubious abstraction—"the markets"— hide the chief lenders to governments. Those are the same global banks that received the government bailouts paid for by massive government borrowing since 2007. "Thieves," mutter the Occupy Wall Street folk— and who can blame them?

The lesson here is that large-scale global banking cannot safely be entrusted to private banks. Their behavior yields socially unacceptable costs. They failed their fiduciary duties, betraying both public and private trust. Their continued existence imposes equally unacceptable risks. Modern societies do not leave military security to private armies; nor education to private schools; nor ports, harbors, and transportation systems to private conveyors; nor control of the money supply to private banks. Governments, enterprises, and households have now become dependent on credit in most advanced industrial economies. The extension of credit ought to be as equally socialized as dependence on credit has become. Lehman Brothers' bankruptcy exposes big global private banking as unaffordable and anachronistic.

Big Finance's Pathology Compels the Logic of Socialized Banking

October 1, 2012

A long string of socially costly misdeeds by major private US banks have been exposed since the current crisis hit in 2007. The latest concerns an obscure enterprise named Mortgage Electronic Registration Systems (Mers).

Founded in 1995, this private company in Virginia never employed more than 50 people full-time. Big private banks (e.g., Bank of America, JP MorganChase) and housing finance companies, like Fannie Mae and Freddie Mac, founded Mers in order to speed the processing of mortgages into mortgage-backed securities (MBS). Investors were willing to buy these new securities (bundles of Americans' mortgages). Most important, US financial institutions wanted the huge profits from producing and trading MBS.

Different local procedures for registering mortgages and processing the paperwork for trading mortgages had been slow and cumbersome across the United States, but financial megacorporations were impatient—so they created this fast, computerized way of registering mortgages and mortgage trades. Mers achieved its purpose during the housing boom that occurred from 1995 to 2007. But when mortgage defaults precipitated the housing crash and then broader economic crises, banks and lenders used Mers to foreclose on defaulted mortgages.

Mers, it now turns out, was lax and loose, as well as fast, in processing foreclosures. Beyond facilitating mortgage transactions, it often represented ultimate lenders (who alone can legally initiate foreclosures) whose exact identities were sometimes questionable. In so doing, Mers violated state laws that strictly regulate foreclosure procedures.

On August 16, 2012, the supreme court of Washington State voted unanimously that Mers had improperly initiated foreclosures on thousands of mortgages. Victims of such foreclosures can now contest them, and other states are moving to do likewise. The already badly depressed housing market has thus been dealt yet another blow—economic uncertainties multiply with the prospect of US courts becoming further clogged by litigation over these foreclosures.

The Mers mess created by profit-driven megabanks is relatively small compared to the other disasters those banks have produced over the last five years. The large private banks were major players in aggressively promoting mortgages to millions who could not reasonably be expected to afford them. These financial institutions took extraordinary and excessive risks (often with other people's deposits) in the new MBS markets and their associated credit default swap markets. We know now that deals between the big banks and the rating companies (especially Moody's, Standard & Poor's, and Fitch) wrongly inflated risk evaluations of those securities. We also know now that insurance megacorporations (especially AIG) could not deliver the insurance protections they had sold to banks and other lenders when mortgages defaulted and MBS values dropped.[14]

The private megabanks' imprudent, often unethical, and sometimes illegal activities were major causes of the global economic crisis since 2007. Conventional economics teaches that banks are financial intermediaries. They connect those with money to save and lend—their depositors and investors—with people and businesses seeking to borrow: a vital economic function. As trustees of other people's money, they are expected to assess, carefully and prudently, the risks of lending that money. When borrowers default, lenders usually bear a significant part of the responsibility for failing to see, evaluate, and avoid such loans. Borrowers, after all, are expected to overvalue their projects, just as lenders are supposed to play the role of skeptical, diligent risk assessors. Collapsed global credit markets in 2008/2009 exposed the private megabanks' colossal failures to perform that role.

In recent months, large US private banks and other megafinancial firms have been caught—and often fined millions—for still other misbehavior. They have imposed illegal extra fees and costs on customers, laundered money from illegal enterprises, and improperly pushed disastrous financial deals on budget-stressed city officials, as in Stockton, California.[15] Last February, five major US banks agreed to pay $25 billion to settle state and federal claims about their "questionable mortgage practices."[16] Major banks will also soon face penalties for their roles in the so-called Libor (London Inter-bank Offer Rate) interest-rate manipulation scandal, exposed last summer.[17]

These unethical and/or illegal and/or self-servingly incompetent actions by Big Finance have proven to be incredibly costly to the entire

14. "The US Sub-Prime Mortgage Crisis Explained," The Casual Truth, available at http://www.thecasualtruth.com/node/262.

15. Eric Schulzke, "Risk and Ambition: Stockton's Bankruptcy a Morality Tale for Cities Around the Nation," Deseret News, September 22, 2012.

16. Aruna Viswanatha, "U.S. Banks Agree to $25 Billion in Homeowner Help," Reuters, February 10, 2012.

17. Charles Riley, "Banks Face Billions More in Libor Losses," CNN Money, July 13, 2012.

world economy. Private profit drove all these bank behaviors and, even when penalized, banks' fines were trivial compared to the profits those behaviors realized. Thus, they continue and extend the list of big private banks' misdeeds. The public fumes, the politicians hype new bank regulations, the courts impose fines … and banks keep finding "new financial profit opportunities."

Big banks' failures raise an obvious question: can finance safely be left in their private hands? If any public enterprises displayed comparably awful records of misdeeds, demands to privatize them would be deafening. Yet neoliberal economic fundamentalism keeps the reverse logic unspoken and, by many, unimagined. Instead, public money and Fed-lowered interest rates keep bailing out and subsidizing the same megabanks that so grievously failed their economic function and the public's trust.

One obvious alternative to this deeply and repetitively dysfunctional private banking system is socialized banking. Once freed from neoliberal fundamentalism, the United States could rationally debate and compare the costs and benefits of private versus socialized banks and various possible mixtures of them. After all, the United States has accumulated experience with the very different kind of banking represented by thousands of workplace and community credit unions. We can also draw upon success for decades with North Dakota's state-owned bank. Other countries' experiences with public and publicly accountable financial enterprises can also help build better financial institutions than we have with big private banks. Another alternative would be to reorganize all banks into workers' self-directed enterprises, where workers and communities affected by bank policies together direct and operate banks.

To ignore alternatives to private megabanks condemns us all to longer lasting, more socially costly, and recurring crises. That is the chief lesson of all the megabanks' misdeeds—from misusing Mers to manipulating the Libor, to utterly inadequate risk assessments of the new century's financial markets.

DEBT

S&P's Judgment on US Debt
Is Substandard and Poor

April 20, 2011

On April 18, Standard & Poor's (S&P), one of three "credit-rating companies" that control that sector of the financial industry, revised its outlook on the safety of long-term US debt to "negative" from "stable." There are only two reasonable reactions to this announcement—although the usual business and political leaders are promoting their usual spins.

We may dispense quickly with the latter since they are not worth the cyberspace they waste. Conservatives "point with alarm"—a gesture they enjoy—at US debt as if it proved, first, general profligacy in the forms of excessive social programs and out-of-control entitlements (Social Security, Medicaid, and Medicare), and second, the "obvious" need to cut current budget deficits by cutting federal spending. These geniuses missed what S&P analyst Nikola Swann wrote or else they found it convenient to speak as if they had no clue about the realities of US debt. As Swann pointed out in the *Wall Street Journal*, from 2003–2008, the US deficit ranged from 2–5 percent of GDP, but it "ballooned to over 11 percent in 2009 and had yet to recover."

In plain English, fast-rising US debt is a direct consequence of the current global economic crisis and the US government's decision to borrow the money it used to bail out the major banks, brokerage firms, AIG, General Motors, and other companies. In plainer English, the conservatives who now dominate both parties are using S&P's negative outlook as a club to make the masses of people pay—in reduced services and entitlements—for the costs of borrowing to bail out major capitalists in crisis.

Now to the two reasonable reactions to the S&P outlook. The first is sheer incredulity. S&P is famous for having issued what Senator Carl

Levin (chair of the Senate investigations subcommittee) recently called "inflated credit ratings" prompted by "rampant conflicts of interest" in the US financial industry. Senator Levin named this company a "key cause" of the economic crisis. That is polite-speak for having published misleading information about credit risks and/or having shown monumentally poor judgment in assessing such risks. So we now should take seriously what this utterly compromised company says? What?!

The second reasonable reaction to the S&P outlook is a yawn. Borrowing to save capitalism and capitalists in crisis has undermined the safety of government debts from Greece to Ireland to Portugal to Hungary, and on and on. Why is anyone surprised that US debt would come similarly into question? In the current fiscal year, with an outstanding US debt just under $15 trillion, the annual projected deficit is to be $1.5 trillion, which adds 10 percent to our debt. Meanwhile, the US projected growth of GDP this year is around 2.5 percent. It takes no special training to worry about a country (that is already the world's largest debtor nation) whose debt is rising four times faster than its wealth.

In November 2010, China's Dagong Global Credit Rating Company (one of that country's major rating companies) downgraded US debt. Should we be grateful that it took S&P only six months to catch up?

Oh, wait … the timing of S&P's announcement was likely not driven by the facts—any more than its credit ratings on mortgage-backed securities proved to be. Since April 18 was the last day to file 2010 tax returns, it was a good moment to spin another scary installment in the conservative campaign to justify cutting government social spending. S&P may be rampant in its interests, but it hardly seems conflicted about them.

"Living Within Our Means" and Standard and Poor's Downgrade

August 8, 2011

The president, senators, congresspersons, media representatives, and many ordinary people speak often, these days, about Washington "learning to live within our means." Last Friday, the private rating company,

Standard and Poor's (S&P), said the riskiness of lending to the United States had risen because the United States was not living within its means (i.e., borrowing too much). Yet the meanings of these two related acts are not what they seem.

"Living within our means," as a rule for the US governments budget, is dishonest, shameful, and hypocritical. First, where was concern about living within our means when taxes on corporations and the rich were cut, especially since 2000? That cut massively reduced the government's "means" to the benefit of the richest few. Back then those same folks promised wonderful economic booms they said would result from the cuts. In fact, we got a terrible global economic crisis and an ever-widening gap between rich and poor in the United States. Yet "living within our means" was barely heard amid the cheers then for tax-cutting on business and the rich.

Second, where was that rule when Washington decided to spend on maintaining an immense military (even as the world's only remaining superpower) or on very expensive wars in Iraq, Afghanistan, Pakistan, and Libya? No, then the talk was only about national security and preventing attacks here.

Third, when banks, insurance companies, and large corporations led the economy into collapse in 2007, they wanted and got trillions in Washington spending to bail them out. No talk then about "living within our means" as federal policy. Saving the economy was all the rage as Republicans and Democrats fell over one another to spend on bailouts.

Only now are politicians concerned over "living within our means." How convenient a phrase to justify and rationalize cutting spending on the middle classes and the poor. How nice for corporations and the rich, and how totally phony. Shame is what belongs on those who use such phrases.

Finally, the phrase nicely evades defining what "our means" ought to include. For example, are the immense multimillion- and multibillion-dollar incomes and wealth of the super-rich part of the "means" the government ought to live "within?" The United States has more than enough wealth to allow the state to tax fairly and perform its proper functions without borrowing. The corporate and rich owners of most of that wealth deny it to the government when there is no direct profit to them. Our national problem is not insufficient means. It is rather a system that allows corporations and the rich to bankrupt the state and then arrange for politicians dependent on them to preach about the state "living within our means." "Hypocrite" is the second word, after "shameful," that belongs to people who say such things.

Much attention now focuses on S&P's announcement on August 5 that it downgraded US debts from AAA to AA+ because it has become riskier for creditors to lend to the United States. Yet it matters little that the two other giant rating companies did not do likewise. Nor is it important that all those rating companies deserve bad reputations because they rated AAA many of the securities that collapsed in 2007/2008 and took an already unbalanced economy into deep recession. Nor does the downgrade impose major cash costs anytime soon.

The S&P downgrade is important because it clarifies and under-scores two key dimensions of today's economic reality that most com-mentators have ignored or downplayed. The first dimension concerns exactly why the US national debt is rising fast. There are three major reasons: (a) major tax cuts especially on corporations and the rich since the 1970s and especially since 2000 have reduced revenues flowing into Washington, (b) costly global wars especially since 2000 have in-creased government spending dramatically, and (c) costly bailouts of dysfunctional banks, insurance companies, large corporations, and the economic system generally since 2007 have likewise sharply expanded government spending. With less tax revenue coming in from corpora-tions and the rich and more spending on defense/wars and bailouts, the government had to borrow the difference. Duh! These are the same three reasons that expose the shame and hypocrisy of those telling the government now to "live within its means."

The second dimension concerns the "deal" just agreed to between President Obama and the Republicans. That deal increases the national debt in the years ahead because it does not alter any of the three major debt causes listed above. The deal reflects the political clout of the corpora-tions and the rich, keeping their tax cuts, subsidies, and main government orders untouched. While the two parties pretend concern about the debt, they debate only how much to cut government spending on the people.

S&P downgraded the US national debt because the government keeps borrowing huge sums. S&P sees a basically political problem looming for the nation's creditors (i.e., owners of US Treasury securities). How long will the mass of Americans accept not only an economic crisis bringing unemployment, home foreclosures, reduced real wages, and job benefits but now also cutbacks in government supports? When will the political backlash explode, and how badly may it impact the United States's creditors?

Will the people demand that their taxes stop going to pay off creditors (corporations, the rich, and foreigners) and be used instead for public services that the people need? The exact same political danger prompted the same rating companies to downgrade the debts of Greece and Portugal. What happened there has now reached our shores, too.

S&P's rating downgrade validated what reasonable observers already knew (given that political backlashes hurting creditors have often happened in recent history). Creditors need to worry about the combination of economic crisis; growing inequalities of wealth, income, and power; and political dysfunction that now defines the United States. The risks of backlash against creditors rise with the national debt. Not to worry is irrational and dangerous for them. Opportunities for political change are mounting for us.

Deficits, Debts, and Deepening Crisis
August 18, 2011

Standard and Poor's downgrades US debt, stock markets gyrate around the world, President Nicolas Sarkozy of France and Chancellor Angela Merkel of Germany hold yet another empty summit, the Chinese and Japanese economies look worrisome. Serious commentators worry about global recession, another global banking collapse, Eurozone dissolution, and austerity programs that only make matters worse. Nouriel Roubini, famed professor at New York University's Stern School of Business asks in an article published in Project Syndicate (August 15, 2011), "Is Capitalism Doomed?" His answer: maybe.

The crisis of capitalism that erupted in mid-2007 now enters its fifth year. It grew out of excessive debts of US households and enterprises (especially financial enterprises) that their underlying incomes and wealth could not sustain. Key to the crisis was real wage stagnation since the mid-1970s. As the cost of the American Dream kept rising while real wages did not, households borrowed (mortgages, credit cards, student and car loans). Debts accumulated on the basis of stagnant real wages. That unsustainable credit bubble blew in 2007. Nothing since has significantly relieved or alleviated that basic contradiction. With high unemployment, total wage incomes have fallen and little extra credit will flow to already over-indebted workers. The crisis deepens as US demand remains hobbled.

Since the 1970s, banks, insurance companies, and hedge funds invented new speculations on the rising debts of US households (e.g., asset-backed securities, credit default swaps). Those financial speculations were even more profitable than the soaring profits of nonfinancial corporations that could keep their workers' real wages flat even as rising productivity delivered ever more product per worker to those corporations. Huge speculative profits prompted financiers to borrow in a self-reinforcing spiral ever further removed from the household debts on which it was based. When that base collapsed as millions of US workers could no longer sustain their debts, so did the financial speculations built upon it.

The wealth and power accumulated by the financial industry since the 1970s secured massive government-funded bailouts after the crisis hit. Recoveries were under way for banks, insurance companies, and larger bankrupt corporations by mid-2009. But no recoveries were provided for real wages, declining job benefits, excess household debts, and falling public services—nor for the unemployed or those who experienced foreclosure.

By bailing out their private financial industries, the United States and other governments took over (nationalized) that sector's bad debts and soured speculations. Governments borrowed to do that, thereby adding massively to national debts. "Recovery" for the financial markets bypassed the mass of people. Economically depressed working classes and increasingly indebted states now combine to unravel even the financiers' recovery.

The trail of failed economic policies undermining a dysfunctional capitalism displays multiple absurdities. Rising household debt had combined with stagnant wages by 2007 to collapse the US housing market, raise unemployment, freeze credit, and cripple state and local finances. As demand for goods and services shrank fast, businesses and the rich stopped investing in production. Their investible funds were idled, and that only aggravated the crisis. The self-regulating, efficient capitalist market system proved to be the myth its critics had mocked. However, the market system did spread the US crisis quickly to Europe and beyond.

As crisis flared in 2008, governments unfroze credit markets by pouring money into tottering banks and insurance companies. Governments printed and created new money to pay for part of these policies; governments borrowed to cover the other part. The governments' creditors included the banks and insurance companies they had bailed out. Governments also borrowed from the companies and rich individuals who had withheld investing in the production of goods and services and had thereby worsened the crisis. The absurdities of such "economic policies" (and their gross injustice) invite grim laughter if only to keep from crying.

But wait, the costly absurdities thicken. Banks and other financial companies that lent to governments got worried about fast-rising national debt levels. The US situation was especially worrisome and culminated in Standard and Poor's downgrade in August. After all, Washington had enjoyed budget surpluses in the 1990s. But then the last decade's massive Bush tax cuts, multiple wars, and then the post-2007 bailouts exploded the US national debt. Politicians who voted for all those budget-busting actions now use the resulting national debt to justify cutting government spending on the mass of people.

Creditors know from history that governments invite political trouble with high and rising debt levels. The interest costs on national debt risk diverting tax revenues to satisfy creditors rather than to provide public services to taxpayers. After four years of economic crisis, populations may not accept reduced government services while more of their taxes flow in interest payments to the banks, insurance companies, and other financial enterprises they blame for the crisis. They may revolt when leaders cut pensions and health insurance "because our nation must reduce its budget deficits and debt."

Those risks drove rating companies to downgrade the debts of ever more "advanced industrial countries." Downgrades signify the historic dangers of this global capitalist crisis. They reflect the absurdities and contradictions of the ineffective, trickle-down policies pursued by governments since 2007.

Across Europe and the United States, all sorts of campaigns seek to prevent or deflect awareness of this systemic crisis of capitalism (when its politics and economics undermine more than reinforce one another). Some aim to redefine the crisis in nationalist terms. For example, the German working class is prompted to blame economic difficulties and/or its government's austerity policies on the Greek and Portuguese working classes and/or their governments' social welfare programs. Other campaigns discover other scapegoats: "the financial industry," "the bankers," or (still more narrowly) the "central bank" are candidates. Texas governor Rick Perry, now running for president, narrowed scapegoating down to one man, the Federal Reserve chairman.

Another diversion from seeing this as a systemic crisis of capitalism asserts that large "emerging" economies—China, India, Brazil, and others—are escaping or even reversing the crisis. However, their profound dependence on trade and capital flows with the United States and Europe should dispel fantasies about their independent development or super-fantasies that their development will revive the United States and Europe. Ever more of this crisis's victims are recognizing the historical roots and systemic contradictions deepening it. Demands for change, organized and disorganized, superficial and systemic, keep building, albeit unevenly, around the world.

Europe's Debt Crisis Deepens

December 22, 2011

Over the weekend (December 17–18), Fitch—the major rating company that, with its fellow majors, Moody's and Standard and Poor's, dominated the business of assessing the riskiness of debt instruments—took a highly publicized step. It downgraded the credit-worthiness of the sovereign debts of many European countries. What a spectacle! These rating companies were distinguished by their laughably inaccurate (to be extremely polite) assessments of the risks associated with asset-backed securities. Those assessments contributed to the economic crisis we are living through. Now the world is supposed to hang on—rather than laugh at—their credit reports.

Europe's debts—and social tensions swirling around them—are clearly problems. Governments collapsing in Greece, Italy, and Spain show that, among other signs of the obvious. The rating companies' downgrades of European debt are rather like downgrading the likelihood of good weather while the rest of us are already rushing to close the windows against pouring rain.

Still worse are the usual media reports and discussions of the Fitch action. They are once again full of eerie references to steps European governments must take "to satisfy the markets." This strange metaphorical abstraction—"the markets"—is portrayed as some sort of Frankenstein monster threatening to eat Europe's children unless the parents support government austerity programs. Those austerity programs are, of course, already making those parents and their children suffer.

Let's take a momentary step back from what is an ideological—or better said, propagandistic—usage of the term. "The markets" is a conceptual device that serves to hide and disguise those particular corporations that stand behind and work those markets to pursue their interests. The politicians' and mass media's language makes it seem as if self-interested pursuit by those corporations were the machine-like operations of some unalterable, fixed institution. We need to remember that markets, like all other institutions, are human inventions filled with a mix of positive and negative aspects and open to change. After all, the mixed effects of markets have made them objects of deep suspicion and skepticism at least since Plato and Aristotle profoundly criticized markets as enemies of community thousands of years ago.

The chief creditors of European governments today are banks, insurance companies, large corporations, pension funds, some other (mostly non-European) governments, and wealthy individuals. When politicians and media speak of the need for European governments to "satisfy the markets," what they mean is to satisfy those creditors. The chief influences among those creditors are the major banks that represent and/or advise all or most of the rest of them. The major European banks were and are the chief recipients of the costly bailouts by those European governments since 2008. Indeed, those bailouts sharply increased the indebtedness of European governments because the latter paid for those bailouts by borrowing.

The bailouts worked in Europe much as they did in the United States. Banks had speculated badly in asset-backed securities and their associated derivatives leading up to late 2008. When borrowers (e.g., mortgagors in the United States) increasingly defaulted on the loans composing those asset-backed securities, the values of the latter collapsed. Banks stopped trusting one another to repay loans between them—central to the global credit system—because all banks knew that they all held huge amounts of asset-backed securities whose values had collapsed. Each major bank feared that others—like itself—might have to default on its debts.

Bank transactions with one another stopped and thereby produced a credit "freeze" or "crunch." In modern capitalist economies, businesses, governments, and consumers have all become more credit-dependent than ever. Such a freeze or crunch therefore threatened wholesale economic nonfunctioning (collapse). The solution was for governments to intervene massively to unfreeze the credit system. They did this on multiple fronts simultaneously, so serious was the crisis.

First, governments lent freely to the major banks that could not borrow from each other. Second, governments guaranteed various sorts of loans and debts so banks that had feared to lend would resume lending. Third, governments borrowed massively so private lenders—especially banks—would have a safe and profitable outlet for their loanable funds. In these ways, as agents of the people, European governments unfroze and rebooted a collapsed private credit system at enormous public expense. They thereby enabled the survival and continued profitability of the banks and their major clients.

Over the last year or so, those banks and their clients—freed by government bailouts from worrying about loans to one another—have begun to worry about their loans to European governments. They fear one thing: aroused and angry publics. People in the streets may not permit their governments to impose "austerity." The people may not accept government cuts in basic public employment and services to save money and pay off creditors that were bailed out at public expense just a short while ago.

So the creditors are now pressing governments to ensure the safety of the national debt (to themselves). The Fitch downgrade is part of that pressure. The references to "satisfying the markets" simply disguise the whole outrageous process. The crisis drama deepens: creditors' pressure on governments increases austerity policies that increase mass opposition that frightens creditors who increase their pressure on governments.

The contradictions driving this vicious cycle agitate all of European society and the global economy interlinked with Europe. European governments fear the creditors and fear their rising domestic oppositions to austerity. They express irritation against Fitch and the other rating companies for making their dilemma worse. They have no solution, bend toward "satisfying the markets," and thus pursue austerity in fits, starts, and retreats. Like animals frozen in the headlights of oncoming disaster, the players in this absurd European drama issue redundant credit reports (Fitch), hold endless and fruitless conferences and summits (Sarkozy, Merkel, et al.), and twitch with anxiety as general strikes proliferate and governments teeter and fall. Meanwhile, phantoms like "the markets" haunt the media analyses and politicians' statements, serving mostly to fragment and obscure what is happening.

Déjà Vu: Germany Tightens Its Economic Power over Europe

August 17, 2015

Germany's leaders herded their European counterparts into imposing harsh austerity on Greece. It was the price, they insisted, that Greece had to pay to receive bailout credits from the European Union, European

Central Bank, and International Monetary Fund (IMF). The Europeans required those bailout credits to be used mostly to pay back loans the Greek government had gotten earlier from private banks (chiefly German, French, and Greek). Those credits could not be used to get Greece out of the 2008 crash that afflicted all of Europe.

Those private banks had gladly and profitably pushed too many loans onto the Athens government for many years. When the 2008 global crash brought forward the moment when the Greek government could no longer carry its bloated, excess private debts, default loomed. Had that happened, those private banks would have required second bailouts (their first occurred in 2008–2009) from their governments. But the speed and generosity of those first bailouts had enraged much public opinion in France, Germany, and Greece. A second bailout, required if Greece had defaulted, would have finished those countries' leaders' political careers. Cleverly, the leaders arranged for those institutions to lend to Greece to pay off its private creditors: no need then for second bailouts.

To cover this maneuver with "public relations" distractions, German chancellor Angela Merkel and others promised to require Greece to undergo a tough austerity treatment, portrayed as economic pain and punishment that Greeks brought on themselves. It was necessary "medicine" that would soon deliver economic recovery. All leaders everywhere promised and still promise recovery to austerity's victims. In fact, since 2010, austerity brought Greece further economic decline, not recovery. Indeed, recoveries proved elusive or painfully slow for most Europeans as they struggled with austerities of varying intensities.

Germany pushed hardest for the harshest Greek austerity. That too was a maneuver for domestic political advantage. Merkel loudly depicted herself as protecting Germans from higher taxes (to pay Germany's share of any future institutions' bailouts of European countries like Greece that did not repay its debts). Merkel and her finance chief rigidly refused to relieve Greece of its debts (even though the IMF and countless experts said openly that Greece's debts were simply "unsustainable" and could never be paid). Merkel's refusal meant that Greeks' tax payments would go not for roads, schools, and hospitals, nor to rebuild a crisis-shattered economy, nor to pay and pension Greek public workers.

Greeks' taxes must instead be used to service Greece's debts to the institutions for limitless years into the future. Merkel's posturing served her domestic political purposes, but at a huge cost for Europe.

The richest European economy—Germany—imposed massive suffering onto one of the poorest economies in Europe. This was to help defray three huge costs associated with the 2008 global capitalist crash for which Greece, a tiny country, bore minimal responsibility. The first cost was a badly imbalanced Eurozone economy leading to 2008. German exports (at carefully managed prices lower than elsewhere in Europe) were financed then by excessive German private bank loans to Greeks and others who purchased those German exports (at the expense of their own countries' producers) while accumulating excess debts. The second cost was the crash itself that brought Greece severe unemployment and economic contraction as revenues from tourism and shipping collapsed. The third cost was the bailout of European (including Greek) private banks and Merkel's maneuver to forcibly convert Greek government debt to private banks into debt owed to the institutions. Denying Greece massive debt relief meant and means heavy austerity.

Alongside the Greeks, many other Europeans now grasp what awaits them too in the "unified Europe" that German leaders are constructing and using. Yet the Portuguese, Irish, Spanish, Italian, and other poorer (relative to Germany and France) people want a differently unified Europe. With troubling historical echoes, German leaders once again seek to force a particular kind of capitalist unity onto Europe. The weapons this time are economic and political instead of military, but they, too, provoke resistance. Europe risks severe divisions and disunity with serious ramifications for the world.

Echoes of Past German Economic Imperialism

In the second half of the nineteenth century, private capitalists in the smaller states that would later become Germany confronted major problems. Those states' politics and cultures still reflected a feudalism that resented and often undermined capitalists. The latter faced tough competition from other, more advanced capitalists and especially the British who dominated world trade. Germany came late to colonialism and kept encountering obstacles from competing colonial regimes, above all the British. Capitalists in what became Germany were also discovering a new and growing threat from their own employees. The latter articulated an anticapitalism from below that envisioned and pursued an alternative, socialist future without private capitalists in it.

The "solution" fashioned by their leader then, Otto von Bismarck, mobilized government support for the growth of German capitalism. Bismarck allied that policy with selective reinforcements of the remaining Prussian and wider German feudalism to build a strong governing coalition. On that basis he sought to blunt the growing socialist workers' movements by constructing the first modern welfare state apparatus. Finally, he forcefully projected a new German colonialism as a major player within capitalism's global imperialist expansion. Holding together this complex set of policies was the glue of intense German nationalism mobilized by Bismarck's wars to unify the diverse smaller sovereignties into one German nation. Yet those wars had other, contradictory effects, including the Paris Commune, which gave a powerful stimulus to socialism and socialists everywhere.

On the one hand, after 1870, Germany became an imperial power on the world stage. On the other, German socialism kept growing. Likewise the competing colonial capitalisms, especially the United Kingdom, also became bigger threats. When this dangerous mix exploded in 1914, the kaiser intensified German nationalism to gain the domestic unity needed to wage war. Germany lost the war, and the Bismarck system dissolved. A socialist and tentatively internationalist Weimar period ensued, but it was hobbled by war debts and oppositions from nationalists determined to revive a German empire.

When the 1930s depression hit Germany, a new nationalist upsurge repudiated the country's history since 1914. The Nazi form of nationalism promised a better, more successful version of Bismarck. It would destroy socialism from below by substituting a fascism from above. A new alliance of private German capitalism, feudal remnants, and a powerful state would hold it all together. Nazi fascism aimed to manage and militarize German capitalism to dominate Europe and regain its lost colonial power beyond.

The Nazis rebuilt German industrial power by means of a state-private capitalist partnership imbued with intense nationalist fervor and fascist ideology. But that proved insufficient to win a second world war or to reconstruct a German empire. Losing the war also split the country in two, as East and West Germany, opposing front-line states in the Cold War. After 1945, the combination of wartime destruction, debt and reparations burdens, and the global capitalist preeminence of the United States overwhelmed West Germany and undermined its reconstruction and growth. West Germany then appealed for and obtained massive debt relief from the United States, United Kingdom, and France in 1953 (precisely the sort of debt relief it now refuses to grant Greece). In exchange, it served as a bulwark against the Soviet Union and Eastern Europe.

Debt relief enabled a German resurgence—celebrated as a self-congratulatory "economic miracle" or *Wirtschaftswunder*. Economic growth funded an expanded welfare state to engage the West German working class as a partner (or at least neutralize it) for Cold War purposes. Again using nationalist imagery, the prevailing ideology defined West Germany as an alliance (not the near merger à la Nazism) of private capitalists, the state apparatus, and labor unions that enabled the latter to claim credit for the welfare state as "social democracy." Germany's Socialist Party dutifully broke with its Marxist past first to join the alliance and eventually become a ruling partner in governing coalitions with German "conservatives."

The post–World War II expansion of the West German economy was export-oriented. German exports remained competitive by deftly using the alliance among capitalists, the state, and unions to organize a kind of unofficial price-and-wage control. This kept German prices from rising as fast as prices elsewhere in Europe, both before and especially after the creation of the common currency or Eurozone.

Effects of the Eurozone

The Eurozone accelerated the boosting of German development at the expense of development elsewhere in Europe. Germany's prices were and remained lower than the rising prices nearly everywhere in the Eurozone. This facilitated German exports, boosted profits from those exports, and began the recycling of those profits through German banks to become loans into the Eurozone. Many countries in the Eurozone were damaged by the competition from German exports yet were also caught up in the euphoria that European unification guaranteed them economic expansion, sooner or later. Thus, they were eager for the expanded loans that German banks were eager to make to other Eurozone governments (e.g., Greece), to banks in Eurozone countries (e.g., Spain) and to firms and individuals throughout Eurozone countries. Neither borrowers nor lenders were adequately careful in assessing the real risks associated with fast-rising private and public indebtedness. Debt papered over growing disparity within Europe much as debt in the United States (e.g., subprime mortgages) papered over the rising inequality generated since 1970 by stagnant real wages coupled with rising productivity and hence profits.

Yet another boost to German economic growth including exports was German reunification in 1990. It delivered to German capitalists a vast new supply of highly trained, industrially disciplined, very productive former East German workers. Best of all, they were used to lower wages than their Western German counterparts. None of Germany's capitalist competitors in Europe, Japan, or the United States enjoyed anything comparable. The latter may have obtained mass immigration of low-wage workers, but they were not as well trained, disciplined, or productive as the former East German workers.

The Eurozone also facilitated German exports outside of the Eurozone. The single currency settled into an exchange rate with other major currencies (e.g., the US dollar, Japanese yen) that reflected all Eurozone member economies. In that way, German exports benefited from a lower relative value of the euro than would have been the case if the old deutschemark currency had remained and reflected just Germany's economic strength and its relationship with trading partners. The other Eurozone members thus subsidized German export success through the Eurozone's exchange rate—much as they also subsidized that success by allowing their price structures to rise relative to Germany's. German banks lent to other Eurozone members the funds that often found their way back to Germany as payment for German exports (much as earlier Marshall Plan loans to Europe found their way back to the United States to pay for US exports).

Profits piled up in Germany in direct proportion to rising indebtedness across the Eurozone. That rising debt masked or at least distracted attention from the underlying, widening inequality within Europe. The basic contradiction—that such German development risked undermining its own conditions—was postponed, its explosive effects delayed. When this unsustainable arrangement reached its limits—when deteriorating economic conditions proved unable to sustain the costs of rising debt—governments, banks, nonfinancial businesses, and individuals faced defaults. The cascading crash of 2008–2009 made the European situation—worse even than the parallel situation in the United States—deeply depressive ever since.

Risks of German Economic Strategy Today

German leaders' pursuit of the basic economic strategy detailed above entails huge risks for Europe and the larger world. First, inside Germany, politicians, media, and others have reverted to depictions of Greeks and other Europeans in poorer countries as lazy, overindulged in their dependence on state supports, and profligate. Workers in these poorer countries are thus differentiated from hard-working Germans and others in richer European countries. Merkel in Germany presided over this sort of nationalistic character assassination in a way reminiscent of Mitt Romney's use of similar rhetoric during the 2012 US presidential campaign. His theme then was that 47 percent (his number) of Americans were lazy and drunk on entitlement to government handouts. He said these Americans voted Democratic to secure their handouts, whereas Romney and Republicans represented the "hardworking" majority. That argument failed to win the election for him, but it did contribute to the dangerous polarizations increasingly besetting the United States since. Where Romney exploited racial stereotypes and income differences, Merkel exploited nationalist stereotypes, quite a policy choice for a German leader given that country's history.

Second, Merkel neatly deflected the economic problems inside Germany associated with precarious jobs, low income, part-time employment, reduced social services, and austerity policies generally. These were ignored in deference to celebrations of the German government's vigilance to not let other Europeans take from them. Or they were recast as problems somehow related to "helping" other poorer Europeans who abused rather than appreciated that help. Moreover, Merkel's line affirmed that Germany's "help" to others was no longer affordable; Germans had done much but no longer could. This sort of argument transformed internal economic problems and policies into failures of others. It converted Merkel's rescue of private German banks with public European money as instead "help" to an inadequately grateful Greece. If German economic policies seemed harsh, that was only because its victims' abusive past behavior left no other choice. Dominant German public opinion comforted itself in these ways.

In the official German statements lies a familiar inability to see, accept, or admit the reality of how Germany interacted with the rest of Europe's economies in the decades leading to the 2008 crash. Those interactions were driven by German capitalist imperatives around revenues and profits. Their self-serving nature relative to many of their European partners was unsustainable in the long term. These interactions entailed a deepening inequality among and within European nations. In all these ways, they undermined the move toward European unity, more so than at any time in the last half century.

German capitalism in its way replicates the fundamental mistake of capitalists elsewhere. It does not know how or when to stop overstepping the limits of what the rest of society will endure and allow. No matter whether opposition comes from Greeks suffering absurd privations; from Germany's only real opposition party, Die Linke; from Pope Francis; or from rising questions and challenges of capitalism per se around the world, German capitalism pushes ahead oblivious. It ignores especially its own past lessons about recasting internal economic problems as the fault of other, lesser people who deserve harsh punishment. Europeans everywhere recoil, again, from German foreign economic policies and their modes of articulation. Their worries about the sort of

European unity Germany's economic dominance will yield are changing into opposition and resistance. Something ominous is under way, and the unfolding Greek tragedy-*cum*-resistance expresses it profoundly.

The Greek Crisis, Austerity, and a Postcapitalist Future

January 15, 2015

[The following interview (conducted by Michael Nevradakis, host of Dialogos Radio in Athens) provides an analysis of the causes of the economic crisis in Greece and in the Eurozone, a debunking of the claims that the Greek economy is recovering, and a proposal for what a postcapitalist future could look like for Greece and the world.]

Michael Nevradakis: Prior to the [presidential] elections, we've heard talk about how the situation in Greece is turning around, that the economy is recovering. How do you respond to this?

Richard Wolff: I respond to it in the same way that I respond to this sort of report that periodically surfaces here in the United States. Here's the way that I would describe it. We have the worst economic downturn in the last seventy-five years, second only to the Great Depression of the 1930s, and we're not yet clear how long this one will last and how bad it will be, so it may even overtake the one in the 1930s; we just don't know.

I would remind everyone that in the aftermath of the Great Depression, with the rise of Keynesian economics, we were told in the economics profession that we had learned the lessons, that we had the mechanisms, we had the research, we had the monetary and fiscal policies and the Keynesian economic theory behind it all to make sure that this kind of economic collapse, cutting this deep, lasting this long, would never happen again. The same people who assured us of that, through the 11 economic downturns that happened in the United States alone between the end of the Great Depression in 1941 and the beginning of this one in 2007, told us, "We have a downturn, but it's not so bad, and we have at least learned the lesson to avoid a really bad one." Well, now we have the really bad one, too. So my first reaction to these conversations about having turned the corner is we're being told that by the exact same people with the exact same level of confidence with which they told us that we would not be in this situation in the first place.

The second thing I would say is this: There has been a recovery. There has been a recovery in the incomes and wealth of the 5 to 10 percent of many of the societies hit by the crisis; stock markets in many countries have recovered; corporate profits have recovered in some parts in both financial and nonfinancial industries—but for the vast majority of people, there has been no recovery. Unemployment is at record highs in many parts of the world. Even for those who have kept their jobs, their jobs have fewer benefits, lower degrees of security, [and] children are having to forgo education or rack up enormous debts to pay for it. Wherever we turn, the basic life condition of the mass of people is poorer than it was five and six years ago.

There is no recovery for the mass of people, and in the end, even those at the top cannot long enjoy a recovery that is denied to the masses below them, even though they refuse to face that reality and therefore suffer the continuation of this crisis. There is a recent report by a leading German economic research institute begging the European Central Bank to pump more money—quantitative easing, they call it—into the European economy to prevent a deflationary downward spiral. Those who are promising recovery [will continue] have a hard time explaining why a conservative economic research institute in Germany should reverse itself and be so anxiety-ridden that this economic downturn will continue for the future.

In your opinion, what led countries such as Greece into the crisis in the first place? Was it simply what we've been hearing in the media that these countries "lived beyond their means" or is there something more that you could point to?

The argument about living beyond their means is somewhere between offensive and silly. Most countries most of the time borrow, and borrow at an increasing pace. They are all "living beyond their means." And they've been doing it in many cases, including that of Greece, for quite a while. The question is not "do they do that?" because they all basically do. Let me remind you that over the last six years, the United States has virtually tripled its outstanding debt [and] is living beyond its means on a scale that could not have been imagined before, so no one is in a position to argue that that's the problem. The United States is doing better than Europe even though it's borrowing more money than the Europeans.

I think the issue in Greece, as elsewhere, has to be explained by a number of conditions that came together. The first problem in Greece was not that they were borrowing too much, but was rather that the lenders to Greece were no longer interested in lending to Greece the way they had been. Many of those lenders had actively pushed Greece into borrowing because they made huge fees off of the national debt of Greece, as they do of most countries. Goldman Sachs helped the Greeks to develop new kinds of accounting that could disguise or misrepresent parts of the borrowing that they were doing, or at least make people think it was less than it was before.

The biggest problem for Greece was the global economic collapse of 2008. Suddenly every major capitalist country, led by the United States, was having to ramp up its borrowing by the hundreds of billions of dollars, and what that meant was that every lender around the world, every bank, every insurance company, every typical lender to a government, suddenly had an immense increase in demand for loanable funds. Many of those borrowers, like the United States, had much higher credit ratings than the Greek government, for all kinds of reasons, and the result was that the lenders saw that they could lend all they want at much lower risk to desperate countries like the United States, trying to dig its way out of a crisis, and so they turned to the Greeks and said, "Why should we lend to you, who are a risk relative to lending to the United States, or Britain, or France, or Germany?" and suddenly the Greeks discovered that their lenders, particularly German and French banks, but others as well, had a more attractive borrower, and suddenly the terms for the Greeks became much more onerous. Interest rates rose, conditions became harsher, and the long-standing pattern of borrowing in Greece was suddenly confronted by a serious change of heart of the traditional lenders.

The second thing, which is just as important, and again, it is true of all countries, not just Greece, is the peculiar political economy of capitalist countries. It works something like this: divide your population into two parts, the mass of working people, the overwhelming majority on the one hand, and the large businesses and the individual rich 5 percent on the other. Each of these groups wants the government to provide them with all kinds of expensive services. Each of them, at the same time, wishes to pay the minimum possible tax burden on themselves, and each of them, using their relative resources, tries to get out of paying taxes. Big corporations and the rich, because of their resources, are able to hire the tax accounts, the lawyers, and they do a much better job of evading taxes than the mass of people.

What the mass of people can do is threaten politically to vote against anybody who raises taxes and for anybody who lowers them and are subject to that kind of persuasion. In any case, what happens in capitalist economies is then that the government and the politicians are placed in an impossible position. They dare not raise the taxes on the masses, because that will cost them votes. They dare not raise taxes on corporations and the rich, because that will make the corporations and the rich support their political opponents and their careers will be over. At the same time, they dare not displease either of the two groups by not providing them with the demanded services and supports and subsidies that they have come to assume.

So what does the government do in that situation? The answer is obvious: It borrows money. By borrowing money, they do not have to raise more in taxes from a population that doesn't want to pay it, and yet they can continue to spend to provide the services that the population demands. And finally, the rich are specifically pleased by this arrangement, because they're the ones who do the bulk of the lending to the government. So they are able to avoid taxation, in which they would have to give money to the government, end of the story, and instead, substitute loans to that government, precisely because they didn't pay the taxes. And that money has to be returned by government to corporations and the rich, and on top of it, paying them interest all the while.

So the corporations and the rich find this a very attractive arrangement; the mass of people continues to get services without having their taxes raised. Everybody wins, ironically, while the government continues to raise more money in debt. To then blame the government as "living

beyond its means," or to not see this mechanism, but somehow to as-
cribe all of this to some character flaw of people is to make it a personal
failing rather than to understand it as a structural and economic arrangement whose irrationality speaks to the absurdity of how capitalist
economies are organized and not to some individual failing.

*What was the role of the euro as a currency, and the Eurozone and its poli-
cies, in creating the conditions that led countries such as Greece, and some of
the other southern European countries, into this crisis?*

I think that the euro, like the whole project of European unification, appealed to all kinds of different groups for all kinds of different reasons. And
this produced the kind of coalition that was able to push it through, to
realize the European community, to realize the single currency, and so on.
But I do believe that the different parts of the coalition that came together
to produce it had very different agendas and very different capabilities for
realizing their agendas. And the result was that the agendas of some were
more than satisfactorily realized, and the agendas of others—partly out of
miscalculation, partly out of being swept up in a kind of euphoria—these
other folks pushed for a reality which has disappointed their hopes.

Let me give you an example: Germany on the one hand, Greece
on the other. For the Germans, the development of a single currency
and a single European market was a dream come true. They knew that
their domestic situation—the workers' councils that mediate the relationship between labor and capital, the ability of that relationship to
keep prices from rising and to give workers job guarantees in exchange
for not pushing wages up and to get the corporations to agree not to
raise prices—meant that as Europe came together and as most other
countries used the conversion of their local currency into the euro as
an opportunity to really raise prices, the Germans would be in the end
the most competitive economy. Not because they are technically more
proficient, but because their domestic increase in prices was kept under
control, while everywhere else, the euphoria of the common market and
currency led businesses and unions to push up prices and wages. So it
was a clever move by the Germans; it created for them an unbelievably
profitable opportunity to export to the rest of Europe, to indeed move

production from countries like Greece and Portugal and Spain back to Germany or to Germany in the first place, to take advantage of the price advantage that German domestic capitalism was able to achieve.

In contrast, Greece and many other Southern European countries saw widespread support for a completely different idea. People there imagined, in the classic mistake of conventional bourgeois economics, that they would benefit by a common currency and a common market because their wages were already lower than those in France, Germany, Holland, and Scandinavia and because they displayed friendly-to-business climates. Many in Southern Europe deluded themselves that the French, Germans, Dutch, and Scandinavians would stand by while their economies were emptied out of manufacturing and many services as producers would leave to take advantage of lower Southern European wages within a unified common economy. Particularly but not only the Germans were busy taking steps to make sure that not only did their industries not leave Germany and Northern Europe for Southern Europe but, in fact, the reverse was happening because of the price advantage that I have explained.

The second mistake the southern Europeans made, including the Greeks, was not to understand that if capitalist enterprises in high-wage parts of Europe, Western Europe and Northern Europe in particular, if they were going to incur the expense of leaving, of moving production, they weren't going to go to Greece and Portugal and Spain. They were going to go to Asia and Africa, which is not that much further but much, much cheaper. Therefore, they're not going to stop halfway in a place like Greece or Portugal; they're going to go much further. In other words, the Greeks didn't understand the larger picture of capitalists moving, particularly to Asia, secondarily to Latin America, and finally to Eastern Europe and Africa, which is a major process of the last fifty years. [They didn't understand] how important that is, and how the competition the Europeans face from the Asian businesses, but also from the United States, which is doing this on a major scale, means that they cannot afford to stop in Greece. So the Greeks thought they would get an advantage, but they made a mistake and pushed for something that wouldn't bring them an advantage and in fact brought an advantage to the Germans and others at the expense of the Greeks, and that is why the experience of unity is so bitterly different for the different parts of Europe, even to the point of threatening the ability of the unity to survive.

Why do you believe there has been such an insistence on austerity on the part of the European Union and the International Monetary Fund (IMF)?

I think they understand that they really have, particularly in their framework, no choice. This is hard, I know, particularly in Greece where I've tried to explain it in the past. Their fear, which is a very real fear—I meet with bankers in New York all the time and I know what I'm talking about—their fear is that countries such as Greece and Portugal will succumb to the pressures of the mass of their people to do something drastic. And drastic means withdrawing from the European Union and trying some other way of proceeding, or, and perhaps I should say and/or, to radically alter their economic systems inside, by basically radically changing the organization of enterprises, the distribution of wealth and income, in order to pursue a radically different economic trajectory, one focused on national rebuilding, one which limits drastically the freedom of capital and enterprise to move and to make investment decisions regardless of the impact on the local economy.

They're very afraid of that. And so what they've decided to do is a different kind of strategy: to try to appeal to the wealthy and to the leaders, the traditional elites of these countries, Greece, Portugal, Italy, Spain, to say look, you're in danger of a wholesale transformation in your own country that will seriously jeopardize everything that you have accomplished and everything you own, and that your best option is to join with us, the IMF, the European Central Bank, the European Community, Germany, France, England, and so on, in an alliance, and that alliance is going to try to get you through this situation by shifting the burden of this economic collapse onto the mass of your people. Tell them a story that their only way out is to become "competitive" and that the only way to become competitive is to lower wages, to lower taxes, and to lower the public services that are paid for out of taxes. To basically go back ten, twenty, thirty, forty years, maybe even more than that, to standards of livings that the Europeans thought they had left far behind, and basically in that way, slowly persuade some businesses to settle in your countries [that] wouldn't have thought of it before—make the wages and the social conditions so poor that you really do become a competitor of an Asia whose wages and taxes are rising, of a Latin America whose wages and taxes are rising; they're going up, you come down, and at some point, you'll be able to get an advantage. That is the real political economy that is being presented here.

And I think the wealthy, the top corporate leaders of Greece and of Portugal, have understood that they will be better off, as they see it, in an alliance with international capital reorganizing their own economies to become "competitive" slowly, than to not cut that deal, to have their own economies go through internal convulsions, where their positions as traditional political elites, as the owners of the means of production, and as the wealthy could very well dissolve in an uprising of either the left or the right or even some combination of them, focused on a national development program that does not give the privileges that have continued to be taken by the elites in those countries.

Have austerity policies like the ones being implemented now in Greece, or the types of policies that are typically championed by the IMF, ever succeeded in helping a country recover from an economic crisis?

The people who make these arguments are also the people who commission and pay for the evaluations. So the answer is: It depends on your point of view. Are there examples that the IMF points to in which austerity drove down taxes and drove down prices and drove down wages in some way that they were followed by upturns in economic well-being? Yes. But of course, the critics point out that wasn't because of austerity; it was for other reasons, or it might even have been despite austerity. It's a little bit like pointing, for example, to Argentina, pointing out that they defaulted on their national debt, ended up paying fifty or sixty cents on the dollar many years later, and yet in the aftermath of that, until recently, they had a pretty good boom going, so they could claim that gee, you know, defaulting is not only not bad, it's good for your economic development, but the critics would quickly point out that Argentina benefited from other things, that its well-being was not because of but despite the default, and so on.

Here's the bottom line: What austerity is about is shifting the burden of an economic crisis from one part of the population to another. The mass of Greek people did not force [Andreas] Papandreou to borrow money. The mass of the Greek people didn't know about or have much to do with fiscal policy at the national level. In fact, governments, bankers, leading industrialists, shipbuilders, the major players of the Greek economy, got together, as their counterparts did elsewhere, to produce the decisions that then, in the wake of the international collapse of capitalism, became unsupportable, producing a crisis in Greece. Once that had happened, there was only one question left: Who was going to pay the cost of all the debt we've run up or all the production decisions we've made that have left us without the capacity to export, with a dependence on imports?

And at that point, as has happened in every country—Greece is in no way unique—the wealthy and the business community went to work, with their resources and their business connections, to make sure that they didn't pay the price. OK, then there were only two other options: If the rich and the wealthy and the corporations don't pick up the cost of the crisis, then either foreign institutions will, like the European Central Bank and IMF and European Commission,. or your own mass of your people. Austerity is the explanation that it's going to be put on the mass of the people, and your own rich folks, your corporations, together with the international organizations, will make sure that happens. When they're asked why, in a period of economic suffering, you would make the mass of people, who didn't cause the crisis and who are already suffering its consequences . . . you can't possibly say, in any kind of honest discourse, well, somebody has to pay and we're not going to do it and the international institutions are not going to do it, so it's got to be the masses.

You can't say that, so here's what you say: You tell a story that yes, this austerity is terribly painful, but there really is no option because the only way out of this crisis is to become "competitive" as a locus of production, "competitive" in terms of the prices of your outputs on the world market, and to get those prices down, and to get production to come here, we have to offer capital internationally very low wages and very low taxes. So you shift the burden of the crisis, which is the point, on to the masses of people, while telling a story which you hope that the media and the professors of economics will take seriously, that this is not only the best way to solve the problem but the only way. None of that is true, but it is the best face they can put on the cost-shifting purpose that austerity serves.

Do you believe that Greece should remain in the Eurozone or should it perhaps return to a domestic currency, and how could Greece even depart from the Eurozone and rebuild its economy with its own currency?

Well, I think the Greeks have to make a decision. And again, this is not unique to Greece at all. The Portuguese have to make this decision; the Spanish have to make this decision, the Italians, and so on. And this decision is really more, in my judgment, about the organization of the economy inside your country. The major question isn't your relationship to the rest of the world. The major question is your relationship to yourself. What is the Greek population going to do? If you continue to permit your huge private companies, shipbuilding and others, and your private banks, to conduct business as usual, to pay the salaries that they do, to give the perks that they do, to organize public policy by working through these people as the crucial middlemen between what the government does and what the larger society and economy had as conditions, then you're stuck. Then you are either going to knuckle under in the form of austerity, or go through basically another kind of austerity, which is what you would face if you quit the euro, if you went back to the drachma [Greece's currency before the euro], if you went back to an independent economy; you'd have to devalue something awful; all your input costs will go crazy; you'd have domestic trouble of the sort you haven't seen in Greece since World War II.

But that's all premised on [leaving the] economy in the basic structure; all the key decisions are made by the major shareholders and boards of directors of leading Greek enterprises. They have long ago figured out how to keep the government from playing a role that threatens them. If you leave all of that intact, and that's a fundamental political and ideological condition, then you're going to face an indeterminate period of time of real economic decline. The decline of Greece as a society, the decline of cities like Athens and Piraeus and all of them, and you're going to become one of the corners of Europe that will be looked upon as [a disaster]. It will be blamed on something in the Greek character, the way you have already seen that done.

Let me warn you, because the United States should be a picture for you to think about: We have, in the United States, the equivalent of Greece. They're called our destroyed major cities. I'm going to pick the most dramatic example, but it is to the United States what Greece is becoming to Europe. The city I have in mind is Detroit, Michigan. Forty years ago it was the center of the automobile industry. Detroit had a population of 2 million people. It was high working-class incomes, highly trade union–organized workers, the United Auto Workers; they produced new music, Motown rock 'n' roll that swept the entire globe as a new kind of culture. They were an economic, political, and cultural mecca, a powerhouse, a success story of modern capitalism. That was in 1970.

So here we are, forty years later, [and] what have we got? The population of Detroit is now 690,000 people. That is, an overwhelming majority of the people left the city; they left behind their homes; they left behind their families; they left behind the schools. The city of Detroit is a wasteland. The majority of its housing is empty. There are fires in large parts of the city every day as abandoned houses go up. One of the largest problems in Detroit today is wild dogs—50,000 dogs. Why? Because the city of Detroit has no money, so it can't hire dog wardens, the people who catch dogs if they don't have an owner and get them off the street. Millions of people can't afford to keep a dog, so they simply let them go, and so what we have is wild dogs roaming the street. I didn't make any of this up. In a very short time, Detroit became a wasteland. The city declared bankruptcy [in 2013] and is now administered by state officials who are all white, in a city that is overwhelmingly black. So you have the economic collapse laid over a racial divide. It is a disaster. Cleveland, Ohio, same thing. Camden, New Jersey, same thing. Youngstown, Ohio, same thing. We have in these areas people, populations as big as Greece, suffering unspeakable, unimaginable long-term economic decline with no end in sight. That is the future of other cities in the United States, and I believe it is the future of Greece.

In a peculiar way, it is even easier in Europe to do it to a whole country, like Greece, than it is to do it to randomly selected cities in the Midwest, the way we do it here in the United States. But if nothing is done to change the internal logic of capitalist development, there is no reason to believe this is going to change anytime soon. Greek wages are not going to go to the level of Indian or Vietnamese or Chinese wages, not for a long time, and those countries are busy using their accumulated wealth to hold on to their industries. They're not going to quickly make capital movable elsewhere. The Greeks have to take control of their own economic possibilities, radically change the way wages and prices are calculated, [and] become "competitive" not by lowering wages but by lowering profits and the returns to capital. That's the way to go, to invest in your own country. Yes, is there a little bit of autarchy here? For sure. But the alternative is to be part of a division of labor on a global scale that assigns to Greece, as it has assigned the same thing to Detroit, and I don't believe the Greek people want or deserve to be put into that situation for decades to come.

In essence, you've made the argument that we should be looking toward a postcapitalist future, not just in Greece but worldwide. What would this postcapitalist future look like and how could it be accomplished?

Yes, you have understood me perfectly well, but let me make one final point about that. In one of my recent radio programs, I talked about billionaires because we have a very useful statistical service here in the United States that keeps track of billionaires, and your [readers] might also be interested to know that we have about 1,600 or 1,700 billionaires in the world. If you put them together, they own together, these 1,600 or 1,700 individuals in the world, as much as the bottom half of the entire population of this planet, some 3 to 3.5 billion people. OK, for me, this conversation about capitalism is over. Any economic system that produces 1,600 billionaires who can together dispose of an equal amount of the property of this planet as the lower half, 3.5 billion people, is an economic system that no longer justifies anyone's support other than those 1,700. Them, I could understand. But this is a system whose success in increasing output is completely offset by its absolutely obscene distribution of wealth, which makes the pharaohs of ancient Egypt look like nothing in comparison. So for me, going beyond capitalism is what we call in the United States a "no brainer." It is something that is, or should be, instant, immediate, and obvious.

To repeat your question, what do you put in its place? Well, for me, the answer is not the traditional socialist focus on collective ownership of the means of production, state enterprise, nor is it substituting government planning for the market, and I will tell you why. I think, after many efforts have been made—the Soviet Union, the People's Republic of China, Eastern Europe, Cuba, Vietnam, and so on—I think it's clear that whatever the achievements of state ownership and planning over private ownership and markets, that proved insufficient. It did not provide a society which the mass of people will see as a desirable, new postcapitalist system to go to, and indeed, those societies were not even able to preserve public ownership and planning, since most of them have more or less collapsed and fallen back to private ownership and markets.

So what is then the missing link? What can we learn from the successes and failures of traditional socialism so that we can better define where we need to go next? And for me, the answer is to understand that we have to transform the organization of enterprises. That is, all of those institutions, whether we call them a company or a firm or an entrepreneur, whatever we want, the way we organize the production of goods and services, the factories, the offices, the stores that produce the goods and services we depend on, they have to be drastically altered.

The way we have it now, the capitalist way, puts a tiny number of people in the position of making all of the decisions. Most business in capitalist societies is done by corporations. Corporations have what are called major shareholders, usually a group of ten or twenty people who own enough shares to be the determining votes on all matters of the corporation. One of the things that shares decide is the board of directors, usually a group of ten to twenty people who make all the basic, day-to-day decisions: what to produce, how to produce, where to produce, and what to do with the profits. So we have organized production so that all the key decisions are made by a tiny group of people, literally twenty to thirty people, at the top of a pyramid. The vast majority of workers, pro-

duction workers, white-collar workers, services, manufacturing, whatever, are excluded systematically from participation in those decisions. If
it's a private enterprise, it's organized the way I just described.

When the state takes it over, as in the Soviet Union, you still have
the gap between the mass of people who do the work and the tiny group
who make the decisions, but what has changed is that the tiny group is
state officials put there by the government or the Communist Party or
whatever ruling groups there are, but you still have an organization that
juxtaposes a small group of decision makers at the top, and a vast mass
of workers excluded from those decisions practically and in actuality at
the other end. And my argument is, therein lies the crucial problem. If
we want economic production of goods and services to serve the people
in each community or in each nation, then we have to put the people
who are to be served in the decision-making position. To make a long
story short, we have to convert from capitalistically organized enterprises into worker cooperative enterprises.

Let me, in a very brief way, give you an idea of what this would
mean. If a factory wishes to close its businesses in Thessaloniki or its
businesses in Cincinnati, Ohio, or in Chicago, Illinois, or in Lyon,
France, or in Dusseldorf, Germany, it would have to be a decision made
by all of the workers there together. One worker, one vote, democratically. In that case, guess what? The factory wouldn't leave; the workers
wouldn't do that because they don't want to move to China or to some
other place and have a job. The whole mobility of production would
have to be organized in a completely different way if workers are to
participate and to do such a thing.

Let me give you another example: If the profits are distributed
democratically—in other words, if all of the profits distributed are distributed by all of the people whose labor helped produce those profits,
namely, all the workers, then guess what? They're not going to give a
wildly disproportionate share of the profits to shareholders as dividends,
just like they're not going to give a few top executives huge pay packages
while the average worker cannot afford to send his kid to school or have
a decent vacation. The single most important cause of unequal wealth
and income is the distribution of enterprise profits. If we change corpo-

rations from the major shareholders deciding on the board of directors and therefore giving the bulk of the profits to themselves, and instead make that a democratic decision, we will have a much less unequal distribution of net revenues in corporations, and consequently, this will be the most serious, sustained, and effective assault toward a direction of less inequality than anything that has been tried in the past. Instead of struggling in every society over the redistribution of income, by converting to worker co-ops, we wouldn't distribute it so unequally in the first place, and that would obviate any need for redistribution.

I could go on, but my answer is this: In addition to social ownership of means of production and proper planning for the economic outcomes we want, we need to democratize enterprises, to finally say goodbye to the capitalist organization of enterprises that has subordinated all of the decisions that enterprises make, that impact the politics, the culture of the whole society, that has subordinated those to what is privately profitable rather than what is socially desirable and sustainable. This has driven us to an impossible situation, and whether we look at it environmentally by the degradation of nature that these corporations have done, or we look at it in terms of social inequality, the time to go beyond capitalism is obvious—it's now, and it's long overdue.

Scapegoat Economics 2015

April 11, 2015

As economic crises, declines, and dislocations increasingly hurt or threaten people around the globe, they provoke questions. How are we to understand the forces that produced the 2008 crisis, the crisis itself, with its quick bailouts and stimulus programs, and now the debts, austerity policies, and deepening economic inequalities that do not go away? Economies this troubled force people to think and react. Some resign themselves to "hard times" as if they were natural events. Some pursue individual strategies trying to escape the troubles. Some mobilize to fight whoever they blame for it all. Many are drawn to scapegoating, usually encouraged by politicians and parties seeking electoral advantages.

For example, Germany's recent history has featured reduced wages (especially via increasing part-time jobs), fewer social welfare protections, major bank bailouts in the crisis of 2008, rising inequality of income and wealth, and austerity policies. Its leaders around Angela Merkel have responded by carefully rescripting their recent financial maneuvers as "Europe's bailout of Greece" in a classic exercise in scapegoat economics. Three institutions (the "troika" of the European Central Bank, the European Commission, and the International Monetary Fund) have lent the Greek government money since 2010. Those loans were used chiefly to pay off the Greek government's accumulated debts to private European banks (including especially German, French, and Greek banks). The "bailout of Greece" was thus really an indirect bailout of those private banks.

Without that indirect bailout, those private banks would have suffered the usual losses that come when banks make loans that cannot be repaid. Those losses would have been costly for shareholders in those banks. The major shareholders among them include some of Germany's richest and biggest capitalists. With their usual political power, they might have gotten the German government to bail them out directly again (since the German government had already done that directly a few years earlier in the 2008/2009 crisis). But such a second direct bank bailout would have been wildly unpopular with German voters and therefore politically dangerous for Germany's top politicians.

Leading German politicians saw the "bailout of Greece" as an opportunity to serve their big-bank supporters with a second but indirect bailout that was disguised as "for Greece." This gambit protected their political careers from voters' wrath while getting all of Europe to share the cost of loans to Greece. German leaders then took the lead in insisting loudly that Greeks pay dearly for Europe's loans. Merkel imposed a crushing austerity regime—with the cooperation of Greece's two mainstream political parties—that shifted massive resources away from Greece's public services for use instead to secure interest on and repayment of the troika's loans.

The opportunism of German leaders was also an exercise in scapegoat economics. German bankers and political leaders—supported by many other European leaders—distracted and deflected their own people's resentments over growing economic problems. Instead of popular anger turning against German, French, and other European bankers, capitalists, their political servant, and the capitalist system itself, it was redirected against Greece and Greeks. German media dutifully led the way in recasting the European loans to Greece (that ended up mostly in private European big banks) as supports for "lazy, overpaid, and over-pensioned" Greeks that were unfair and costly burdens for hard-working German and other European taxpayers.

By means of this heavily staged public "Greek" drama, Germany added international economic scapegoating to the domestic scapegoating already widespread in Europe. It had repeatedly targeted communities of immigrants. Typically, the immigrants first arrived to provide employers (who often encouraged immigration) with lower paid workers and thus higher profits. Then when the inevitable next capitalist business-cycle downturn arrived, the resulting discontent of unemployed and recession-burdened people was deflected and turned against immigrants. They were blamed as if they "took away jobs" from nonimmigrants rather than unemployment being the periodic burden, for immigrants and nonimmigrants alike, imposed by the profit-driven, fundamentally unstable capitalist system.

The United States has repeatedly displayed the same blame game with immigrants and with ethnic minorities. In the wake of the crisis since 2007, it is extending domestic scapegoating to still others. Governors now increasingly attack state employees, their unions, and pensions as if they, rather than the crisis, had suddenly become the economic problem. Mayors across the country do the same to municipal workers. Of course, both state and municipal budget problems since 2007 are primarily the results of high unemployment and reduced consumer spending. In short, it was and remains the crisis since 2007 that played and plays the key role in cutting governments' tax revenues and hurting government budgets. Growing and more effective tax-evasion strategies of business and the rich have had the same effect. Responding to lowered tax collections, politicians fearful of damage to their careers refuse to raise tax rates. Instead they embrace spending cuts that they justify by means of scapegoat economics.

Thus they demonize public employees as lazy, greedy, overpaid, underworked, and over-pensioned—all remarkably similar to German depictions of Greeks. Governors practice scapegoat economics by promising to protect "the public" from tax increases by "not pandering to" public employees and their unions and by "reining in" their pensions. Those politicians act as if public employees and their pensions were suddenly the problem rather than a dysfunctional economic system. They similarly miss the stark reality of the dysfunctional political system they operate: It cuts government help to people in economic crises just when they need it most. Instead, US political leaders, like their German counterparts, use scapegoat economics to justify their selective spending cuts.

Scapegoat economics this time also serves capitalism's global relocation. For decades, existing factories, offices, and stores have been moving from old capitalist growth centers (Western Europe, North America, and Japan) to new centers (e.g., China, India, Brazil). Similarly, enterprises are growing more in the new rather than the old centers. Headquarters sometimes remain in the old centers even as enterprise facilities locate elsewhere. Jet travel, computers, and telecommunications make all this manageable. The capitalist competition that impels this relocation also means that the old centers lose many well-paid occupations with ample benefits and job security. Workers in places like Germany and the United States are increasingly forced to settle for lower paid, insecure jobs with fewer benefits. While jobs and wages grow more quickly in the new centers, wages there remain so low that huge profits reinforce capitalism's global relocation.

As capitalists relocate, populations everywhere must adjust to and accommodate all the usually attendant frictions, sufferings, and costs. In the old centers, unemployment and lower-paid jobs undermine governments' tax revenues. Given resistance to tax increases, governments turn increasingly to expenditure cuts in their accommodation to capitalism's relocation. This often worsens unemployment and wage rates. More important, it further depresses mass standards of living. Consumption, household finances and relationships, marriage and career decisions: All are caught up painfully in the adjustment process. The same applies, likely more traumatically, to capitalism's new centers. There, formerly agricultural and rural people are transformed quickly into industrial and urban populations living in extremely overcrowded and poorly provisioned slums.

Capitalism's relocation is socially disruptive in yet another basic way. It deepens economic inequality at both poles. Profits rise and wages stagnate in the old centers. Employers distribute the rising profits chiefly to shareholders and top executives and secondarily to upper management and professionals helping them operate corporations. An often spectacular growth in income and wealth inequalities afflicts the old centers. In the new centers, arriving capital makes partnerships with local capitalists and government officials. The latter become extremely wealthy more quickly than local wages rise, and so inequalities of wealth and income deepen in the new centers, too.

The gains and losses of relocating capitalism are very unequally distributed in both its old and new centers. This only aggravates the social tensions already emerging from the many adjustments and accommodations people are forced to make. Suffering from personal, financial, and community losses, individuals and groups often feel betrayed by "their" political and economic organizations. In the United States, for example, many working people believe that the Democratic Party and labor unions had promised to "protect" them but failed to do so, especially in the crisis and debt-funded bailouts since 2007. They have come to fear that now they will be required to absorb the costs of dealing with those debts by being subjected to austerity policies while "others" get protected from those policies. Feeling betrayed or abandoned by their traditional political representatives, many become susceptible to a new politics organized around scapegoat economics.

As exemplified by new Republican governors in the upper Midwest sensing electoral opportunity, this politics appeals to voters by promising to "protect" them from austerity policies (in the United States, unlike Europe, "austerity" is not the name used). This means, first and foremost, that voters will be spared tax increases. These are demonized as always and necessarily "bad" economics for everyone. But the Republican governors now go further and promise to protect voters also from spending cuts by making sure that those cuts focus on "others." Enter scapegoat economics. The governors find "others" to be scapegoated in response to crisis-driven and capitalist relocation–driven declines in tax revenues. First of all, those others are—you guessed it—the traditional targets: those on welfare, in inner cities, immigrants, and so on. The often racist overtones of such appeals are only too well known. Nowadays, the second set of those "others" has come to include public employees, their unions, salaries, and pensions. To secure their careers, politicians promise voters to protect them by cutting government spending on both sets of scapegoated others.

When it works, such politics sets one part of the population suffering from capitalist relocation, crisis, and austerity policy against another part. This permits big banks, large corporations, and the rich, who own and direct them—those with the most responsibility for causing the crisis—to escape paying for it. They escape in part because their wealth and power made sure that they benefited first and most from the government bailouts in 2008 to 2010. They also escape because scapegoat economics enables them and their political friends to shift the burden of paying for the crisis onto certain of its victims while "protecting" other victims from further victimization. Perhaps capitalism inherited scapegoat economics from prior economic systems, but capitalism's crises keep renewing that ugly injustice.

Greece Needs Our Solidarity in Its Struggle Against Austerity
July 3, 2015

Not for many years has the issue been posed as clearly as it will be on July 5 in Greece's referendum: European capitalists, the political leaders whom the capitalists' money controls, and the austerity they impose will be judged by the people most savaged by that austerity.

The Greek people were informed that the financial maneuvers made by Europe's biggest banks, biggest industrial capitalists, and the usual political elites (shamefully including Greeks and "socialists") in 2008–2009 would absolutely require massive losses of Greek jobs, incomes, property, and financial security for many years to come. Recycling former British prime minister Margaret Thatcher's words, they were told "there is no al-ternative." Other Europeans (and Americans, and others, too) were told the same, although their austerities were less bleak (so far).

After all, slaves had to suffer from the mistakes of their masters and the crises of slave systems—and likewise serfs had to suffer from their lords' mistakes and feudalism's crises. So workers must now absorb the costs of capitalism's crises and capitalists' mistakes (including the documented crimes of the biggest banks). Workers must suffer the capitalists' use of the state to bail themselves out of their crisis and then, through austerity policies, to shift that bailout's costs onto the general public. This, the Greeks were told, is what must be.

The Greeks have thus provided a convenient but urgent test case. European leaders believe that workers in capitalism's old centers (Western Europe, North America, and Japan, especially) now must accept declines in their standards of living. Capitalism is abandoning them to make higher profits in Asia, Latin America, and elsewhere—capitalism's new centers. Savaging the Greek workers' standards of living (and, if needed, a few other countries' workers' too) teaches a double lesson. The first is, "decline is your future—get used to it." The second is, "be glad your decline is—deservedly—not as bad as that of the Greeks."

From 2008 to 2012 the Greeks followed their conventional leaders in accepting this dictated decline. They were told the austerity would be temporary, bitter medicine needed for recuperation. But the decline only got worse, and promises of recuperation came to be exposed as empty.

Syriza's rise to victory in 2012 represented both the Greek people's partial awakening to the reality of what was happening to them and their determination to stop and reverse their economic decline. The January to June 2015 negotiations between the Syriza government and the European leaders completed the Greek people's awakening. In response to the European leaders' mantra of "there is no alternative," Syriza and its Greek supporters answered, "alternatives are always there." It's just that conservatives cannot see or imagine them.

The referendum on July 5 will express the results in Greece of a contest between capitalism's management and plans for European society (economic decline for capitalism's old centers, disappearance of former "middle layers," their major cities' transformation into playgrounds for capitalism's richest, etc.) versus what Europe's working classes will permit. It will show Europe its future. If the Greek people vote no—their refusal to cooperate with capitalism's plans—then a new political landscape will emerge. In Europe and likely beyond, the new twenty-first-century struggle will pit new forms of socialism against forms of capitalist barbarism. If the Greeks vote yes, they will embolden European capitalist leaders to push austerity further until the next working-class resistance arises and mobilizes sufficient support to finish what Syriza began.

Solidarity from others oppressed by austerity policies everywhere is Greece's greatest need now. Real solidarity will also help mobilize the forces everywhere that are coming to realize the deepening costs and injustices of accepting capitalism's continuation.

Deficits, Debts, and Demagogues

April 11, 2012

Government budget deficits and the national debt are occasions more for demagogues to preach than for serious analysis. The usual suspects, conservatives and liberals, are gearing up for the election. Each side uses the large federal budget deficits and fast-accumulating national debt to beat its tired ideological drums. Conservatives insist that deficits and debts require huge cuts in government jobs and job benefits (especially pensions) and in social programs (especially Medicare and Medicaid). Liberals push for less drastic cuts in federal employment and programs because "the economy still needs stimulus." Liberals promise that when prosperity returns and Washington's tax revenues rise, we can painlessly use them to reduce the accumulated debt.

The two sides have been promoting these positions for decades, long before the current deficits and debts arrived. The latter are just opportunities exploited by both sides to repeat old sermons to their faithful. However, there are important political lessons to learn by connecting deficits and debts to the demagogues using them these days.

What are the actual causes of recent years' high deficits that have boosted the national debt? The first cause is the capitalist crisis. When millions are fired, their lost income means lower individual income taxes flowing to Washington. When businesses lose sales, their incomes also drop and thus also their income tax payments to Washington. Lower sales mean lower sales taxes flowing to state governments. Our collapsed housing market lowers property values, and that drops the property taxes on which local governments depend.

Second, even as government revenue shrank because of the crisis, Washington undertook extremely costly bailouts of large banks and other corporations as part of stimulating a crisis-ridden capitalist economy. Washington also sent more money to states and localities to offset a part of their revenue loss because of the crisis. Crisis-induced revenue losses plus crisis-induced expenditure increases are the major causes of today's large deficits and national debt increases.

The third major cause of federal deficits and debts has been huge reductions in corporate income taxes and individual incomes taxes on the richest Americans. At the end of World War II, for every dollar paid to Washington in individual income taxes, corporate profits' taxes amounted to $1.50. Today, the ratio is very, very different: for every $1 paid in individual income taxes, corporations pay $0.25. Despite the effects on statistics of S corporations and other tax loopholes for businesses and executives, the bottom line shows a massive shift of the federal tax burden from business onto individuals. Over the same period, the top rate of the federal individual income tax fell from 94 percent to 35 percent: a massive federal tax break for the richest Americans.

The result was and remains obvious: The middle of the income distribution—the majority that is not rich and not (or not yet) really poor—had to pick up the burden. No wonder that a majority of the population is upset, angry, talks endlessly about "tax revolts," and deeply distrusts politicians of all stripes who imposed the twin massive tax shifts upon them. The majority correctly fears being driven down into the mass of the poor. As that process unfolds, the majority becomes increasingly resentful and angry and looks for whom to blame.

The job of the demagogues is to deflect that anger onto a credible scapegoat. Their goal is to protect corporations and the rich (a) from the return of the tax rates they paid in the past, (b) from paying for the crisis since 2007 that they helped cause, and (c) from paying for the government bailouts they demanded and received and that saved them from very serious crisis-induced problems.

The demagogues' preferred scapegoat is the public sector of our economy. So they attack government employees and the public services they provide. Chief among their current targets are the pensions paid to retired public employees. These are denounced as primary causes of the deficits of local, state, and federal budgets. Democrats and Republicans agree to cut those pensions as a way to reduce the deficits.

Yet this scapegoating is easy to expose. Public employee pensions have not risen in any dramatic way over recent years, so they could not and did not cause the government budget deficits to zoom upward. Those pensions did not cause our national debt suddenly to soar. Capitalism's second-worst crisis in seventy-five years and the government's bailout program for large corporations and the stock market—that's what caused the deficits and the exploding national debt.

Attacking workers' pensions is preferred because it protects corporations and the rich from blame in this time of mounting economic difficulties for most people. It pits government workers against private-sector workers. Attacking public workers' pensions undermines retirement programs to which they contributed, benefits they accepted in place of wage increases from their employer. Conservatives use lower pensions in the private sector to argue for parallel reductions in public employees' pensions; next they will use reduced public pensions as arguments to lower private-sector pensions.

Cutting public employees' pensions makes workers pay for a crisis they did not cause and for the massive government bailouts they did not get. How convenient for corporations and the rich that Democrat and Republican demagogues are "concerned about the problem of government pensions." Instead of scapegoating public workers, they could remember the lessons of the last time US capitalism crashed.

In the 1930s Great Depression, powerful unions and socialist and communist parties got the government to raise taxes on corporations and the rich. Those tax revenues helped fund a New Deal for most Americans by (a) creating the Social Security system for the millions over sixty-five, (b) creating the unemployment compensation system for the millions without jobs, and (c) creating and filling over 12 million federal jobs.

As corporations and the rich rolled back the New Deal over recent decades, they created conditions for another massive crisis. Now, they aim to turn their crisis into another chapter in that rollback. When capitalism delivers these results, it has outlived its usefulness for all but the few beneficiaries of that system.

THE SO-CALLED RECOVERY

Recovery? What Recovery?

July 28, 2011

The so-called economic recovery since mid-2009 was chiefly hype, a veneer of good news to disguise and minimize the awful underlying economic realities. The few (large corporations and the rich) who bear much of the responsibility for the crisis made sure that the government they finance used massive amounts of public money to support a recovery for them. The mass of the population was excluded from the government-financed recovery for the few. We now have the summary official statistics to expose this grotesque injustice.

In economics, as in other fields, pictures and graphs are sometimes worth more than a thousand words. So it is with a summary graph prepared by a group of economists at Northeastern University in Boston.

Their short report[18] exposes the basic lie in claims by politicians, media spokespersons, business leaders and others that the US economy has been in an economic "recovery" since early 2009.

What did recover in the United States, partly or wholly, were only corporate profits (especially those of banks) and the stock markets. Figure 6 (the report's chart 14) shows three vertical bars indicating the size of profit and stock recoveries from the second quarter of 2009 through the first quarter of 2011.

Figure 6. Percent Changes in the Indices of Corporate Profits, Stock Market Prices, Selected Hourly/Weekly Wages, and Aggregate Employment from 2009 II to 2011 I (2009 II–100)

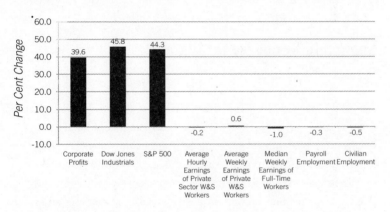

Source: Andrew Sum and Joseph McLaughlin, "Who Has Benefitted from the Post-Great Recession Recovery? A New Look at the Growth Performance of Jobs, Wages, Corporate Profits, and Stock Price Indices During the First Two Years of Recovery," Center for Labor Market Studies, Northeastern University, Boston, Massachusetts, May 2011 (Chart 14, p. 8); available at http://bit.ly/1QhG8EG.

What did not recover by the first quarter of 2011 is shown by the

18. Andrew Sum and Joseph McLaughlin, "Who Has Benefitted from the Post-Great Recession Recovery? A New Look at the Growth Performance of Jobs, Wages, Corporate Profits, and Stock Price Indices During the First Two Years of Recovery," Center for Labor Market Studies, Northeastern University, Boston, Massachusetts, May 2011; available at http://bit.ly/1QhG8EG.

five remaining bars in the chart. Those tiny bars show what happened to payrolls and employment. From the depths of the crisis in early 2009 until mid-2011, there has been absolutely no recovery in wages or jobs for US workers.

The crisis of the capitalist system in the United States that began in 2007 plunged millions into acute economic pain and suffering. The "recovery" that began in early 2009 benefited only the minority that was most responsible for the crisis: banks, large corporations, and the rich who own the bulk of stocks. That so-called recovery never "trickled down" to the US majority: working people dependent on jobs and wages.

The countless claims of "recovery" as if it were a general economic event spread across the entire US economy are lies. They hide the tragic truth of ongoing economic crisis for the many.

Economic Recovery for Whom?

March 7, 2012

We expect ever-grosser competitive lying from the presidential primary candidates. We should expect no less from the media "analysts," politicians, and academics competing for big business favors. With those expectations, we might be less disappointed by what we get.

These days, the hype about "economic recovery" is intense. Obama pitches it as a reason to reward him with campaign donations and votes. The money should flow in from the business community that wants badly to hide the fact that recovery has—from the beginning of this crisis—been only for them at the expense of recovery for everyone else. They need a president who hypes "recovery" as if it's about helping everyone in some general or "fair" way. The votes should come, Obama's team calculates, because average people are becoming increasingly desperate. They want someone in power who might help them even just a bit.

The Republicans had planned to use the economy against Obama (as he did against them in 2008). The recovery hype drove them to emphasize instead contraception, religion, and the ever-popular Iran bashing. By abandoning their attacks on "Obama's bad economy," Republicans leave the field to those hyping recovery.

The major media take their cues from politicians and their orders from the megacorporations that own them. Mainstream academics, lowest on the public relations hype totem pole, celebrate recovery, too. Then they remember they are supposed to be independent thinkers, so they find something about "the recovery" to "debate." That turns out to be, yet again, whether government interventions help or hinder economic recovery. In reality, big business leaders and the top politicians they control collaborate ever more closely for their mutual benefit. To the mainstream academics falls the public relations task of pretending that big business and the government are adversaries.

However convenient to some, to speak of economic recovery today is false. There is no general improvement in economic conditions, let alone the sustained, self-reinforcing economic upturn that the word "recovery" is supposed to mean. Here is what we know early in March 2012. The "good" news is about unemployment (slowly declining for a few months), retail sales (slowly rising), and especially sales of automobiles (rising quickly). It is also about corporate profits (high) and General Motors (GM) profits (record high). Finally, the stock market had a nice upturn over recent months as well. That's pretty much it for the good news.

Here's the "bad" news. Housing prices are falling again (their much-hyped "recovery" earlier during the crisis turned out to be false). Manufacturing was down in the latest reports, while consumer spending and construction spending were flat. Consumer debt is rising again. The largest city bankruptcy in US history has been announced for Stockton, California (population 300,000). State and city services across the country continue to be cut. Real wages and job benefits keep trending down.

A closer look at the good news raises even more doubt about "recovery" than the bad news does. Let's focus on those robust car sales and the hiring back of some laid-off auto workers. Consider just two facts. First, the average age of cars on the roads in the United States today is 10.8 years, making them the oldest fleet since the records began many years ago. People are not buying cars because they can afford them. Rather, their old cars now cost too much to repair too often. What they borrow to spend on car replacement now will require spending less on everything else in the months ahead. Second, hiring more auto workers will have a much smaller impact on the US economy than rehiring used to. That is because the auto industry bailout deal with the unions allows GM, for example, to hire "new" workers at $16 per hour, half of what they used to pay for the same jobs.

Looking closer at high corporate profits shows that they come more than ever from overseas activities of US corporations. Indeed, the country's sad condition and worse prospects are why so many US corporations place their hopes and investments outside the United States.

The truth about "economic recovery" is that for the mass of people, it is untrue. For the top 10 percent and especially the top 1 percent— those who brought global capitalism into crisis in 2007—recovery has been real. They got the huge bailouts from Presidents Bush and Obama. They got the trillions in government loans at low interest that they lent back to the government at higher interest rates. (So much for how profits are capitalists' rewards for "taking risks.") To pay for its expensive bailouts (hyped as "stimulus plans"), the US government chose *not* to tax big businesses and their rich executives. Doing that, we were told by business and government alike, might "hamper the recovery."

So the government borrowed trillions to "fund the recovery." From whom? From the same banks, insurance companies, large corporations, and rich executives whom the government had bailed out and *not* taxed. When those creditors began to worry that the US government's debt was becoming too high to sustain, they demanded that government cut back public services and use the money instead to pay interest and principal back to those creditors. And so it does.

"Recovery" is a recurring hype for a grotesquely unjust economic system. It is dusted off and reused whenever possible to cover the basic policy shared by both major parties in the United States during major capitalist crises: help those at the top so maybe it will "trickle down" to everyone else. "Recovery" is the go-to word when business and government impose conditions to make the United States more profitable, especially for big business. Those conditions now include declining real wages, job benefits, and public services for most Americans. They also include the huge numbers of personal and small business bankruptcies that cheapen the costs of secondhand equipment; empty office and retail space and professionals (accountants, lawyers, etc.) desperate for work.

After Five Years: Report Card on Crisis Capitalism

July 9, 2012

After five years of crisis—with no end in sight—it's time to evaluate what happened, why it happened, and what needs to be done. One key cause of this crisis is the class structure of capitalist enterprises. I stress that because most treatments miss it. By class structure, I mean enterprises' internal organization pitting workers against corporate boards of directors and major shareholders. Those boards seek first to maximize corporate profits and growth. That means maximizing the difference between the value they get from workers' labor and the value of the wages paid to workers. Those boards also decide how to use that difference ("surplus value") to secure the corporation's reproduction and growth. The major shareholders and the directors they select make all basic corporate decisions: what, how, and where to produce and how to spend the surplus value (on executive pay hikes and bonuses, outsourcing production, buying politicians, etc.). Workers (the majority) live with the results of decisions made by a tiny minority (shareholders and directors). Workers are excluded from participating in those decisions: a lesson in capitalist democracy.

US capitalism changed in the 1970s. The prior century of labor shortages had required real wage increases every decade (to bring in immigrant workers). In the 1970s, many capitalists installed labor-saving computers, while others relocated production to lower-wage countries. Demand for US laborers fell. Simultaneously, women moved massively into wage work as did new immigrants from Latin America. The supply of laborers in the United States rose. Capitalists no longer needed to raise real wages, so they stopped doing so. Since the 1970s, what capitalists paid workers stayed the same. Meanwhile, computers helped labor productivity rise: What workers produced for capitalists to sell kept increasing. Surplus value (and profits) therefore soared (e.g., stock market boom, rising financial sector) while the wage portion of national product/income fell.

By making these changes, US capitalism provoked a classic contradiction for itself. It paid insufficient wages to enable workers to purchase growing capitalist output. The solution, led by the fast-growing financial sector, was twofold. First, it cycled rising corporate profits partly into major new consumer lending (mortgages, car loans, credit cards, and later student loans). Rising consumer debt sustained growing mass consumption despite stagnant wages and so postponed an otherwise certain economic downturn. Second, financiers promoted profitable new investments for corporations and the rich (securities based on consumer debts and credit default swaps that insured such securities). Financial corporations displaced nonfinancial corporations as dominant in the US economy. Financial transactions based on consumer debts built on stagnant wages (the ultimate means to service that debt): those fruits of capitalist decisions brought the 2007 crash. (What is widely known as the crash of 2008 technically began in the fourth quarter of 2007.) The crisis nightmare began: a cyclical downturn coupled to long-run decline in workers' purchasing power.

As the crisis deepened, capitalists and mainstream economists insisted that it was "only a financial problem"—credit had frozen because banks did not trust one another and stopped lending. The credit freeze would be "easily managed" by federal bailouts of financial and a few other corporations (e.g., General Motors) deemed "too big to fail." Dutiful politicians funded those bailouts with massive government borrowing from (rather than taxing) the large cash hoards accumulating in the hands of banks, large corporations, and the rich. They hoarded, they explained, because lending to or investing in the economy they had crashed was "too risky." Instead of making their hoards available to individuals and businesses that might have revived the economy, financial capitalists lent them to the government to bail out those same capitalists: a lesson in capitalist efficiency.

As government debts soared to bail out global capitalism, financial capitalists began to worry about overindebted governments. Those governments' citizens—especially where traditions of anticapitalist criticism were strong, as in Greece—might balk at servicing debts that resulted from capitalism's failures, not theirs. So financial capitalists demanded ever higher interest for lending to such governments. They also demanded the imposition of austerity programs. Public employment and services were to be slashed. The money thereby saved would instead guarantee interest and repayment of those governments' debts. Major leaders dared not suggest—let alone raise—significant taxes on corporations and the rich as an alternative to government borrowing or austerity. In this way, the costs of economic crisis and bailouts were shifted onto national populations via unemployment, home foreclosures, and austerity: a lesson in capitalist justice.

Let's summarize: (1) capitalists decided in the 1970s to computerize and increasingly relocate production overseas; (2) that enabled them to impose wage stagnation and greatly increase surpluses and profits; (3) financial capitalists lent to consumers and built a speculative bubble based on consumer debt; (4) when rising consumer debts exceeded what stagnant wages could afford, the system crashed; (5) capitalists got trillion-dollar bailouts while lending government the money for those bailouts; and (6) now, capitalists make entire populations pay for the crisis and bailouts by directing politicians to impose austerity. This capitalist system not only fails to "deliver the goods," it dumps ever more outrageous bads.

Nor are solutions available in New Deal–type regulations and Keynesian deficit spending as promoted by economists Paul Krugman and Robert Reich. While the New Deal reduced capitalist excess and eased mass suffering (neither happens now), it never overcame the 1930s Depression (World War II did). Capitalism's costly cycles were never stopped (eleven downturns occurred after 1941 and before the 2007 crash). Moreover, President Roosevelt's insufficient New Deal regulations and taxes on corporations and the rich were undone after 1945 as capitalists funded the politicians, parties, lobbyists, and think tanks that shaped legislation and public opinion. A new New Deal now (green or otherwise) would have poorer and shorter-lived economic results. Capitalists now have greater financial resources and decades of experience in blocking and undoing limits on their wealth and freedom.

After five years of crisis, it has become clear that any real solution for capitalist crisis must include changing the class structure of capitalist enterprises and thereby their directors' decisions. Those are twin obstacles to ending capitalism's repeated crises and their immense social costs. The necessary change would reorganize the production of goods and services. Instead of undemocratic, hierarchical capitalist corporations, workers would collectively become their own board of directors and make all the key decisions themselves. Had workers' self-directed enterprises replaced capitalist enterprises in the 1970s, real wages would not have stopped rising thereafter; jobs would not have moved out of the United States; a consumer credit explosion would not have happened—and so on.

Workers' self-directed enterprises would have their problems, too. We cannot exchange an inadequate capitalism for some pretend paradise. America can, however, do better than a capitalism whose failures were already many and deep before exploding into this latest severe crisis. We ought finally to dare to think so, say so, make the needed changes, and move forward.

Recovery Hype: American Capitalism's Weapon of Mass Distraction

September 27, 2013

From President Obama on down, defenders of the status quo insist that the US economy has "recovered" or "is recovering." Some actually see the world that way. They inhabit, imagine they inhabit, or plan to soon inhabit the world of the infamous top 1 percent. Others simply seek security in life by loyally repeating whatever that 1 percent is saying.

Here is the "recovery" that they see. The top 1 percent of income earners in the United States took 19 percent of the national income in 2012, the largest share since 1928. That 1 percent also saw their average income rise by 31.4 percent from the current crisis's low point in 2009, through 2012. The top 1 percent certainly enjoyed a recovery.

In total contrast, income for the other 99 percent rose by an average of 0.4 percent during the same period. Many of those people actually saw their earnings drop. That was not a recovery, not even close. For the vast majority of Americans, the recovery hype is just a weapon of mass distraction. From 2007—the last year before the current recession hit—until now, US Census Bureau data show that the median income of Americans has dropped from $55,627 to $51,017 (i.e., nearly 10 percent), with no recovery evident.

Yes, the stock markets and profits for large banks and corporations have recovered, more or less. That explains the good fortune of the top 1 percent. Their incomes depend heavily on the health of those parts of the economy (especially interest, dividends, and capital gains).

But the 99 percent depend mostly on wages and salaries. High unemployment keeps their income hobbled, as does the persistent shift in the United States from jobs with high pay and good benefits to jobs with neither.

Hyping a recovery helps politicians boost their popularity (or at least slow its decline). It also serves to give masses of people with growing economic difficulties the impression that "other people" are experiencing a recovery. So they blame themselves (their age, skill set, education, and so on) for missing out. The recovery hype thereby functions as a massive "blame-the-victim" program, in which a dysfunctional capitalism escapes criticism, while its victims instead turn criticism inward upon themselves.

Hyping recovery pleases those seeking reassurance about the state of capitalism. They want to hear that it is—or will shortly be—the secure, near-perfect economic system they always thought and said it was. They want to see the system's flaws, imperfections, and ongoing crisis—stressed by capitalism's critics—as merely minor and passing irritations. Calming references to recovery—used often and said as authoritatively as possible—nicely suggest that capitalism is either healing itself or being healed by a benevolent government.

Academic economists, with careers built celebrating capitalism's efficiency, growth, and optimality for everyone, need urgently to hype recovery just as they have long hyped capitalism. They want to escape the ridicule of agitated students who keep taking on more crushing debt to pay for school, while their job and income prospects deteriorate.

These students turn a critical eye toward the economic system and quickly discover the rich and diverse literature of criticism of capitalism.

Why, they increasingly demand, have their teachers never taught them about all that? Mainstream economics professors fear the exposure of their long-standing intolerant exclusion of most strong critics of capitalism from teaching and research opportunities. Students are beginning to demand the open, balanced education long denied them. They want to hear and read the academic critics alongside the academic celebrants of capitalism; they want to decide for themselves which perspective—or combination of perspectives—to use and develop.

Hyping recovery is also supported from darker, more cynical motives. Leaders of large corporations who have already moved many of their operations out of the United States call the current situation a "mature" economy. This euphemism reflects their sense that rapid growth now happens more outside the United States than inside and, therefore, higher profits beckon overseas where wages and taxes are lower. They want to keep freely relocating over the coming years with minimal opposition as they depart.

The leaders of these companies especially prefer to be less heavily invested here when the American working class is realizing that the capitalism that raised their wages across earlier decades of growth is fast departing for more profitable opportunities abroad. That departure abandons the American working class to steady decline—as countless indicators show, among them falling real wages, reduced public services, and high unemployment.

Business leaders and their elected friends fear workers' rage and resentment should they be able to identify who and what did them in. Hyping recovery provides "delaying cover" as businesses executives relocate their facilities abroad, their homes and offices inside "gated communities," and their workplaces into "heavily secured enterprise zones."

Many mass media corporations render the service of hyping the recovery eagerly to their advertisers. These advertisers wish to avoid association with bad news that might distress audiences. The mainstream media therefore offers up infotainment with economic recovery "highlights." They also emphasize reports about countries whose experiences with the global economic crisis are worse than that of the United States.

For example, immense attention focuses on Greece and Spain, rather than Germany or Sweden. The crisis has been far, far less damaging in the latter than in the former or in the United States. Likewise, when the mass media here cover the high unemployment rates in certain European countries, they often conveniently omit that unemployment there does not affect citizens' health insurance coverage, pensions, or most public services and subsidies as negatively as it does in the United States.

The recovery hype performs the same service of mass distraction in this crisis as the accumulation of consumer debt provided since the 1970s. From the 1970s to the economic collapse in 2008, household debt accumulation distracted American workers from the stagnation of their real wages. As the requisite accumulation demanded by the American Dream slipped increasingly out of reach of wages and salaries, it was acquired instead through borrowing. Eventually, rising household debt levels could no longer be sustained by wages and salaries that had stopped rising.

Crisis ensued. Since 2009, the recovery hype has replaced debt accumulation as the chief distraction, sustaining the illusion that capitalism adequately serves the 99 percent.

Why Debates over the Fed's Interest Rate Miss the Point

October 3, 2015

Sometimes public debates focus on important social issues; at other times, debates distract from them. Disputes over whether the Federal Reserve should raise interest rates illustrate that second sort. Yes, "serious people" take strong positions for or against interest rate hikes. They sharply question one another's motives to spice up what passes for mainstream media economic news. But it is not the debate we could and should have, not even close.

Both sides of that debate celebrate capitalism. They differ only on how best to have government serve the reproduction of capitalism: by leaving it alone, by intervening intensely, or somewhere in between. These days they hassle over raising, lowering, or retaining current interest rates. The possibility that capitalism—rather than the Fed or interest rates—might be the problem troubles none of these folks. It does not occur to them. Nor is that surprising given the monotonous mantra of academic economics departments and the journalists and politicians trained by them. The orthodox economics professoriate treats capitalism as so wonderful and "optimal" (among their favorite words) that questioning it brings only the momentary scowl of a teacher/priest dismayed by a student's/acolyte's failure to grasp essential, universal, absolute truth.

Yet capitalism is a system of stunning and endlessly recurring instability (named everything from "adjustments" to "disturbances" to "cycles" to "crises," depending on perspective). Recurring economic downturns have plagued the last 250 years of first European and then global history. Before and after John Maynard Keynes, efforts to prevent or overcome that instability while retaining capitalism have all failed. That is why we are now in the badly lingering grip of the latest "crash" in 2008.

That is also why the Fed lowered interest rates so far and for so long that we now debate whether and when to raise them. For it turns out that the Fed's "low interest rate policy response" to the 2008 crash set in motion consequences that frighten many observers. Thus, they fear the uncertainty troubling investors who hesitate because they do not know when, how fast, and how far rate increases will go. They worry about speculation fueled by cheap loans at historically low interest rates. And they agonize over the risks of inflation if and when low interest rates plus the increased money supply accompanying them were to start a spiral of asset purchases. Those policy consequences might be, they warn, worse than the instability that provoked the interest rate reductions. In short, capitalism's instabilities provoke policy instabilities, and both incur massive social risks and costs.

Yet such is the fealty of debaters to capitalism's "optimality" that no comparison of its instabilities versus alternative systems can enter the mainstream of professional economics discourse. We few dissenters among academic economists merely irritate our colleagues. More effective are the voices coming from outside professional economics. First and foremost are the angry masses who cannot escape poor job conditions and prospects, poor incomes and disappearing benefits, a lack of job security, and unsustainable debts. As they get excited by Bernie Sanders and, in another way, by Donald Trump, and in still other ways by Pope Francis's statements on economics, they undermine the self-confidence of a rigid academic economics and the journalists and politicians who recycle it.

Let me here anticipate a criticism of where this article is going. Moving beyond capitalism, critics may insist, is at best a long-term goal, not something applicable or relevant to solving the immediate problems of the current capitalist downturn and what policy actions the Fed should take in response. On the bases of just such reasoning, past responses to capitalist cycles—large as in the 1930s and small as in the 1980s—have always been limited to what Congress did with fiscal policy and what the Fed did with monetary policy. They mostly brushed away systemic analyses or systemic change as solutions.

Yet neither fiscal nor monetary policies nor combinations of the two accomplished the second of the twin goals every president promised those policies would achieve: exit from economic crisis and prevention of future crises. Given all the crises we have had—plus now the extreme one since 2008—debates should have included admissions of the policies' failures and explorations of system changes that might achieve crisis prevention. Instead, mainstream debates have largely been limited, yet again, to disputing specifics of the Fed's monetary policy.

An economic system grounded on worker co-ops as the chief form of enterprise organization, and thereby exerting democratic control over government policy, would function differently. It would not likely sit by and allow the simultaneous emergence of unemployed workers, unutilized productive capacity, and unmet social needs for output—the way capitalism routinely does. It would mobilize private and government resources immediately to resolve any unwanted interruption in production. It would match hours worked to output wanted—with due deference to the natural environment as well as workers' needs for rest, relaxation, and nonproductive activities. Everyone would have equivalent hours worked, so no "unemployment" would ever need to exist.

In short, business cycles of the sort endemic to capitalism would disappear with capitalism itself. Decisions in enterprises and in residential communities would be governed conjointly through democratic assemblies of workers and community residents. No subset of the population—for example, major share owners and the corporate boards of directors—would any longer make the key economic decisions (what, how, and where to produce and what to do with enterprise profits). Their self-interest could no longer shape politics and culture by using or withholding the productive property they own and control. The norms of capitalism today—and especially its instability—would vanish with the transition to a system of economic democracy based on worker co-ops.

A few paragraphs hardly suffice to explain and defend a transition from capitalism to an alternative system. But they are enough to expose the utter inadequacy of a debate now—eight years into capitalism's second-worst crisis among so many—pretending again that system change is not worth discussing, examining, or debating.

Capitalism and Its Regulation Delusion

October 15, 2015

Volkswagen (VW), we now know, systematically evaded pollution control regulations. For years it defrauded 11 million buyers of its diesel engine vehicles, fouled the planet's environment, and thereby damaged the health and lives of countless living organisms. Regulation-defeating deception gave VW diesel autos competitive advantages over other companies' diesel products and thereby enhanced its profits, the driving purpose of capitalist corporations.

VW's was hardly the only socially destructive mockery of regulation. Ford and other auto companies had earlier done the same as VW, got caught, and paid fines. Other auto companies have not (yet) been caught, but similar evidence has surfaced about diesel vehicles produced by Mercedes-Benz, Honda, Mazda, and Mitsubishi.[19] Exposures and punishments, if and when they occur, clearly fall far short of dis-

---

19. Damien Carrington, "Four More Carmakers Join Diesel Emissions Row," *Guardian*, October 9, 2015.

suading major capitalists from evading regulations. Thus, we now know that General Motors and Toyota did not follow regulations recently requiring notification of government agencies after crashes, injuries, and deaths associated with ignitions and airbags.

As products using computer devices increase, they spread opportunities for similar evasions of regulations. New mechanisms have enabled electrical appliance makers to falsify regulated energy-use tests.[20] Capitalist competition and profit were motivators in these and many other regulation evasions. The problem is endemic, for example, in the food and drink industry.[21] Since 2008's global capitalist crash, the world has learned of parallel failures of financial regulation with horrific social consequences. Nor is the failed relationship of capitalism and regulation only a US problem; it is global.[22]

The history of regulation follows the same well-worn path in many industries. First, corporations deny the negative effects of their products or technologies when victims or critics expose them. Usually after many profitable years, corporate denials no longer succeed as social movements demand regulations and legislators begin to respond. Then lobbying, bribery, and public relations campaigns press legislators (in the following order) to do nothing, do the minimum, do the minimum later, phase the minimum in over many years, and provide for industry self-regulation. The resulting legislative struggles take time and thereby allow additional years of profitable unregulated production.

If corporate obstruction eventually fails, legislation creates an agency empowered to regulate certain practices, enterprises, and/or industries. Immediately the affected capitalist corporations commence new evasive actions. They lobby, bribe, and/or fund public relations campaigns to (a) get their friends into top agency positions, (b) shape exactly how regulations will work, (c) limit the agency's budget to per-

---

20. Jad Mouawad, "Beyond VW Scandal: Home Appliance Industry no Stranger to Tricks," *New York Times*, October 9, 2015.
21. Duncan McNair, "Horsemeat Scandal: A Year On, Nothing Has Changed," *Telegraph*, January 14, 2014.
22. Prem Sikka, "Scandals and Regulation Lead to an Auditing Merry-Go-Round," *Conversation*, May 18, 2015.

form regulatory duties, and (d) attack any agency official or activity unacceptable to them. Taken together, these tactics commonly result in "regulatory capture," a common term now among journalists, academics, and the informed public. From being objects of regulation, capitalist corporations turn the tables and capture the regulators. The crooks control the police chief.

All the above takes time, enabling many years of corporate profits at massive social expense. Occasionally, after all that, if social activism prevails and exposes gross abuses (despite the mass media also controlled by corporate capitalism), real regulation can begin. Then the regulated corporations resort, as VW did, to outright regulatory evasion that gains them yet more profitable years. If caught, corporations' fines, lawyers, and damaged reputations will incur costs that are tiny relative to many years of big profits. The exposed, socially destructive product or technology will then often be abandoned—usually with publicity pretending that capitalists acted from a sense of social responsibility. They then often recoup the costs of that publicity by raising the prices of whatever products they decide to produce next.

Capitalists abandon the exposed products and technologies because (a) their profitability was compromised once regulation actually set in, and (b) new products and/or new technologies open vistas of higher profits for the years between their introduction and when long delayed regulation finally arrives (if it ever does). Then this absurd delusional tragedy of capitalist production and regulation plays yet again with the new products and/or new technologies. Their social costs will soon emerge, generating victims and critics. Capitalists will show us again that they are driven by profits; caring for the social or natural environment is secondary or absent. Still, some people will again prefer regulating the existing system rather than face the underlying problem: capitalism's intrinsic incentive to cheat for profits no matter the social costs.

Regulation thus represents an enduring delusion (much like taxes on profits that show parallel histories of corporate opposition and evasion). Whether it be "self-regulation," performed by capitalist enterprises or industry organizations, or regulation by government, both amount to applying bandages when the problem is a deep cancer. Regulations do not successfully correct or repair an increasingly dysfunctional (for the 99 percent) capitalism. The endless dialectic of capitalism and regulation teaches those not lost in ideological apologies the necessity of system change.

The fundamental contradiction between capitalism and regulation can be overcome if profit and competition stop functioning as the drivers and standards of enterprise success. They must be demoted to become no more than two among many dimensions of enterprise to be considered in reaching the key decisions about what, how, and where to produce and what to do with enterprises' net revenues. Likewise, the decision makers need to be changed from the capitalist norm. Instead of the tiny minority (major shareholders and the boards of directors they choose) making all the key enterprise decisions, decision making needs to be democratized. Enterprise decisions need to be made conjointly by all enterprise participants and by residents of residential communities that interact with the enterprises (much as political decisions in those communities must likewise be conjointly achieved). The resulting decisions will reflect and serve the working and residential communities. No longer will they serve and reflect primarily the tiny minority that now governs the economy so undemocratically.

Then the conditions will be in place to support production and regulation operated by and for the same communities. The notion of government by, of, and for the people will finally have acquired its necessary economic basis, as capitalism joins its predecessor economic systems (slavery, feudalism, and so on) as part of the past we will have moved beyond.

Part III: Crisis Politics

The capitalist crisis since 2007 was so deep, global, and long-lasting that it threatened to prevent "politics as usual." It suggested to some that we might need to relearn political lessons from the last major capitalist crash, the Great Depression of the 1930s. To others it brought ominous suggestions and signs of "class war." Major political parties and groups berated one another using poorly understood economic concepts (e.g., deficits, debts, debt ceilings, federal budgets, Keynesianism). Countries moved toward the breakup of their constituent regions, dangerous migrations and wars proliferated, and old political loyalties frayed or vanished. What politicians and events left unspoken was often more important than what was said. The basic issue was how to cope politically with a crisis far deeper and more difficult to end than any major political formation had foreseen.

The essays in Part III aim to show the economic goals pursued by major political forces as they contended for power and to manage the crisis in their differently preferred ways. The essays also seek to expose goals pursued by these same forces as they avoided and kept silent about key political dimensions of the crisis. In the midst of the crisis (autumn 2011), the explosive emergence of Occupy Wall Street altered political conditions above all by successfully inserting the "1 percent versus 99 percent" into world discussions of the crisis and the capitalism it reflected. One result was to open a much wider space for criticism of capitalism—and for conceptualizing the deepening crisis as a symptom of capitalism's flaws and inadequacies.

The essays in Part III work within and further develop that space. They also begin to engage the diverse tendencies and targets among those whose criticisms of the crisis have broadened into criticisms of capitalism as a system. Different positions have begun to emerge on the roles and powers of the Federal Reserve, the relevance of the New Deal political realities to current conditions, and whether austerity as a government policy or capitalism itself is or should be the main issue now.

GOVERNMENT INTERVENTION

Government Economic Intervention for Whom?

January 25, 2011

No one in the US government campaigns these days for the direct government hiring of the many millions of unemployed and underemployed people—even though those millions suffer the resulting losses of income and self-esteem; they become burdens on their families, friends, and neighbors; and their reduced purchasing hurts countless others who work to produce what the unemployed and underemployed can no longer afford. Even though the last president faced with huge unemployment created 11 million federal jobs between 1934 and 1941, any comparable government step is off the agenda of Democrats and Republicans now.

The conventional explanation—or better, excuse—for this inaction is ideology: the government, we are told, ought not to intervene in the economy because the private sector does all that better and cheaper. Before taking this seriously, even for an instant, consider two economic interventions our government is now undertaking. The US government's National Institutes of Health has unveiled its plan to form a new National Center for Advancing Translational Sciences. Its official purpose is to have the government undertake research to find new drugs because the private sector is not doing enough of that, according to the Institutes of Health director, Francis S. Collins. He says: "I am a little frustrated to see how many of the discoveries that do look as though they have promising therapeutic implications are waiting for the pharmaceutical industry to follow through on them." All this is reported in a front page story in the *New York Times* (January 23, 2011) that explains this government intervention as aimed to offset and compensate for the private drug makers' decision that work on new drugs is not profitable enough to warrant their investment.

In other words, because the private sector fails to do something deemed socially important, the government is stepping in to do that itself. Note the disparity. The massive unemployment and underemployment of workers by private capitalist employers is likewise socially important and is likewise something the private sector is failing to do because it is not profitable. Yet no direct government hiring of unemployed and underemployed workers is under way or planned. How revealing.

For the second example (also reported in the same issue of the *New York Times*), let us turn to the joint news conference by President Obama and China's president, Hu Jintao. There Mr. Obama said, "We want to sell you all kinds of stuff ... planes ... cars ... software." Later the two presidents announced $45 billion in export deals with China for US corporations. This was nothing less than direct economic intervention to aid corporations. Much public money has been and continues to be spent in all sorts of ways to support US government agencies' work to expand export markets for US corporations in China and elsewhere.

Evidently the US government does not believe in leaving the promotion and advertising of US goods abroad to the private sector that receives all the revenues from export sales. It feels that the private sector's performance is inadequate, so the government must supplement, at public expense, insufficient private outlays for promotion with direct, publicly financed promotion. Yet we have no direct hiring to supplement the private sector's inadequate employment of workers. Again, how revealing.

The issue is not and never has been about whether to have the government intervene directly in American capitalism. The issue has always been for whom and in whose interests does the government intervene (and choose not to intervene).

This Is No Bailout for Main Street America

February 9, 2012

Big announcements of breakthrough legislative deals during election campaigns should be taken with huge grains of salt. Generally more rhetoric than reality, they sometimes contain real concessions made by politicians seeking votes. So it is with the Washington announcement of $25 billion to help homeowners.[23] Something significant is happening, but it lies below the surface of the headlines.

Typically, modern governments intervene in two ways when—as has been true since 2007—free-enterprise capitalist economies produce particularly bad versions of their recurring economic "downturns." One economic policy is aptly called "trickle-down" economics. It involves throwing heaps of money at the top of the economic pyramid—to mammoth banks, insurance companies, and other corporations at or near economic collapse. Policy makers hope that such help for these institutions will revive their activity and thereby trickle down—as credit and orders for medium-sized and small businesses, and then, finally, to jobs and maybe wage increases for the majority of workers.

The alternative is "trickle-up" economic policy. It involves government financial aid aimed chiefly at helping the mass of workers. That policy's goal is for the assisted workers to resume purchasing, which will, in turn, boost business revenues and so rebuild prosperity.

The historical record is quite clear: trickle down is no better or more effective a policy to end deep recessions and depressions than trickle up. In the last great capitalist downturn of the 1930s, the Roosevelt administration first tried trickle down. Its poor results, coupled with profound political pressures from below—the Congress of Industrial Organizations (CIO) membership drives that brought new millions into labor unions and the surging socialist and communist parties—forced President Roosevelt to add major trickle-up policies. They worked better, but not well enough to overcome the Great Depression.

---

23. Dominic Rushe, "Obama Welcomes $25bn Mortgage Settlement for Homeowners," *Guardian*, February 9, 2012.

Of course, large corporations, their shareholders, and stock markets prefer trickle down. They get bailed out and they "recover" while the rest of us watch to see what may or may not trickle down. The US working class has been waiting for over four years. Precious little has yet trickled down. The majority of citizens prefer trickle up and for parallel reasons. Which kind of policy prevails depends on which side wields more power over the policy makers.

Under Bush and Obama, trickle down has dominated overwhelmingly since the current crisis began in 2007. There were a few trickle-up measures: modest individual income tax cuts, repeated but very ineffective efforts to help those subjected to foreclosure, and extensions of unemployment compensation benefits. However, they were utterly dwarfed by what the Treasury and the Fed poured out in trickle-down bailouts. By 2011, it was clear that the Bush-Obama trickle-down policy had failed to end this second-worst economic downturn in a century.

The Obama team was beginning to learn what the Roosevelt team had learned sooner in their Great Depression. It turns out that bailouts for the top of the economic pyramid, which never trickle down, leave an economically depressed mass at the bottom. Governments that also try to pay for trickle-down policies by imposing "austerity programs" on the bottom only make matters worse. Sustained depression at the bottom eventually threatens the top—first economically and then also politically.

That happened sooner and more powerfully in the more depressed and more politically mobilized conditions of the 1930s. But the Tea Parties and the Occupy Wall Street movement, in their radically different ways, suggest something comparable unfolding now in the United States. In Europe, the process is further along, as the Greek example shows.

The Obama team began in 2011 to supplement a wholly inadequate trickle-down approach with some limited trickle-up elements. The biggest of these have been the reductions in the Social Security deduction on paychecks. Another small step is this week's modest help for homeowners facing foreclosures. It will not help the majority of those in such danger—for example, the 50 percent of mortgages owned by Fannie Mae and Freddy Mac are ineligible. It will help the rest, but not much.

Consider simply that the negative equity of US homeowners is estimated now at $700 billion. That is how much more they owe on their homes than those homes are worth. This new bill proposes $26 billion in aid for that problem. No such timidity attended the trillions provided for the trickle-down bailouts since 2007. The banks are happy with this proposed settlement's low cost to them.

While the government's help to homeowners is far from adequate or just, it represents a partial and late recognition of trickle-down economics' inadequacy as policy. It further concedes the need for some trickle up. What happens next depends on the evolution of this crisis and of the political forces gathering strength.

Those factors will determine how long the beneficiaries of trickle-down economics can sustain the policy's dominance and continue to shift its costs onto the mass of people through austerity programs. Those same factors will also determine whether we see a further shift to trickle-up economics—or a more basic challenge to an economic system whose instability is so severe and so socially costly.

Ghost of New Deal Haunts Democrats' Agenda, but It's Time to Summon FDR

October 10, 2012

While George W. Bush's absence was obvious at the 2012 Republican convention, so was another president's absence at the Democratic convention. Mitt Romney banished Bush because his last year, 2008, linked Republicans in office with economic crisis and big bank bailouts: not a vote-getting association. The Democrats banished President Franklin Delano Roosevelt, but for a different reason, and in a different way. They feared reminding people of what FDR did the last time US capitalism crashed. President Barack Obama and most Democrats are so dependent on contributions and support from business and the rich that they dare not discuss, let alone implement, Roosevelt-type policies. Obama's convention speech passingly referred to FDR's "bold, persistent experimentation." Obama said nothing about what FDR actually did in the last great collapse of capitalism, nothing about his policies' achievements or their shortcomings.

What FDR accomplished needs rescue from banishment by Obama and Democratic leaders. In the deep 1930s Depression, FDR massively assisted average Americans. He created the Social Security and unemployment compensation systems that directly helped tens of millions. His federal jobs programs provided jobs and incomes for additional tens of millions from 1934 to 1941. These "stimulus plans" helped average citizens with financial supports, jobs, and paychecks. Those citizens then spent on goods and services that realized profits trickling up for businesses. FDR's trickle-up economics worked—far from perfectly, but better for most Americans than Bush's or Obama's policies.

Leading Democrats today lack the courage even to propose what FDR did. Obama keeps offering incentives for the private sector to hire more, but that policy failed over the last five years to return employment to precrisis levels. Obama refuses to expand Social Security as an anticrisis policy. Instead, Obama and the Democrats pursue chiefly trickle-down policies: bail out banks and select megacorporations, boost credit and stock markets with infusions of cheap money, and hope something trickles down to lift average peoples' incomes. Despite five years of failed trickle-down economics, Democrats today still fear to consider FDR's alternatives, acting as if they never happened.

Powerfully organized worker demands caused FDR's conversion to trickle-up economics. Stunningly successful Congress of Industrial Organizations (CIO) unionization campaigns in the 1930s coordinated with rising memberships, activities, and influences of socialist and communist parties. These forces demanded and obtained direct help for the mass of people, while some among them also advocated basic social change as the best crisis solution. Obama and most Democrats try to repress emerging parallel forces such as Occupy Wall Street. They simultaneously excuse their weak, so-called moderate policies by blaming the supposed lack of public support for more progressive policies.

FDR leveraged and channeled organized worker pressures into a grand social compromise, his New Deal. It pleased majorities of the American public and of capitalists and the richest 5 percent. That won him repeated re-election. The New Deal got corporations and the wealthy to finance Washington's provision of help to average Americans in exchange for the CIO, socialists, and communists muting demands within their ranks for system change. By warning capitalists and the rich that his New Deal was their only alternative to revolution along Soviet lines, FDR split their ranks and won support from many. He likewise got most in the CIO, socialist, and communist parties to marginalize their anticapitalism in return for a real social safety net. FDR never persuaded all capitalists and all the rich; serious, determined opposition arose. Likewise, dissenting socialists and communists persisted in fighting for basic economic and political changes. However, FDR's New Deal social compromise prevailed.

Corporations and the rich thus paid high taxes and made large loans to finance Social Security, unemployment compensation, and federal jobs programs. From the 1940s to the 1960s, corporate income tax rates and tax rates on high-income individuals were much higher than they are today. FDR took the money his policies needed from corporations and the rich. That's where the money was then, and that's where it is now. But unlike FDR, today's Democrats have no plan or program to get it. So discussing what FDR actually did was banished from their convention.

Choosing trickle-up economics to cope with capitalism's crash was key to FDR being reelected three consecutive times. No other president in US history had such success. After FDR's death, Republicans moved to limit presidents to a maximum of two consecutive terms. Like FDR, Obama rode a capitalist crash into power, but Obama risks being ridden out because of failed economic policies. Yet Democrats dare not offend their financial backers to follow FDR's way or even acknowledge its relevance.

The New Deal also had flaws that enabled it to be destroyed. Those capitalists and rich individuals who never welcomed the New Deal were determined to undo it once the war ended in 1945. Because FDR's compromise had preserved the capitalist system, shareholders and the boards of directors they selected kept their positions inside the structure of corporations. There, they retained the incentives and accumulated the power and resources to undermine the New Deal and its major supports. Sometimes these enemies of the New Deal shaped government policies: for example, to eradicate communist and socialist parties (e.g., through McCarthyism) or to weaken unions (e.g., through the Taft-Hartley Act). Sometimes, corporate owners and leaders directly funded foundations, think tanks, and organizations molding public opinion. Dissenting socialists and communists had warned about FDR's grand compromise: by leaving enterprises in the hands of major shareholders and their boards of directors, the New Deal signed its own death warrant.

By the 1980s, corporations and the rich had sufficiently weakened labor and the left to more openly dismantle what remained of the New Deal. Market deregulation, tax cuts, neoliberalism, neoconservatism, and privatization were the new era's processes and watchwords—with Ronald Reagan as mascot. Because they developed no effective counterstrategy to affirmatively defend what the business community and the rich assaulted, Democrats lost parts of their electoral base and thus strengthened the Republicans. Keeping FDR's achievements away from their 2012 convention marked another step in the Democrats' decline.

FEDERAL RESERVE

Ben Bernanke's Silence Speaks Volumes

February 9, 2011

Federal Reserve Chairman Ben Bernanke's testimony before the House budget committee largely repeated what he has been saying recently.[24] It was interesting only for its likewise repeated silences which, as so often, spoke loudly. The biggest silence concerned taxing corporations and the rich in the United States.

Many sentences were devoted to the burdens of the huge deficits being run by the US government, to the need to reduce those deficits. Otherwise, Bernanke warned, lenders might one day stop providing

---

24. Richard Blackden, "QE Safeguarded 3m American Jobs, Says Federal Reserve Chief Ben Bernanke," *Telegraph*, February 9, 2011.

those immense flows into the US Treasury. But not one word about reducing the deficit by taxing large corporations and the rich.

One day before that testimony, Britain's chancellor of the exchequer announced a modest tax increase on banks in the United Kingdom: a "fair contribution," he said, "to our recovery." No such idea, let alone any action, in the United States.

Instead, we hear pronouncements like Bernanke's that reflect the belief that cutting outlays is the only way to go. The debate then becomes about which outlays to cut. Bernanke makes clear his preferred cuts lie in healthcare. Note that the United States already spends more than other developed nations for poorer healthcare outcomes as measured by national health statistics. Bernanke says nothing about lowering government outlays by reducing the profits of drug makers and healthcare providers. Nor do the possible impacts of reduced healthcare on the well-being and productivity of the US workforce merit any comment or concern from Bernanke.

It is worth remembering that when the United States borrows trillions of dollars to cover deficits, a significant portion of that borrowing comes from the large corporations and richest individuals who lend to the government the money that, apparently, they did not have to pay in taxes to that government. I can see the desirability for them of lending at interest rather than being taxed. The matter looks otherwise from the standpoint of the rest of us. Silence on taxation of corporations and the rich should be exposed and opposed for the blatant ideological bias it represents.

Another deafening silence concerned the matter of states and cities. Their currently projected cuts in public services and employment will damage education, infrastructure maintenance, and countless social services. Their effects will overwhelm the far smaller initiatives that Obama announced in his State of the Union message and which will only be realized in part given the split political control of Congress. Like Obama, Bernanke had nothing to say or offer on the dire crisis of state and city budgets.

Last, consider the silence on unemployment. Bernanke did explain that the current rate of job creation, if maintained, would mean many more years of high unemployment. No word was uttered about even the vaguest idea of government job creation—again, a silence, as if that idea or program did not exist (despite massive evidence to the contrary provided by FDR in the 1930s).

Taxing large corporations and the rich would have its effects on the larger economy, positive and negative. In any rational debate, those effects would have to be weighed and considered against the positive and negative effects of the alternatives, including those used since this crisis began and those now projected. Instead, we have silences from Bernanke and from Obama, silences that close and narrow, rather than open and widen, discussion over the nation's crisis and future.

Bernanke's Speech Was Only a Minor Footnote to Enduring Crisis

August 27, 2011

If Americans expected some sign of dramatic policy initiatives from Federal Reserve Chairman Ben Bernanke, they were disappointed in yesterday's speech. If they expected a serious assessment of the costs of the failed "recovery program" to date as the basis to argue for a change in approach, they were disappointed. If Europeans hoped for a strong signal that the United States would coordinate policies with them and provide some tangible supports to their struggles with this same economic crisis, they were disappointed.

Instead, Bernanke repeated how confident he was in the basic strengths of the US economy while acknowledging that the recovery so far had been less than he had hoped for and that eventual recovery would continue to be "slow." He chided Congress and the president for not using more expansionary fiscal policy and leaving too much of the burden of overcoming crisis on the Federal Reserve. He reiterated promises of very low interest rates for banks to borrow from the Fed for the next two years.

This all amounts to more of the same policies we have been seeing. The Fed has evidently decided not to change course, despite those policies' poor performance since the crisis hit in 2007. "Trickle-down" is indeed the right name for this program: shovel help to the financial top of the economic pyramid and hope it trickles some of its loot down to the mass of businesses and individuals. The immense cash hoards now accumulating in US banks and corporations stand as strong testimony—alongside so much other evidence—that trickle-down economics is failing yet again.

Bernanke admitted what every observer knows, that the US housing market's current double dip into a second downturn is making economic matters worse. Yet nothing was offered there except ominous references to things eventually improving. They are ominous because "eventually" is a euphemism for the following: let housing prices drop until they are so low that even the falling wages of the US working class will enable some uptick in housing purchases (and so an end to falling home prices). Meanwhile, the millions of US residents who invested their only wealth in their homes will have lost a major part of that wealth and thereby hobbled their economic futures and further stalled economic "recovery."

Bernanke's words amount to condemning the housing market and, thus, the economy as a whole, to enduring a rough economic cycle in the usual capitalist way. That is, let the system cut wages enough (by lasting high unemployment, above all else) and cheapen the material costs of business enough (bankrupt businesses must unload tools, equipment, space, etc., at fire-sale prices) to make it once again profitable for capitalists to hire workers and set up or expand businesses. Then those workers may earn enough to afford the cheapened homes, and so on.

The policy options that Democrats and Republicans so loudly debate function mostly to distract people from the ongoing capitalist cycle's social costs. Their debates—like most media coverage of them—are wordy displays that blow smoke above the hard reality. What we are actually doing is waiting for economic destruction to cut deeply enough so that the profit motive can revive the economy it first knocked down.

The economic crisis that exploded in the United States spread destructively by way of the market system that links the United States to Europe. Now the economic problems inside each area have become mutually aggravating. Bernanke might have proposed more or better collaboration among central banks to manage their common problems and risks. Some concrete initiatives might have calmed capital markets at least a bit. Instead, silence: another opportunity was thus missed.

Europe's government debt problems are intertwined with its dysfunctional private banks as they try to impose counterproductive austerity regimes on European populations. They want the heavy costs of failed trickle-down policies to be borne by those populations. European leaders hope their masses will not explode in revolt before the profit motive can kick in to revive the system and "grow European capitalism's way out" of the looming dangers. Bernanke's speech suggests that he and the Fed share the same hope for the United States. His speech reveals the underlying plan: everyone should wait patiently and suffer the losses until a genuine recovery "eventually" arrives.

Janet Yellen and I Were Taught to Revere Capitalism. But It's a Failing System

February 4, 2014

Janet Yellen, the US Federal Reserve's new chair, and I were graduate economics students around the same time at Yale University. The professor who shaped the macroeconomics we learned was James Tobin. He taught us to be Keynesian economists: that is, to accept capitalism as the sole object and focus of our studies, to celebrate it as the best possible system, and to preserve it against its own serious faults. Keynesian economics teaches that to secure capitalism's blessings requires systematic government intervention in the workings of the economy.

Yale doctorates during those years certified that we had learned how the monetary and fiscal policies offered by Keynesianism composed the government's optimum tools of economic intervention. Central banks (in the United States, this meant the Federal Reserve) would administer monetary policy. This meant manipulating the quantity of money in circulation and interest rates. Legislatures and executives would administer fiscal policies, namely, manipulating tax rates and government expenditures. The goals of both monetary and fiscal policies would be to prevent private capitalism's instability (its recurring swings between sharp upturns and downturns), or at least to ensure the downturns were short and shallow (unlike the long and deep 1930s Great Depression that inspired Keynes's work).

Successive chairs of the Federal Reserve sought to manipulate the nation's monetary system to those ends, so far as possible. Whatever their party affiliation (Bernanke is a Republican, while Yellen is a Democrat), they coordinate their monetary policies with the fiscal policies pursued by the sitting president and Congress. Indeed, policy differences have been limited and rarely arose among them in their shared quest to manage capitalism's inherent and immensely costly instability. Thus, from the standpoint of economics, the two parties are better understood as two wings of one capitalist party in the United States sharing virtually dictatorial political influence.

The Federal Reserve has needed to "manage" the monetary system also by bailing out collapsed financial firms on occasion, and much of the entire industry since 2007 (at a historically unprecedented clip costing trillions).[25] Nor did the Fed ever prevent capitalism's cycles. The official downturn measurer, the National Bureau of Economic Research, lists a dozen capitalist swoons since the end of the Great Depression: on average, one every five years.

The Fed claims that its interventions likely made downturns less awful than they might have been. Bernanke the Republican Fed chair aimed for that, Yellen the Democrat agreed as vice-chair, and now she will continue to aim for that as the new chair. If ever the phrase "same-old, same-old" applied, it does so in this nonevent of musical chairs at the Fed.

After Yale, Janet Yellen and I took different paths in our approaches and experiences working within US capitalism. Ever the liberal Democrat, she endorses capitalism despite its cyclical and colossal waste of resources and the human tragedy this imposes across the globe. No courses at Yale troubled Yellen or me with any analyses of how exploitation lies at the core of capitalist production. We were never taught that the majority of

---

25. The Week Staff, "The Federal Reserve's 'Breathtaking' $7.7 Trillion Bank Bailout," *The Week*, November 28, 2011.

industrial workers produce more value for employers than what employers pay them. We were prevented from encountering arguments examining how this idea of "more" (or, in economic terms, of a surplus) contributed fundamentally to the systemic inequalities that define capitalist societies.

No irritating Marxism was allowed to disturb the deep, unquestioned political tranquility that professors embedded in Yale's graduate economics curriculum. The celebration of the free competitive market, although often extended rhetorically to the free marketplace of competing ideas, was suspended in the case of Marxian concepts and analyses of capitalist economies. The latter were systematically excluded at Yale as at most US universities then and ever since: no free marketplace of ideas there.

Like Bernanke, Yellen will do her job as best as she can. No thought about alternatives to capitalism will likely occur to her. She and the Fed's board of governors will consider no policy responses to the current system's grotesque flaws and injustices that entail changing the system. No free marketplace of competing ideas at the Fed either. She will, like her predecessors, transfer the deep political conservatism of her graduate economics education in the United States to her policies.

Critics have attacked the Fed since its inception a century ago because of its structural (and extraordinarily cozy) entwining of government regulation and the banking industry it presumably regulated. Just as important, however, are the conceptual continuities between mainstream economics as academic discipline and as governing policy ideology. What threatens those continuities now is the emerging dissent to mainstream academia and the widening disconnect between the Fed's policy universe and most people's lives.

The global capitalism into which Janet Yellen and I graduated with new PhDs in the 1970s proceeded ever since to illustrate growing inequality of income and wealth across and within most economies, which has contributed to mounting social unrest, conflict, wars, and unspeakable social tragedies. Since 2007, the global economic meltdown has reminded everyone of capitalism's vulnerability to the kinds of economic catastrophes that marked the 1930s. Gradually before and quickly since 2007, interest in Marxian and other critiques of capitalism and in socialist as well as other alternative economic systems has been rekindled.

Yellen and I had the same economics education and have experienced the same global capitalist development since, yet we have responded very differently. The same systems generated contradictory outcomes. Capitalism's dysfunctions have led me to appreciate and independently learn what Marxian economics has to teach me, outside of Yale's mainstream economics. Yellen and her cohorts avoided and bypassed all that.

Convinced that we can do better than capitalism, many have analyzed the incipient alternatives emerging from capitalism's deficiencies, such as cooperatives and workers' self-directed enterprises. For us, Occupy represents a powerful surge against capitalism, yet another sign of the waning tolerance for a system that Yellen will try to preserve.

DEBT CEILINGS AND BUDGET BATTLES

Budget Battles: Sound, Fury, and Fakery

April 15, 2011

Weeks of highly publicized debates—some in Congress, more in the mass media—brought Republicans and Democrats to a budget deal. To maximize public attention, they threatened a possible government shutdown. Both parties said that large government deficits and accumulated debt were "serious problems." They agreed that solving them required only spending cuts, not revenue increases. In unison, they repeated, "we" must "learn to live within our means."

In fact, both sides never actually engaged the deficit and the debt. They limited themselves to purely cosmetic, symbol-laden cuts (Republicans) and refusals to cut (Democrats). Aiming at the 2012 election, both parties used the deficit and budget debates purely to impress their voters.

Basic numbers tell the true story. The current (fiscal year 2011) budget spends about $3.5 trillion while receiving $2.0 trillion in tax revenues. The difference of $1.5 trillion (the equivalent of $1,500 billion) is this year's deficit. The US Treasury must borrow that from whoever will lend to the US government. After much hot air, Republicans and Democrats reached a "historic compromise," namely, a spending cut of $38 billion. That will reduce this year's deficit from $1,500 billion to $1,462 billion, an economically insignificant sum. The sound and fury of Washington's debates signified that nothing was to be done about the actual deficit.

Republicans pretend to be deeply troubled by huge government deficits run up in recent years. They conveniently forget why those deficits soared: capitalism's crisis increased unemployment (and thus cut income tax receipts) and Washington's response was to borrow trillions and spend them on bailing out banks and credit and stock markets. Republicans revive their old mantra: reduce deficits by cutting "wasteful spending" and "government mismanagement," which turns out to mean the social programs they don't like. Republicans hope to cash in politically on popular upset over the crisis's costs and the government's unfair and ineffective response.

Democrats pretend to be as troubled by deficits as Republicans. They parrot Republicans in denouncing wasteful government spending and mismanagement. However, they champion fewer spending cuts than Republicans, hoping thereby to cash in politically on popular support for helpful government programs needed especially in hard times. Democrats are also loudly oppositional where that might appeal to their voters (e.g., saving Planned Parenthood from cuts).

Democrats and Republicans did not even discuss, let alone agree on, tax increases on the wealthy or on corporations as ways to cut deficits. At the same time, their proposals for cutting spending were economically insignificant. In short, the two parties' deficit-reduction campaigns were fakes.

What difference do deficits make? When the government's tax revenues fall short of its expenditures, it must borrow the difference. That borrowing adds to the country's total accumulated debt. As a result, next year and thereafter, government spending will have to pay interest on this year's borrowing. That means using a portion of its tax revenues in the future *not* to provide public services or help people, but instead, to pay interest on its borrowing this year.

Deficits matter because they divert tax revenues away from serving most taxpayers to enriching Washington's creditors instead. They also matter when Republicans and conservative Democrats use deficits and government debts as excuses to cut government programs they oppose.

Conservatives fear and oppose government economic interventions other than those that support and protect business interests. When most recessions hit, conservatives want tax cuts for business and little more. When major recessions hit, they want massive government bailouts of businesses. If those require deficits, the conservatives support them (they backed the Bush and Obama administration bailouts from 2008 to 2010). They only turn against deficits later, once business profits are restored, and then demand cutting government economic interventions that benefit other than business interests.

Liberals and Keynesians usually favor government deficits during recessions. They want the government to spend not only to soften hardships during economic downturns but also to compensate for businesses' hesitancy to invest in poor economic conditions. Otherwise, liberals fear that crises may turn people against the capitalist system and/or to extremist politics. Thus, Paul Krugman angrily urges President Obama to increase rather than limit government spending and not worry about deficits. In such enthusiasms, liberals and Keynesians underestimate the real costs of deficits and who will likely have to pay for them.

The problems with these liberals' logic are many. First, if the government taxed corporations and the wealthiest individuals more, it could maintain high spending without having to incur huge deficits. One recent calculation showed that if corporations and individuals earning over $1,000,000 per year paid the same rate of taxes today as they paid in 1961, the US Treasury would collect an additional $716 billion per year.[26] That would cut the 2011 deficit by half and likewise

---

26. Chuck Collins, "We Don't Need to Shut Down the Government: Tax the Wealthy and Deadbeat Corporations to Close Budget Gap," AlterNet, April 7, 2011.

its interest costs. Second, consider who lends to the US government. Major creditors include the People's Republic of China, Japan, large corporations, and wealthy individuals in the United States and abroad. The greater our deficits, the more of everyone's taxes go to pay interest to those creditors. Third, consider the basic injustice of deficits: (1) Washington taxes corporations and the rich far less than it used to in, say, the 1960s; (2) Washington therefore runs a deficit; and (3) the US Treasury then borrows from corporations and the rich the money that the government allowed them not to pay in taxes.

The bottom line: US capitalism collapsed into dependence on massive government support in 2008 and since. Beyond providing immense, open-ended guarantees for the debts of defunct banks, insurance companies, and so on, government support to business included trillions spent on bank and corporate bailouts. The government chose to pay for most of that by massive borrowing (rather than raising taxes on corporations and the rich—not even on those corporations that government funds saved from certain bankruptcy). That is why those huge bailouts required correspondingly huge deficits.

On April 13, Obama suggested a small tax increase on rich individuals (raising the top bracket from 35 to 39 percent compared to the 91 percent it was in the 1960s) and an end to certain corporate tax loopholes. If ever enacted into law, those suggestions together would not change much. They would yield less than $100 billion per year. That would cut the 2011 deficit, for example, by a mere 7.5 percent. Moreover, more "historic compromises" with Republicans will only further reduce (or eliminate) even these modest tax burdens on corporations and the rich.

Both parties in Washington have supported and sustained massive ongoing deficits supporting a crippled, state-dependent capitalism. Those deficits will continue to raise our national debt and continue to be used as excuses for cutting government services to people. Fake debates around deficits should not distract us from what capitalism has demanded and obtained from both of its parties or from the urgent need to build a real opposition to them both.

Fiscal Cliff Follies: Political Theater Distracts from Key Problems with the Fix

January 4, 2013

The last-minute deal reached in the final hours of 2012 continues the sham political theater that dominated the mass media for months. One phony issue was a "stalemate" between the parties. In fact, they achieved and sustained consensus all year. Both parties agreed to raise taxes and cut government spending. The fiscal cliff did that and so did the last-minute deal. In Europe that policy is called "austerity." Republicans and Democrats merely bickered over details of austerity: who would be taxed how much more and who would obtain how much less government spending.

Europe's austerity policies since 2010 worsened the economies of Greece, Britain, Portugal, Spain, Ireland, and Italy. They likewise provoked the most massive and coordinated protests of the last half-century. Capitalism itself is among the protests' targets. The United States in 2013 thus looks set for perhaps Occupy Wall Street Round 2.

The last-minute deal also continues the parties' shared program of shifting the costs of the crisis and the government bailouts of banks, large corporations, and the stock market onto the mass of the citizens. Thus—despite President Obama's gross exaggerations—the tax increases "on the rich" have meaningless impacts on the distribution of wealth and income and on the deficit. For example, income taxes on couples earning over $450,000 per year will rise from 35 percent to 39.6 percent of the portion that exceeds $450,000. That will yield extra tax revenue to Washington amounting to less than 4 percent of its 2012 deficit.

At the other end of the income and wealth spectrum, all US workers subject to the payroll tax on their incomes (around 150 million workers) will see the rate rise from 4.2 percent to 6.2 percent in 2013. For couples earning $50,000 per year, that means an additional $1,000 will be withheld from paychecks. That is meaningful for them and for the economy confronting $1,000 less that each such couple will spend.

Republican leaders hype how they saved the rich from bigger tax increases desired by Democrats and maybe lessened the deficit. Democratic leaders will hype how they made the rich pay higher income taxes while maybe lessening the deficit. In honest discussions, the "maybe" must be inserted because the deficit depends more on how the economy evolves in 2013 than on these relatively less significant tax rate changes.

For example, consider this likely economic scenario across 2013: Tax increases agreed upon in the last-minute deal help drive the economy into its second downturn since 2007—just as austerity policies did in Britain. This second US downturn increases unemployment, enterprise cutbacks, and bankruptcies. These all reduce Washington's tax revenues while requiring greater social spending (on unemployment insurance, food stamps, welfare, Medicaid). Reduced tax revenues combined with increased spending would enlarge the deficit in 2013 from what it was in 2012 no matter the outcome of the fiscal cliff follies.

Liberals and Keynesian economists have responded to the Fiscal Cliff theatrics with another kind of folly. They stress "economic growth" as better strategy than austerity. By growing the economy, the higher GDP would reduce the deficit without higher tax rates hurting citizens, and government spending cuts damaging the economy. (Recall this ancient notion: People will suffer a smaller piece of the economic pie if the pie is growing.) To grow, liberals want more stimulus spending by Washington. They admit that will worsen the deficit in the short run. But they insist that the resulting growth will reduce unemployment, enterprise cutbacks, and bankruptcies. Those reductions will boost government tax revenues while decreasing needs for government social spending. Growth would thereby erase the initial deficit (needed to fund the stimulus), and could reduce the deficit beyond that.

Liberals and Keynesians promoting growth strategies avoid dealing with how the profound inequalities of capitalism help cause economic crises, bailouts, and both parties' commitments to austerity politics. It was the wealth and power of large banks, corporations, and Wall Street that obtained their unprecedented government bailouts, thereby hugely increasing government deficits. Once bailouts restored corporate profits and stock markets, those same large banks, corporations, and Wall Street use their wealth and power to reduce government spending (chiefly on social programs) to deal with deficits. With or without economic growth, US capitalism's performance is now more subordinated to a tiny rich minority than at any time since the last economic crisis (1930s) imposed by that same minority.

Extremely unequal distributions of wealth and income among individuals, and among enterprises, enable the richest and largest to manipulate the economy and control the political parties. Thus they kept down wages to zoom profits, especially since the 1970s; they reduced business tax rates and top income tax rates dramatically across those same years; and they likewise cut government regulation of their business practices. The result was global capitalist crisis. Yet their economic and political power got the government to bail them out first, foremost, and to the exclusion of most others.

Growth inside the United States is no longer their priority. They now invest chiefly in industries expanding abroad. For them, the United States has become a "mature" market—business-speak for an economy expected to grow slowly if at all, weighed down by masses of people with declining job and income prospects. Neither large corporations nor our richest citizens (chiefly major corporate shareholders and directors) want to pay taxes to sustain such masses of people. They prefer austerity: Keep tax increases down and shrink costly government supports for the masses "unfortunately" marginalized by US capitalism's development.

Explanations of Keynesian theory and celebrations of economic growth miss 2012's real lessons. The key problem is an economic structure disinterested in a democratically focused way out of economic crisis and decline for the population as a whole. It is not realistic to propose policies that ignore that structural disinterest. Counterposing growth to austerity policies distracts attention from struggles to change an economic system—and especially the structure of its enterprises—whose concentrated wealth and power sustain socially destructive policies. Those struggles are key to realistic political agendas for 2013.

Economic Policy Debates: Theater of Distraction
July 29, 2013

Endless debates over austerity versus stimulus policies agitate governments. Which is "the correct" one to escape global capitalism's ongoing crisis? The debates proceed as if official policies were key to ending crises. But the politicians' fights over policies are mostly distractions from the main events: how crises usually end themselves and their immense social costs.

In the United States, Republicans promote policies that prioritize national debts as "the" economic problem. Enlarged debts, they assert, prevent businesses from making investments that "create jobs." Republicans therefore demand austerity policies—chiefly cutting government spending—to reduce national debts and thereby exit crises. Democrats—at least those who still differ from Republicans—promote policies that prioritize reducing unemployment. They want increased government stimulus spending even if national debts rise. That spending, they argue, will boost demands for goods and services, thereby creating jobs and pulling the economy out of crisis. Democrats denounce austerity for worsening crises, while Republicans denounce rising national debts for worsening crises.

Actual government policies usually oscillate between these two anti-crisis policies or combine them in "grand compromises" amid politicians' self-congratulations. Similar policy theater makes headlines in other countries. Government leaders act roles as economic problem solvers, as if their policies determined the outcomes of crises. Indeed, the same basic policy battles, oscillations, and compromises have been repeated during each recurring business downturn in capitalist countries since 1929.

The reality of crises is quite different. Government policies actually are rather tangential, their impacts minor. Capitalism usually self-corrects its inherent, recurring downturns by depressing its production costs. The downturns usually end after and because unemployment and business cutbacks drive down labor and other production costs. When those costs fall sufficiently for capitalists to see profits from growing or starting their businesses, they invest. Resumed investments lift production and employment out of crisis. Meanwhile, heavily publicized debates over alternative economic policies rage in government, media, and the academic circles. They distract the public from the immense social costs of how capitalism actually overcomes the cycles it reproduces: by unemployment and business cutbacks.

When a capitalist economy enters another cyclical downturn (nothing has yet worked to prevent them), many immediately affected capitalists reduce output, cut input orders, and fire workers. These actions distribute and deepen the downturn across the economy. Fired workers buy less and thereby hurt other capitalists, who cut their payrolls, and so on. Reduced input orders from initially affected capitalists do likewise. Labor and product markets spread capitalist downturns. The depth and duration of each crisis vary with the particulars of these enterprise–market interactions.

Capitalist downturns include the mechanism that usually ends them. Deepening unemployment drives increasingly stressed workers to seek or retain jobs by accepting lower wages. Unemployment also enables employers to cut job benefits and job security. Pensions become less secure or smaller, or they simply vanish. Medical insurance coverage narrows, raises workers' co-pays, or both. Vacations are shortened, job protections shrink, and so on. Capitalist downturns drive down employers' labor costs.

Downturns also diminish employers' other costs. Capitalists reducing production cut demands for productive inputs. That often depresses those inputs' prices. Enterprises bankrupt by downturns often sell their used equipment and tools at low prices. Downturns lower demand for factory, office, and store space, and thereby their rental rates; by likewise lowering demands for legal, architectural, cleaning, and other services, prices of the latter usually fall.

Eventually, reduced costs of workers, inputs, and required services induce profit-driven capitalists to resume or increase investment. Capitalist downturns usually produce the conditions for subsequent upturns and vice versa. We insert the term "usually" in the sentences above because sometimes a downturn's speed and spread are so great that capitalists fear to invest even as costs decline. Then downturns persist and often become depressions.

The social costs and pains of capitalism's self-negating downturns are mostly borne directly by the masses of the unemployed, their families, and their neighbors. Homes are foreclosed; educations troubled, interrupted, or abandoned; marriages and households destroyed; and so on. Because unemployed workers, bankrupt enterprises, and reduced production all cut tax flows to federal, state, and local governments, they in turn cut many public services just as social needs for them rise. Government budgets are strained because downturns reduce revenues while raising mandated outlays for unemployment compensation, food stamps, and other "safety net" items won by workers' struggles in past capitalist downturns.

Many people subjected to capitalist downturns sooner or later question the system. Can societies do better than a system that imposes recurring downturns and their associated suffering and immense costs? Capitalism's defenders have rarely engaged such questioning. Instead they offer some comfort and much distraction in response to pressures from downturns' victims. Comfort takes the form of unemployment compensation, food stamps, and welfare. Distraction takes the form of public theater: well-dressed politicians inside imposing government buildings urgently debating economic policies as journalists and economists declare those debates to be important.

Even after capitalist downturns end, the political theater continues. Austerity's champions insist that their policies ended the downturn or would have done so sooner if only they had been adopted. Stimulus advocates make parallel claims. More government spending does at least modestly counter or moderate economic downturns, while austerity usually worsens them. Nonetheless, the old debate persists. Capitalism's downturns keep recurring and with them the need to distract those suffering the attendant pains and costs.

Downturns underscore capitalism's wastes, inefficiencies, and injustices for millions. Unemployed workers suffer alongside unused raw materials, tools, equipment, and workplaces, while urgent social needs for the outputs they might have produced go unmet. In such conditions, opportunities arise to challenge the system and its supports. One such support is the distracting theater of policy debates over austerity versus stimuli. The main strategic issue ought not to be which policy will overcome crisis. Rather, it should be the reasons behind retaining a system that imposes repeated downturns on everyone and so unjustly distributes their immense social costs and wastes.

POLITICAL ECONOMY OF PARTISAN "DEBATES"

Ongoing Crisis and Liberal Blindness
June 6, 2011

The double dip of this crisis is upon us. The latest data agree: the housing market has been in full double-dip mode for five months as home prices keep declining. The foreclosure disaster keeps increasing the combination of homeless families and empty homes. Think capitalist efficiency. Unemployment rose back above 9 percent again. The average length of unemployment is now 39.7 weeks, the longest since these records began in 1948. Investments by businesses are decelerating and governments keep dropping workers.

Over 20 million workers are unemployed or underemployed. Over a quarter of the nation's productive capacity remains unutilized, gathering rust and dust. Annual output of $1 trillion is lost by wasting these resources. Think capitalist efficiency again.

The so-called recovery benefited US banks, larger corporations, and the stock market. It bypassed everyone else and is now over. Still wondering what hit them, victims of the crisis—the mass of working people—now face paying for that recovery. "Their" government borrowed massively to bail out the corporations. That boosted the national debt. And that now "requires" cutting government spending by "absolutely necessary" reductions in government jobs, services, Social Security, Medicaid, and Medicare. What money the government saves by cutting public services it can then turn over to the corporations, the rich, and the foreign governments (led by China) who lent it the funds to produce that short-lived recovery (for them).

Paul Krugman is better than most mainstream economists. He pushes his liberal views against most of that mainstream. But Krugman shares the classic liberal blindness. Accounting for today's economic wreckage, he worries about "fatalism." The problem for him is subjective. People—Krugman likes to obliterate differences with that term— accept that "recovery from financial crisis is usually slow." Krugman admits that previous governments similarly responded to crises slowly because of their shared "fatalism and learned helplessness." What he proposes instead is the usual liberal set of economic solutions as "obvious": aggressive fiscal policy (bigger deficits), aggressive mortgage debt reduction (mechanism unspecified), and so forth. The people should do these things because not doing them is "simply crazy" and because "fatalism … is the main enemy of prosperity."

Krugman argues that the grotesque injustice of the government's response to crisis is caused by a psychological disposition—fatalism— ascribed to the people. That's like Keynes blaming capitalist crises on the problem of making investment decisions faced with uncertainty about the future—we all struggle with uncertainty, right? Liberals like Krugman avoid locating economic problems in the core capitalist structure of production—in struggles between employer and employee.

Krugman does not explain why "fatalism" keeps following crises. He does not ask, let alone answer, what structural factors might explain that. Instead he wants smart people to correct the mistaken fatalism afflicting lesser minds. Condescension toward those he disagrees with reinforces his point that lack of smarts explains fatalism. Governments' slow responses to capitalist crises reveal stupidity.

Here is the explanation Krugman lacks. Capitalism has always been unstable. Governments have never prevented the boom and bust cycles despite nearly every leader having promised, as each cycle's downturn hit, not only to get through it "but also to make sure to prevent the next one." Of course, governments could rush in and offset cycles with massive programs of public employment and public investments. Liberals often urge that. But governments refuse unless massive pressure from labor unions and socialist and communist parties from below force partial and temporary steps in that direction (as happened with President Roosevelt after 1933).

Capitalism's instability arises in good part from struggles between employer and employee. Crises arise when enterprise profits do not suffice for employers and their shareholders. They then reduce production, fire workers, and cut their purchases of inputs. These steps reduce other employers' profits who react likewise. Spiral into recession ensues. Capitalism long ago evolved a way to manage its inherent instability. As unemployment grows and lasts, the jobless become willing to work for less than before, driving wages down. As businesses fail, the resulting glut of secondhand machinery and equipment, and empty factory and office space drives down those business costs. Eventually, when the labor and materials costs have dropped enough, employers see sufficient profit possibilities. Their investments resume and therewith the bust phase gives way to the boom phase.

Why should government intervene in capitalism's method of self-healing from its interminable instability affliction? After all, for most capitalists the decline of business costs constitutes an attractive method of coping with crises. Likewise most capitalists do not welcome the precedent set if governments intervene to rescue the masses from the system's dysfunction. And capitalists most certainly do not want to pay the costs of such government interventions.

So capitalists have good, structural reasons—grounded in their positions inside the enterprises they run—for opposing liberal solutions to the immense social costs of capitalist crises. Fatalism is not the cause of the problem. It is merely the outward, superficial face of the political system's unwillingness to contest the message coming from its chief patrons, capitalist employers.

When mass suffering in protracted downturns threatens to move toward attacking the system itself, capitalist employers—and hence their government—sometimes recognize the need for a small and temporary dose of the liberal solution. Even then, government action has less to do with the fiscal stimuli liberals endorse and more with a different task: shifting mass suffering and anger away from anticapitalism and toward celebration of benevolent government. That is what FDR accomplished by establishing Social Security and unemployment insurance in the 1930s.

Liberalism's outdated antipathy to Marxism—and ignorance of the new developments in Marxian thinking of recent decades—is its key problem, a debilitating legacy of the Cold War. That antipathy and ignorance undermine liberalism's capacity to think its propositions through, to ground them in economics and history, and to explain the key "whys" needed to shore up its arguments about what is happening, what should be happening, and why those two diverge.

The Truth about "Class War" in America

September 22, 2011

Republicans and conservatives have done us a service by describing federal policies in terms of "class war." But by applying the term only to President Obama's latest proposals to raise taxes on the rich, they have it all backward and upside down. The last fifty years have indeed seen continuous class warfare in and over federal economic policies.

But it was a war waged chiefly by business and conservatives. They won, and the mass of middle-income and poor Americans lost. Obama's modest proposal for tax increases on the rich does not begin a class war. On the contrary, it is a small, modest effort to reduce the other side's class war victories.

Big business and conservatives have worked to undo the regulations and taxes imposed on them in the wake of the Great Depression of the 1930s. Then, an upsurge in labor union organization (the Congress of Industrial Organizations sweep across basic US industries) and in socialist and communist parties membership gave President Franklin Delano Roosevelt the support and the pressure to tax business and the rich. He took their money to pay for the massive federal hiring program (11 million federal jobs filled between 1934 and 1941) and to start the

Social Security Administration, among other programs. He regulated their business activities to try to prevent devastating capitalist depressions from recurring in the nation's future.

Since the end of the Great Depression—and especially since the 1970s—the class warfare waged by business and its allies (most conservatives in both parties) was successful. For example, at the end of World War II, for every dollar Washington raised in taxes on individuals, it raised $1.50 in taxes on business profits. In contrast, today, for every dollar Washington gets in taxes on individuals, it gets 25 cents in taxes on business. Business and its allies successfully shifted most of its federal tax burden onto individuals.

Over the same period, the tax rates on the richest Americans fell from 91 percent in the 1950s and 1960s and 70 percent in the 1970s to the current low rate of 35 percent. The richest Americans won that spectacular tax cut. Middle- and lower-income Americans won no such cuts, while paying a higher proportion of their income for Social Security that the rich were required to do.

In plain English, the last fifty years saw a massive shift of the burden of federal taxation from business to individuals and from rich individuals to everyone else. Class war policies? Yes, but a war that victimized the vast majority of working Americans.

Republicans and conservatives carefully avoided using "class war" to describe those tax-shifting achievements over the last half-century. They wanted us to believe that all they cared about was economic growth and job creation. But when President Obama now proposes modest increases in tax rates on rich individuals ("modest" because they don't begin to return to the tax rates in the 1950s, 1960s, and 1970s), the Republicans and conservatives howl "class warfare." Obama claims that higher taxes on the rich reduce the need for spending cuts that would slow growth and increase unemployment.

Republicans and conservatives argue that raising taxes on corporations and rich individuals punishes those who create jobs and thus will hurt efforts to reduce unemployment. Neither logic nor evidence supports their arguments. The US Federal Reserve recently reported a record quantity of cash on the books of US businesses (hoarding over

$2 trillion). Despite the currently very low taxes on businesses and the rich, that cash is *not* being invested and is *not* creating jobs. Nor is it being distributed to anyone else who is spending it, either. Washington could tax a portion of that cash and spend it to stimulate the economy. That would be especially effective if the taxed cash were spent to hire the unemployed rather than leaving the cash idle in businesses' hoards.

Billionaire investor Warren Buffett upset many of his fellow super-rich individuals by a *New York Times* op-ed that he wrote (published August 14, 2011). It explained that he had never met any serious investor who decided about investments based on tax rates. Rather, the prospects of profits and sales made the key difference to investors. Buffett urged higher income taxes on rich Americans like himself partly because those higher taxes would not negatively impact job creation in the future just as it had not done in the past. He implied that it was becoming dangerous for capitalism's survival to keep providing the minority of rich people with lower federal tax rates than the middle and lower income majority paid.

Economists know that a long time—usually years—separates making an investment and reaping the profits from selling the output of that investment. Anyone making an investment today cannot know what tax rates will be in the future. They may be higher or lower or the same as they are today. That's why investors' decisions depend far more on real costs today and estimates about future sales, markets, and prices in the future than on speculation about future tax rates. The claim that tax increases today will cut investments thinly disguises an effort to lower taxes on business and the rich now.

History reinforces the same point. In the 1950s and 1960s, tax rates on corporations and the rich were much, much higher than today. Yet those years had lower unemployment and higher rates of investment and growth than today. Low tax rates on businesses and the rich do not create jobs.

Struggles over taxes always pit business and the rich against the middle-income earners and the poor. Each side seeks to shift the tax burden off of itself and on to the other side. "Class war" in that sense is nothing new. Accusing only one side of waging that war is ignorant at best and dishonest at worst. No one should be fooled. Today, business and the rich are waging class war yet again to avoid even a small, modest reverse in the huge tax cuts they won in that war over the last half-century.

The Political Economy of Obama's Reelection

November 14, 2012

Capitalism's crises, especially when deep and long-lasting like today's, polarize its politics. Left and right are reinvigorated by improved opportunities to advance their respective economic agendas. The middle, long in power and deeply complicit with capitalism, gets blamed for the crisis and its social costs. The resurgent right uses the crisis to advance classic demands on behalf of business and the rich for yet more wealth, income, and freedom from government regulation and taxes. The resurgent left uses the crisis to argue that capitalism's injustice, inefficiency, and waste show the need for transition beyond it. The middle tries to hold on, hoping that capitalism's intrinsic instability, its recurring cycles, will produce an upturn before the people abandon the middle. Such an upturn could "stabilize" politics, undermine the appeal of the left and right, and be credited to the middle's policies. This struggle of right, left, and middle provides an entry point into the political economy of President Obama's reelection.

Political polarization caused by capitalist crises is clearest today in the economy most damaged so far. Greece's two main parties of the middle alternated power for decades, but they suddenly dropped to a combined 35 percent of the vote in the 2012 elections. Left and right parties surged into sudden political prominence. They are winning mass support as people abandon the political middle. They resent the crisis and bailouts chiefly of banks, corporations, stock markets, and the rich. They hate austerity policies that shift the costs of crisis and bailouts onto them by cutting public jobs, services, and supports just when they are most needed.

A parallel drama unfolds in the United States. The crisis since 2007 produced a resurgent right in the tea parties. They blamed the crisis on poor people abusing credit, immigrants abusing US law, and institutions and governmental economic interventions. A few criticized Wall Street but quieted when reminded about the right's chief financiers.

Thus the resurgent right married social concerns (e.g., oppositions to abortion, birth control, gun control, church-state separation) to enthusiastic support for capitalism.

Tea party members expressed that marriage by reviving old tirades against "socialism." They secured financing not only by carefully avoiding any critique of capitalism, but also by insisting that capitalists would resume prosperity and growth if freed of government regulations and taxes. The right sought to use the crisis to advance the classic capitalist agenda of maximizing wealth, income, and freedoms for the corporate elites and the richest 1 percent to 10 percent of individuals.

The left in the United States lacks the right's financing opportunities. It also inherits the last fifty years of state persecutions and corporate attacks that destroyed once-strong political parties (populist, socialist, and communist) and labor unions' former militancy, size, and power. A resurgent left slowly and arduously regathers people and resources to organize itself into a social force. Occupy Wall Street (OWS) thus emerged only years after the tea parties in the United States, and after a resurgent left arose in Europe. OWS was far less organized and financed than either of them. Its nonetheless astonishing growth demonstrated the vulnerability of the middle (traditional Republican and Democratic establishments) and the powerful potential of a new left.

The middle, as servant/guarantor of capitalism, fundamentally opposes an anticapitalist left. The middle likewise fears that the right's program could generate a popular backlash threatening capitalism. Occupying the middle in US politics (as traditional Republicans and Democrats always have), Obama's job is to protect the economic status quo and manage crisis turbulence like a steady pilot. He works to undermine the appeal and/or organizations of both resurgent right and left while waiting/hoping for the capitalist cycle's next upturn. Upturns happen when wages and costs fall far enough to offer profit opportunities that induce capitalists to invest again.

President Obama offers "hope and wait" for an upturn while not significantly increasing taxes or regulations for corporations and the rich. That is what the political middle does. Obama's slight increase in regulation (e.g., the Wall Street Reform and Consumer Protection Act, a basic regulatory response to collapse of 2007–2009 and various scandals thereto attached) and merely talking about raising the richest individuals' tax rates further galvanized the right and its financing. Obama had taken such small steps to counteract left accusations that the costs of crisis and bailouts were being shifted onto average people through mass unemployment, home foreclosures, and austerity policies. Crises polarize by making the political middle increasingly difficult to hold.

Because of the tea parties' size and financing, Obama tried to accommodate, moderate, and compromise more than repress them. That cost him the enthusiasm of his supporters since 2008. Because of the ultimately greater threat of OWS's mass appeal and because the OWS organization and financing were weak, Obama repressed more than accommodated it (coordinated mayors bulldozed encampments, police harassed, etc.). That produced a deeper enmity whose consequences will soon unfold.

The resurgent right captured control of a significant portion of the Republican Party. It forced the Romney campaign to waver between middle and right. Thereby the right's interpretation of the causes and cures for the economic crisis became the major challenge to the middle. While Romney wavered, Obama championed the middle. Meanwhile, a repressed OWS (and others such as the Green Party) could not make candidates contend with interpretations of the crisis as the product of a capitalism sacrificing the 99 percent for the benefit of the 1 percent.

The 2012 election thus tested what the resurgent right could achieve when functioning as a massively funded, major component of Romney's campaign. Obama's victory shows that the right lost to the middle; too many voters rejected its analyses and programs. Without a seriously contending left, the 2012 majority preferred the middle, despite having lost confidence in it continuously since 2008.

The crisis continues and may worsen over the next year or two. The economic decline that helped produce OWS has deepened (e.g., average real weekly wages fell 2.5 percent from October 2010 to October 2012). The right just suffered a defeat. The middle weakens further as economic recovery remains elusive. The resurgent left in Europe grows and strengthens. Many conditions for a resurgence of OWS or its reincarnation are in place.

Class War Redux: How the American Right Embraced Marxist Struggle

December 19, 2012

Conservatives and Republicans used to keep quiet and private about their views on classes and class war in the United States. They ceded those terms to leftists and then denounced their use. The United States was, they insisted, a mostly "classless" society, civilization's pinnacle achievement. We were a vast majority of wondrously comfortable and secure consumers.

Workers or capitalists, like classes, were antiquated, disloyal, and irrelevant concepts. True, a few fabulously rich people were visible (most likely film or sports celebrities or "entrepreneurial innovators"): their antics and luxuries were fun to mimic, admire, or deplore. An annoying and assuredly small underclass of the poor also existed: most likely, persons "destroyed" by drugs or alcohol.

However, over recent decades, that approach has given way to a harsher view of US society and the world beyond. At first, in their homes, country clubs, and unguarded moments with friends, conservatives and Republicans redefined their prime political enemy as the "moochers." Those people—Republican presidential nominee Mitt Romney called them "the 47 percent" always voting Democrat—depend on government handouts and vote accordingly to secure those handouts.

Moochers include welfare recipients, the poor receiving Medicaid, students getting subsidized college loans, illegal immigrants, and, sometimes, also those "entitled" to get Social Security and Medicare benefits. They are all society's real "exploiters," using government to tax the other 53 percent of the people for the funds doled out to the 47 percent.

Conservatives and Republicans are thus classifying the population into two key subgroups. Gone are images of the United States as one big happy middle class. Instead, one class, self-defined as the upper 53 percent, comprises self-reliant, hardworking taxpayers: true social givers. The other class composes the lower 47 percent: takers who give little as long as dependence saps their creativity and responsibility.

Romney's campaign showed that conservatives and Republicans increasingly use this class analysis to understand society and construct their political programs. Romney's campaign also proved the increasing determination of conservatives and Republicans to pursue class war explicitly in these terms. Romney later confirmed publicly what had been exposed in his private appeal to wealthy funders.[27]

A chief Romney adviser, Stuart Stevens, wrote: "On 6 November, Romney carried the majority of every economic group except those with less than $50,000 a year in household income. That means he carried the majority of middle-class voters."

Warren Buffett, the multibillionaire, says that because "his class" is winning, economic inequality is becoming dangerous. He thus wants rich Americans to be taxed more. He presumes—like most Democrats—that class and class conflict are terms that will repel Americans and persuade them to support Buffett's tax reform proposals.

That presumption is flawed. The political terrain has shifted.

Conservatives and Republicans see advantages in becoming open class warriors. They invite the voting population to join them in fighting the class war. Their program: to liberate the hardworking, self-reliant class (those earning over $50,000) from ruinous taxation. To that end, they will reduce and eventually eliminate handouts to the dependent clients of an overspending state controlled by those clients' votes.

Republicans promise to end "abusive" taxation and other government programs redistributing wealth and income from the upper 53 percent to the lower 47 percent.

This class war aims to eradicate its enemy. The dependents will lose the government handouts that destroyed their self-reliance, creativity, and responsibility. Forced to become independent, like the 53 percent, they will abandon the Democrats and secure Republican victory. This politics—designed to eradicate the enemy—replicates the strategy deployed earlier against another Democratic voter base, organized labor, after it returned Franklin Roosevelt to office four times.

---

27. Douglass Daniel, "Mitt Romney: Obama Won with 'Gifts' to Blacks, Hispanics, Young Voters," *Huffington Post*, November 14, 2012.

After this class war succeeds, government will return to its "original purposes" of military defense, law enforcement, and little more. The lower 47 percent will be freed from debilitating dependence to resume the happy middle-class existence that is the social optimum.

That this class narrative is not evidence-based or factual is beside the point. Of course, vast tax reductions go to corporations and the richest citizens, just as vast subsidies do, and likewise, laws enabling monopoly pricing, tax evasion, and so on. Corporate profits and individual wealth depend on government, too. The class warfare narrative of the US right proceeds anyway, because it plausibly promises tax cuts as relief for Americans in worsening economic difficulties.

To the extent this class war from above succeeds, Democrats will weaken, and government assistance for the poor and working class will atrophy. Such austerity will deepen resignation, bitterness, and depoliticization for many.

However, austerity also generates another kind of class war, in which classes are defined differently. These new class analyses, discourses, and struggles are initiatives emerging in and around the Occupy Wall Street movement in the United States—and analogous anticapitalist movements elsewhere. They borrow, but also depart from, earlier socialist traditions.

The exploited class (workers) produces the surplus value appropriated by the class of exploiters (capitalists). The capitalists then use that surplus to control politics and thereby sustain a social system that serves them primarily. Champions of the exploited class aim to change the system by ending the division between worker and capitalist inside the enterprises.

Unlike what happened in the Soviet Union and the old socialist world, the focus is now less on changes in property ownership and in the relation of markets to planning. Instead, the emphasis falls more on changing the organization of production, replacing the top-down, undemocratic dictatorship inside capitalist enterprises with the horizontal, workers' self-direction of cooperatives. The new model of industrial or enterprise organization is not the Soviet state enterprise but rather the typical worker cooperatives that constitute the Mondragon Cooperative Corporation. The democratization of enterprises would enable reduced income and wealth inequality and all the political and cultural inequalities that flow therefrom.

How political struggles have changed! Conservatives and Republicans pursue one kind of class war to destroy Democrats and the welfare state with austerity programs. The Democrats weakly resist and mostly "compromise" to survive in that class war. Meanwhile, capitalism's ongoing crisis and austerity programs provoke another, different class struggle.

Pompous predictions that class struggle was a passé concept have been proved wrong. Quite the contrary, right and left place multiple, contested class analyses and struggles at the center of politics today.

Critics of Capitalism Must Include Its Definition
May 26, 2015

Most business leaders, mass media, politicians, and academics keep defining capitalism, the main economic system in today's world, as markets plus private ("free") enterprises. That definition is wrong. Definitions matter more now than ever as people increasingly question, challenge, and want to move beyond capitalism.

Consider the twentieth-century revolutions that overthrew a capitalism they defined as markets plus free enterprises. In Russia and China, they replaced private, free enterprises with socialized (state-owned and operated) enterprises and replaced market mechanisms of distribution with central state-planned distribution. They called that "socialism," thinking they had abolished and gone beyond capitalism. However, their socialism proved unable to sustain itself and mostly reverted back to capitalism.

One reason those revolutions failed to go beyond capitalism was those revolutionaries' definition of capitalism and socialism. That definition crucially shaped their strategies for and very conceptions of revolutionary social change. Since that definition still shapes debates over and strategies for social change today, it urgently needs to be criticized and set aside.

Because capitalism is so regularly defined as "a market system," we may consider first the actual nonequivalence of capitalism and markets. Capitalism became the dominant economic system in England in revolt against feudalism there in the seventeenth century. Capitalism spread from England to the Western European mainland and thereafter to the rest of the world. However, capitalism was neither the first nor the only system to utilize markets as its means of distributing resources and products. In the slave economic systems that prevailed in various times and places across human history, markets were often the means of distributing resources (including slaves themselves) and the products of slaves' labor. In the pre–Civil War United States, for example, masters sold slaves and cotton produced by slaves in markets. Thus, the presence of a "market system" does not distinguish capitalism from a slave system.

The same logic applies to feudalism. In many times and places across European feudalism, for example, products of feudal enterprises (called "manors") were sold in markets to serfs and lords of other manors. During the twentieth century, feudal *latifundias* in Latin America sold their products on world markets. The presence of a "market system" does not distinguish capitalism from feudalism. Even the presence of a particular market—for wage labor, for example—is no definite marker of capitalism's presence. Economic history displays various examples of slaves and serfs having some or all of their labor power exchanged in markets for money or other commodities.

A parallel argument applies to "free enterprise." The capitalist enterprise is more or less "free" to set the prices, quantities, and qualities of its outputs; organize its labor processes; choose among available technologies; and distribute its profits. But much the same has often applied to slave plantations and feudal manors.

Likewise, capitalism has persisted when markets were subordinated to other mechanisms of distribution. For example, during World War II, ration cards distributed by the US government fundamentally displaced the market system for distributing many goods. Capitalism also can and has coexisted with "unfree" enterprises. In August 1971, President Richard Nixon took away the freedom of capitalist enterprises to set prices or wages. Capitalism elsewhere has often continued despite markets and enterprise freedoms being variously abrogated or suppressed for differing lengths of time.

Whatever distinguishes capitalism from such other systems as slavery and feudalism, markets and free enterprises are not it. Nor will competition or the extent of government intervention serve to differentiate capitalism from other systems. The competition among capitalist enterprises had its parallels in competitions among slave plantations, feudal manors, feudal guild workers, and so on. Competition varies in its forms and intensities among capitalist enterprises depending on the context and conditions of each industry across time and space. The same is true for competition among noncapitalist enterprises.

Finally, government intervention into an otherwise "private" sector of the economy has also been a variable feature of all economic systems. In some slave systems, slaves were chiefly privately owned, while in others, states owned and worked many slaves. In Europe, the absolute monarchies toward the end of feudalism were states owning huge numbers of subordinated serfs alongside the privately run feudal manors of such kings' subjects. Shifting constellations of private versus state production units characterize noncapitalist as well as capitalist systems.

So then how should we define capitalism to differentiate it from alternative economic systems such as slavery, feudalism, and a postcapitalist socialism? The answer is "in terms of the organization of the surplus." How an economic system organizes the production, appropriation, and distribution of its surplus neatly and clearly differentiates capitalism from other systems.

In slavery, one group of persons, the slaves that are others' property, performs the basic productive labor. Slaves use their brains and muscles to transform objects in nature into what masters desire. Masters immediately appropriate their slaves' total output, but they usually return a portion of that output for the slaves' consumption. The excess of the slaves' total output over what they get to consume (plus what replaces inputs used up in production) is the surplus. The masters take that surplus and generally distribute it to others in society (e.g., police and army, church) who provide the conditions (security, belief systems, etc.) needed for this slave organization of the surplus to persist through time.

Feudalism displays a different organization of the surplus. Serfs are not property as slaves are; lords do not immediately and totally appropriate what serfs produce. Instead, serfs and lords enter into personal relationships entailing mutual obligations (in European feudalism: fealty, vassalage, etc.). In medieval Europe, lords assigned land parcels to serfs, whose labor there yielded outputs. Feudal obligations typically included either (a) serfs' laboring parts of each week on their assigned plots and keeping the proceeds and laboring other parts of the week on the lord's retained land, with the lord keeping the product of that labor ("corvée"); or (b) the serf delivering to the lord as "rent" a portion of the product (or its monetary equivalent) from the land assigned to and worked by the serf. Corvée and rent were forms of Europe's feudal surplus.

Capitalism's organization of the surplus differs from both slavery's and feudalism's. The surplus producers in capitalism are neither property (slavery) nor bound by personal relationships (feudal mutual obligations). Instead, the producers in capitalism enter "voluntarily" into contracts with the possessors of material means of production (land and capital). The contracts, usually in money terms, specify (a) how much will be paid by the possessors to buy/employ the producer's labor power, and (b) the conditions of the producers' actual labor processes. The contract's goal is for the producers' labor to add more value during production than the value paid to the producer. That excess of value added by worker over value paid to worker is the capitalist form of the surplus, or surplus value.

While the capitalist, feudal, and slave organizations of the surplus differ as described above, they also share one crucial feature. In each system, the individuals who produce surpluses are not identical to the individuals who appropriate and then distribute those surpluses. Each system shares a basic alienation—of producers from their products—located at the core of production. That alienation provokes parallel class struggles: slaves versus masters, serfs versus lords, and workers versus capitalists. Marx used the word "exploitation" to focus analytical attention on what capitalism shared with feudalism and slavery, something that capitalist revolutions against slavery and feudalism never overcame.

The concept of exploitation serves also to differentiate socialism clearly from capitalism, feudalism, and slavery. In a socialism defined in terms of surplus organization, the producers and the appropriators/distributors of the surplus are identical; they are the same people. In such socialist enterprises, the workers collectively appropriate and distribute the surplus they produce. They perform functions parallel to those of boards of directors in capitalist corporations. Such "workers' self-directed enterprises" (WSDEs) are unlike slave, feudal, and/or capitalist enterprises. WSDEs represent the end of exploitation.

Significant conclusions follow. Soviet socialism from 1917 to 1989 did displace private in favor of social ownership of means of production and markets in favor of central planning. It did not displace the capitalist organization of the surplus in favor of WSDEs; surplus producers and appropriators in state enterprises were not made identical.

Workers produced and others—the Soviet Union's Council of Ministers and their appointed state officials—appropriated and distributed surpluses generated in state industrial enterprises and on state farms. The Soviet definition of socialism did not focus on the organization of the surplus. Most socialists over the last century, pro- and anti-Soviet alike, used the same definition. In the nineteenth century, Marx and Engels saw the seizure of state power as a means to transition from capitalism to socialism. In the twentieth century, state ownership of the means of production and state central planning became the definition of socialism itself: the end, not just the means. That problematic definition of capitalism and its difference from socialism remains prevalent to this day.

The twentieth century's major experiments to establish socialism would have ended differently had organizers defined capitalism and socialism differently. Their policies might then have replaced not only private with social property and markets with central planning, but also exploitative with nonexploitative organizations of the surplus. As ground-level organizations, WSDEs might have secured a democratic accountability of socialist governments and thereby the survival and development of socialist economies.

The surplus-focused definitions of capitalism and socialism are available to social movements today as they engage and contest economic systems. Or those movements can stay enmeshed in old, endlessly recycled debates between more (Keynesian and welfare statist) versus less (neoliberal) government intervention in capitalist economies. Will the movements keep limiting their goals to expanded government regulation of, and intervention in, economic systems where capitalist organizations of the surplus continue to prevail?

Or will social movements—increasingly facing a hostile global capitalism—seek alliances with advocates of system change by establishing enterprise democracy through WSDEs? Such political questions become urgent as more people than ever question capitalist globalization and capitalism generally.

Cooperatives of all kinds, including worker cooperatives, have a long, complex history. In many parts of the world today, they have carved out an acceptable—on condition of remaining a relatively small—place in otherwise capitalist economies. They rarely confront capitalism as an alternative economic system, likely fearing capitalism's probable reaction.

Confrontation—putting WSDEs forward as a systemic alternative to capitalism—could take may forms. For example, labor unions could add the establishment of worker coops to their strategies vis-à-vis capital. When employers demand concessions by threatening to close enterprises, move them abroad, and so on, unions could refuse and proceed instead to establish worker coops if and when the employers actually abandon enterprises. To take another example, localities could campaign for use of eminent domain to address both unemployment and poverty by organizing and supporting worker coops. Extreme poverty was not an obstacle to the formation and successful growth of the worker coops formed by the Catholic Priest Arizmendi in Mondragon, Spain, in 1956. Indeed, long-lasting poverty within capitalist Spain prompted the decision to organize enterprises instead along democratic, cooperative principles that proved the basis for Mondragon's phenomenal growth through to the present. High school, college, and university curricula could include both abstract discussions on how the United States might do better than capitalism and offer practical courses for establishing worker coops.

Most important would be if progressive political forces saw gains from allying with, helping build, and undertaking mass political and ideological support for worker coops. The latter could then provide a crucial communication bridge between the left and the daily struggles of workers in their enterprises, both those still capitalist and those that are WSDEs or becoming so. Workers already in WSDEs and those working for transition to WSDEs could also provide economic and political supports to left political initiatives and campaigns. In return, the left could mobilize for legal and other changes to provide worker coops with the needed legislative framework, capital, and markets. Mass political campaigns eventually secured the Small Business Administration for small businesses and various levels of political supports for minority and women-owned businesses. WSDEs could benefit from parallel administrations assisting them.

Eventually, when WSDEs had become widespread enough and an allied left had grown enough, they jointly could offer the American people a real choice never before available. They might choose an economy based on capitalist, top-down hierarchical enterprise organization or one based on WSDEs, or some mixture of both. If fair and open, I have little doubt where that vote would point.

US Politics' True Bipartisan Consensus: Capitalism Is Untouchable

October 22, 2013

The economic aim of both major US political parties is, in the end, the same: to protect and reinforce the capitalist system.

The Republican Party does so chiefly by means of a systematic, unremitting demonization of the government. They blame it for whatever ails the capitalist economy. If unemployment grows, they point to government policies and actions and attack particular politicians for what they did or did not do to stimulate the economy, directing criticism away from the employers who actually deprive workers of their jobs.

Republican solutions for capitalism's ills always involve reducing the government's demands on private capitalists—lower their taxes, deregulate their activities, and privatize government production of goods and services. Their program for the future is always: free the private capitalist system from government intervention and you will get "prosperity" and growth.

The Democrats protect and reproduce the system by assigning to the government the task of minimizing the problems that beset capitalism. So, for example, they want the business cycles that are an inherent affliction of capitalism to be foreseen, planned for, minimized, and overcome by government intervention. This is the underlying purpose of Keynesian economics and the monetary and fiscal policies it generates.

Beyond cycles, capitalism's more long-term problems, such as tendencies to produce great inequalities of income and accumulated wealth, lead Democrats to propose very modest government redistribution programs. Minimum wages, progressive tax structures, food, housing and other subsidies, and freely distributed public services exemplify Democrats' band aids meant to protect capitalism from its own potentially self-destructive tendencies.

From the GOP, you will hear denials that such self-destructive tendencies even exist. Economic problems always reduce to pesky and unwarranted government tampering in the free market. The few Republicans who will admit that capitalism is responsible for its own ailments also see capitalism as a fully self-healing system. The best solution for capitalism's problems, they insist, is to let the system function and correct them. Anything else will just make matters worse.

Most Democrats will paint Republicans as slavish servants of short-sighted corporations and the few whom they make rich. These, say Democrats, threaten capitalism's survival by failing to utilize government solutions to problems that consequently become worse and increasingly dangerous, putting the whole global economy—and capitalism's reproduction—at systemic risk.

Republicans will disregard Democratic economic policy as steps toward what they call "socialism": socialism defined as government ownership and operation of what should be private enterprises.[28]

Neither party, though, has figured out how to prevent capitalism's business cycles. Both consistently fail to make sure that cycles they failed to prevent would be shallow and short. So today, Republicans blame the crisis since 2007 on government over-regulation and interventions in the housing and finance markets (and they blame Democrats for cham-

---

28. Michael McAuliff and Sara Kenigsberg, "Obamacare Is Socialism: Reps. Louie Gohmert, Steve King Attack," *Huffington Post*, March 27, 2012.

pioning those policies). Democrats blame the crisis on too little regulation of those markets and insufficient redistribution (and—you guessed
it—they blame Republicans for opposing those government policies). In
short, crises, like everything else, are just opportunities to be explained
and exploited politically to advance each party's characteristic policies
and their electoral strategies.

In what were "normal times," US capitalism would reproduce itself
with nice, calm oscillations between Republican and Democratic presi-
dencies and congresses. For the minority of Americans who legitimately
cared about which party was in or out, their interests focused on issues
usually disconnected from any structural debate about the capitalist economic system. These included local and regional issues; foreign policy;
and social issues like sexuality, access to guns, flag-burning, and draft
protests. Capitalism rolled along, in part, because both parties functioned as alternative cheerleaders for it, treating it as beyond criticism.

Recent political gridlock and shutdowns suggest a "new normal"
has arrived. Political combat between the parties has become more intense and intractable, because capitalism has changed since the 1970s.
By then, the post–World War II boom in Western Europe, North America, and Japan—and also anxieties about the Soviet Union, China, and
their allies—had lofted real wages and government-funded social services far above their levels in capitalism's global hinterland, especially
Asia, Africa, and Latin America. Capitalists in Western Europe, North
America, and Japan were therefore eager to evade both the high wages
and the taxes they faced.

Major technical breakthroughs at the time made evasion possible.
The ubiquitous availability of jet travel made movement around the
globe much easier, cheaper, and faster. Computer and telecommunications advances enabled enterprise headquarters to monitor, command,
and control production facilities anywhere on the planet. It suddenly became practical to move production and distribution sites from locations
of high wages and taxes to locations of poverty and weak government.
Sharp competitors led the way as first manufacturing and then service
jobs were increasingly "exported" or "outsourced." Laggards suffered and
so learned the importance of following their more nimble competitors.

Most Republicans and Democrats facilitated the process by end-lessly promoting "free trade" and arguing that any constraints on free enterprises' relocations were unthinkable, inefficient, and (other syn-onyms for) "really bad." As more and more jobs left the United States, and formerly prosperous cities and states entered long-term declines, the two parties blamed their favorite targets: one another.

The idea that capitalism and capitalists were the problem was some-thing neither Democrats nor Republicans allow into their debates and talking points. Yet it was precisely capitalists' profit-driven, self-interest-ed decisions to move that have caused our economic problems. And so they remain.

Part IV: Crisis Responses, Going Beyond Capitalism

From the Occupy Wall Street movement to winds of change agitating students and a reduced labor movement to recent new electoral initiatives, responses to the crisis have notably contained significant, albeit still minority, impulses to move beyond capitalism. This crisis of capitalism—like its parallel in the 1930s—is thus generating tendencies to see the solution to these recurring crises in system change. So far, it is many people's consciousness that is moving in that direction and making that direction increasingly explicit. No organized movements to embody and publicly express that consciousness have yet arisen to parallel what grew so dramatically from below in the 1930s.

The essays in Part IV explore the obstacles encountered by those making systemic critiques of the crisis and working toward system change as the needed solution. They seek to contribute to such critics' understanding of the deepening crisis and, by refuting alternative explanations for major events and moments of the crisis, to build the critical movement's confidence in its own positions. By entering the debate over what kind of system change is to be the strategic goal, these essays engage classic disputes within the left about what postcapitalism could or should be.

Economic democracy has been a lively ghost lurking behind and around the history of modern capitalism since it spread from England in the seventeenth and eighteenth centuries. It has been capitalism's "other," that shadow the system could never quite shake. Capitalism's crises always revived and renewed social interest in economic democracy. The depth and length of the current crisis, occurring within a longer-term relocation of capitalist growth to new areas and away from its original bases in Western Europe, North America and Japan, provides conditions for the ghost to achieve its realization. Transition within the enterprises that form the production core of modern capitalism—from their hierarchical, top-down capitalist structures to an egalitarian, democratic, cooperative structure—is the system change increasingly captivating thoughtful critics of the current crisis. The essays in Part IV explore the case to be made for that transition as the best response to what strikes ever more people as an unacceptably dysfunctional capitalism.

THE OCCUPY MOVEMENT

Occupy Wall Street Ends Capitalism's Alibi

October 4, 2011

Occupy Wall Street has already weathered the usual early storms. The kept media ignored the protest, but that failed to end it. The partisans of inequality mocked it, but that failed to end it. The police servants of the status quo overreacted and that failed to end it—indeed, it fueled the fire. And millions looking on said, "Wow!" And now, ever more people are organizing local, parallel demonstrations—from Boston to San Francisco and many places between.

Let me urge the occupiers to ignore the usual carping that besets powerful social movements in their earliest phases. Yes, you could be better organized, your demands more focused, your priorities clearer. All true, but in this moment, mostly irrelevant. Here is the key: if we want a mass and deep-rooted social movement of the left to reemerge and transform the United States, we must welcome the many different streams, needs, desires, goals, energies, and enthusiasms that inspire and sustain social movements. Now is the time to invite, welcome, and gather them, in all their profusion and confusion.

The next step—and we are not there yet—will be to fashion the program and the organization to realize it. It's fine to talk about that now, to propose, debate, and argue. But it is foolish and self-defeating to compromise achieving inclusive growth—now within our reach—for the sake of program and organization. The history of the US left is littered with such programs and organizations without a mass movement behind them or at their core.

So permit me, in the spirit of honoring and contributing something to this historic movement, to propose yet another dimension, another item to add to your agenda for social change. To achieve the goals of this renewed movement, we must finally change the organization of production that sustains and reproduces inequality and injustice. We need to replace the failed structure of our corporate enterprises that now deliver profits to so few, pollute the environment we all depend on, and corrupt our political system.

We need to end stock markets and boards of directors. The capacity to produce the goods and services we need should belong to everyone—just like the air, water, healthcare, education, and security on which we likewise depend. We need to bring democracy to our enterprises. The workers within and the communities around enterprises can and should collectively shape how work is organized, what gets produced, and how we make use of the fruits of our collective efforts.

If we believe democracy is the best way to govern our residential communities, then it likewise deserves to govern our workplaces. Democracy at work is a goal that can help build this movement.

We all know that moving in this direction will elicit the screams of "socialism" from the usual predictable corners. The tired rhetoric lives on long after the cold war that orchestrated it fades out of memory. The audience for that rhetoric is fast fading, too. It is long overdue in the United States for us to have a genuine conversation and struggle over our current economic system. Capitalism has gotten a free pass for far too long.

We take pride in questioning, challenging, criticizing, and debating our health, education, military, transportation, and other basic social institutions. We argue whether their current structures and functioning serve our needs. We work our way to changing them so they perform better. And so it should be.

Yet for decades now, we have failed to similarly question, challenge, criticize, and debate our economic system: capitalism. Because a taboo protected capitalism, cheerleading and celebrating it became obligatory. Criticism and questions got banished as heresy, disloyalty, or worse. Behind the protective taboo, capitalism degenerated into the ineffective, unequal, crisis-ridden social disaster we all now bear.

Capitalism is the problem—and the joblessness, homelessness, insecurity, and austerity it now imposes everywhere are the costs we bear. We have the people, the skills, and the tools to produce the goods and services needed for a just society to prosper. We just need to reorganize our producing units differently, to go beyond a capitalist economic system that no longer serves our needs.

Humanity learned to do without kings and emperors and slave masters. We found our way to a democratic alternative, however partial and unfinished the democratic project remains. We can now take the next step to realize that democratic project. We can bring democracy to our enterprises—by transforming them into cooperatives owned, operated, and governed by democratic assemblies composed of all who work in them and all the residents of the communities who are interdependent with them.

Let me conclude by offering a slogan: "The United States can do better than corporate capitalism." Let that be an idea and a debate that this renewed movement can engage. Doing so would give an immense gift to the United States and the world. It would break through the taboo, finally subjecting capitalism to the critiques and debates it has evaded for far too long—and at far too great a cost to all of us.

How the 1 Percent Got Richer, while the 99 Percent Got Poorer

October 26, 2011

The just-released Congressional Budget Office (CBO) report, "Trends in the Distribution of Household Income Between 1979 and 2007," supports a basic claim of the Occupy Wall Street movement sweeping the country: that deep economic inequality is corrupting politics, culture, and American society as a whole.

CBO reports are almost universally considered and relied upon as epitomes of nonpartisan research. Simply put, the CBO report shows that over the last quarter century (1979 to 2007, to be exact), the top 1 percent of income earners enjoyed far, far bigger real income gains than the other 99 percent. As a result, the share of total income earned by the top 1 percent rose dramatically—doubling from 10 percent to 20 percent—at the expense of falling shares of income for all of the other 99 percent of the US population.

No wonder the Occupy Wall Street movement showed genius in crafting and adopting the slogan "We are the 99 percent." No wonder that an October 2011 *New York Times*/CBS News poll showed a majority of Americans expressing sympathy with the Occupy Wall Street movement barely five weeks after it was born—a stunning achievement relative to comparable mass movements in US history.

The CBO numbers teach some basic lessons. First, the last thirty years of ideological preaching about the superiority of private, deregulated, market-driven capitalism served to enable and mask one of the largest and fastest upward redistributions of income in modern history. The gap between the tiny rich minority and everyone else widened dramatically. The CBO report thus documents the actual class war over recent decades: the real winners and losers. The report thereby exposes the absurdity of the recent bleats from the 1 percent denouncing modest efforts to limit their huge gains as—horror of horrors—"class war."

Second, the CBO report shows that the US government's transfer payments (social welfare supports for the poor, Social Security and Medicare spending, and so on) did not offset the upward redistribution of income to the richest 1 percent. Nor did the federal tax structure. The 1 percent used its growing wealth to make government taxing and spending policies aid, rather than constrain, the class war they pursued so systematically. The CBO report concludes that the top 1 percent was the only portion of the total income-earning US population to experience a sharp rise in its share of the total US income taking into account all federal transfers and taxes. Indeed, the top 1 percent's share of income rose further after all transfers and taxes are taken into account than before taking them into account. Federal spending and taxing policies were thus complicit in furthering this last generation's sharp turn toward greater income inequality.

Third, the CBO report documents that alongside the staggering fact and impact of the current economic crisis—the second major collapse of capitalism in the last seventy-five years—there was the preceding and equally staggering fact of massive upward redistribution of income. How are these two facts related? The answer is not difficult to discern.

The 99 percent were falling ever further behind the top 1 percent. The latter's exploding luxury consumption shaped tastes and standards defining the "American Dream." With real wages stagnant in the United States since the 1970s, the 99 percent tried to reach or keep the dream by sending more family members out to work more hours, and borrowing ever larger amounts, over the last twenty-five years. Eventually, their exhaustion and stress from increased work, coupled with unsustainable levels of accumulated household debt (for homes, college expenses, automobiles, and credit cards), brought the economy to the brink of crisis.

Meanwhile, the speculative excesses of the 1 percent who were enjoying unprecedented income and wealth gains took the US economy over the brink. Such consequences of a falling share of the national income for 99 percent of the US population were key contributors to the current crisis—and are key contributors to its depth and duration. In sum, the last generation's upward redistribution of income helped cause the current global capitalist meltdown.

To fully appreciate the social impact of the fast-deepening income inequality, it needs to be seen alongside the equally fast-deepening wealth inequality in the United States. If citizens here possess any appreciable wealth, it takes the form of their homes. US housing prices have fallen through the crisis (since 2007). Over the same time, the rising use of home equity as collateral for loans has cut the portion of home values owned by occupiers, while raising the portion owed to banks. The combination of falling home prices and falling owners' equity in those homes yields another massive upward redistribution of wealth. That is because stock markets "recovered"—thanks to massive infusions of government money into financial institutions. Wealth in the form of stocks and bonds thus rose relative to wealth in the form of home ownership. Stock and bond ownership is highly concentrated in the United States, much more so than home values. The result is deepening inequality of wealth distribution alongside greater income inequality.

The claims and promises of US capitalism to be an engine that builds and sustains a vast "middle class" and that constantly "delivers the goods" seem more hollow today than ever. Questions, criticisms, and opposition bubble up across the country. The CBO report reflects, as well as documents, the underlying economic realities. However inadvertently, it thereby supports the rising tide of protest.

The Originality of Occupy Wall Street
November 11, 2011

The political movements of the left that I have participated in over many decades were almost always focused on or prioritized particular issues (e.g., wars, civil liberties, civil rights, poverty, collective bargaining) and/or particular subsections of the population (e.g., African Americans, women, gay people, immigrants). The authorities almost always took advantage of that focus to separate and isolate the movement from society generally. They were often successful. Even when the authorities failed to provoke general hostility to the movement, they were able to prevent the development of more than a general sympathy for it.

In the short history of Occupy Wall Street (OWS) and its spread to date, I am struck by its impressive insistence on remaining a movement around a very general and inclusive critique of an unjust economy (99 percent against 1 percent) that has corrupted much of US politics and culture. The net result is a built-in systemic critique, sometimes explicit (remarkably often named as capitalism) and almost always implicit. The hesitation to choose among and focus on specific demands reflects the wisdom of maintaining the broad, systemic critique. The taboo against systemic critique—a legacy of postwar anticommunism—seems to be broken. Nonetheless, the struggle to select and prioritize specific demands needs to take time and great care, especially if that struggle is to be accomplished without losing the invaluable systemic critique and demand for change. Most other movements of the left could not accomplish that (to their detriment and often destruction).

In its short history, OWS seems already well along in discovering and instituting a new kind of leadership system and organization. The task is daunting and its accomplishment has likewise eluded most left movements in the past. The polarities to avoid are (a) purely horizontal collectives lacking the coordination and shared focus without which massive duplications and wastes of energy and effort breed disorientation and demoralization, and (b) conflict-ridden power concentrations that dissipate and de-energize general initiative and enthusiasm. Here too, interesting explorations of how to navigate between these polarities are under way in OWS. The US left is littered with the debris of movements that crashed on these polarities and/or atrophied from settling into one or the other.

OWS is rooted in the mass disaffection felt about the basic political economy of the United States. Those dominating economics, politics, and culture seem determined to keep the society moving in just those directions that will deepen that disaffection and thereby strengthen OWS. Income and wealth inequality, alienation from politics, deteriorating job, and educational and retirement opportunities all conspire to recruit for OWS. The increased stresses and strains of personal life and relationships do likewise. OWS has already managed to exert combined political and personal attractions on a broad public.

Since 2007, the United States has been engaged in this sequence of social events: a capitalist crisis, a trickle-down economic recovery program (that helped the top but never trickled down to anyone else), and an austerity program to pay for that trickle-down program. Europe experienced a parallel engagement. However, Europe had much more viable and intact labor unions and anticapitalist political parties and party factions. They enabled the mobilization of Europeans against austerity programs and in some cases also against the trickle-down policies and crisis-ridden capitalism that produced austerity programs. They also reaffirmed and reinforced existing organizational patterns that did not attract much of the new energy emerging on the left.

In contrast, the United States has taken longer to react and respond. Yet therein lays an important dialectic of opposites. Precisely because the United States has long-declining and therefore weak labor unions and no significantly influential anticapitalist parties, opposition to the crisis-trickle-down-austerity sequence takes much longer to form and mobilize. People in the United States have to rebuild old shells of organization from the bottom up or build altogether new organizations. Yet with this difficulty comes a certain distance from and relative freedom to consider, evaluate, and pick carefully among the many old habits, presumptions, and organizational forms and styles that have demonstrated their strengths and weaknesses in and for left movements.

In Europe, those oppositional forces that seek to start afresh and independent of the older movements—for example, the various "indignant" groupings—slip quickly into disunity and tension with the existing left organizations. This weakens and divides the left just when the opposite is needed most. In the United States, OWS may well be able to avoid that problem precisely because of the old left's long period of decline and demoralization.

The stunning growth and social influence of OWS in its few weeks of existence augur well for its survival and maturation.

Harvard Students Join the Movement

November 13, 2011

Over the last ten days, Harvard students twice stopped business as usual at this richest of all US private universities. An Occupy Harvard encampment of tents followed a large march of many hundreds through the campus protesting Harvard's complicity in the nation's extreme inequality of income and wealth. A week earlier some seventy students walked out in protest of Harvard's large lecture course in introductory economics. They too explained that they were acting in solidarity with Occupy Wall Street (OWS) movements. They specifically criticized the narrowly biased economics they were learning that both reflected and reinforced the inequalities and injustices that fuel the OWS movements. The walkout in the economics lecture deserves our special attention.

That walkout responds to (a) the quality of capitalist development in the United States for the last quarter century, (b) the complicity of university economics departments in systematically hiding or rationalizing that development, and (c) the new space and support for long-overdue criticism of capitalism opened by the OWS movements.

In the early 1960s, I sat as a student in that same Harvard large lecture class. With many fellow students, I grumbled then at its narrow, technical celebration of the status quo. The interests we brought to the course—to understand the causes of economic instability (recessions, depressions, inflations, crises), how economic change shapes political and cultural history, why so many are poor and so few rich, and what alternative economic systems might be preferable—were largely evaded, ignored, or trivialized. Without an OWS movement, we did not walk out. We sat and endured. Most of us resolved to avoid further economics courses. Introductory economics mass lectures turn few students into economists or even economics majors. They are one-semester immersions in the ideological celebration of capitalism. Harvard's introductory course was and is no exception.

The professor who prompted the student walkout, N. Gregory Mankiw, is a well-known mainstream celebrant of private capitalism. He dutifully opposes government economic intervention (except when needed in crises to reestablish conditions for resumed reliance on private capitalism and its wondrous efficiencies). He evidently found the alternatives to capitalism so uninteresting that he wasted no time or effort to learn or teach about them. The profession rewarded Professor Mankiw with a prestigious Harvard professorship. The political establishment made him an advisor to President Bush and now candidate Romney. The economic establishment blessed him with a lucrative contract to write a major introductory textbook.

Professor Mankiw lectures in a huge hall to many hundreds of students. They also attend small classes taught by graduate students. This arrangement—typical at many universities—involves one or two weekly lectures by the professor and one or two sessions with graduate student instructors. Besides being a student in such a class at Harvard, I later served as just such a graduate student instructor at Yale. Over the last thirty-five years I also taught exactly such a large introductory economics lecture course at the University of Massachusetts, Amherst, almost every year. It is a pedagogical nightmare that I know from every vantage point.

What students learn in a huge anonymous lecture course is far, far less than could occur in a small classroom with intensive interaction between a skilled teacher and a few students. Imposing teaching duties on graduate students struggling with their own courses and dissertations leads to very mixed (I am being polite here) educational results. Remember too that neither professors nor graduate student instructors in the US system are ever required to study the subtle art of teaching. Most professors are rewarded far more for publishing and university administrative services than for teaching effectiveness. Graduate students are likewise rewarded far more for their coursework than for assisting in the teaching of undergraduates. The enduring pedagogical failure of these large lectures does lower the university's cost of "teaching."

This system's utterly predictable result is that large introductory lectures are awful compared to what introductory courses could and should achieve. The few exceptions depend on rare individuals who care and learn how to teach even under such adverse lecture conditions. We usually remember them.

Whether consciously or not, the seventy Harvard students were protesting the failures of their education as well as of the larger society. They balked, for example, at how Mankiw's economics handles the inadequacy of their lecture course itself. In the Mankiwian view, one high-priced professor teaching hundreds is much more "efficient" than having him interact with a few in a seminar setting. The bottom-line-driven desire of Harvard to save the costs of the small classes actually needed for quality education is neatly obscured by concentrating on quantity: counting "educated" students as so many beans or peanuts produced by one professor. Such fetishizations of quantity are hallmarks of mainstream economics.

The protesting Harvard students also found Mankiw's economics minimally useful for understanding the actual economy they and their families engage daily. Celebrating capitalism is not the same as understanding it, let alone evaluating its strengths and weaknesses. In this the protesting students ironically share the view of business. Long ago, business in the United States also realized that the celebration of capitalism performed by economists like Mankiw was not very useful for (and often contrary to) teaching how capitalist enterprises and markets actually work. So they developed a second, alternative track for studying economics. It would focus on analyzing the actual workings of the economic system and leave the celebratory work to the economics departments. That alternative track is called business schools.

It is a good sign that today's Harvard students include many who recognize the important political and ideological breakthrough accomplished by the Occupy movement. It is an even better sign that they are determined now to join and further its central goal of exposing and opposing the profound inequalities and injustices of the current system. And it is perhaps best of all that they take the struggle to one of the chief ideological apologists for that system, mainstream economics.

Criticism, Violence, and Roosting Chickens

November 16, 2011

The 99 percent offered criticism of the 1 percent. They exposed and made clear what most Americans know. They struggled peacefully to inform and mobilize public opinion. They won huge numbers of hearts and minds. The 1 percent in the United States did what their counterparts in Tunisia, Egypt, Bahrain, and other countries did earlier this year. First, they tried to deny the 99 percent the media access needed to reach the people. That failed. Then, they tried scattered police intimidation and pressure to stop the criticism. That failed. Then, Democratic Party operatives tried to convert the Occupiers to become Obama enthusiasts for next year's election. That failed, too.

So now, the weapon of criticism wielded by the 99 percent suffers the countercriticism of violence by servants of the 1 percent. No one will miss which side resorted to organized, massive violence so early and so unnecessarily in this conflict. As in Iraq, Afghanistan, and elsewhere, US government agencies cover their failure to win hearts and minds by resorting to violence. Chickens raised abroad return home to roost as they often do. Consider the image: New York Police Department machines and personnel destroy the free library that had functioned so well in Zuccotti Park.

New York has acquired a newly renamed mayor: Mubarak Bloomberg. Situated atop the 1 percent, he gave the order to "clear and clean" Zuccotti Park. This mayor, who presides over some of the world's filthiest tunnels and stations—that daily threaten the public health of millions of subway riders—suddenly acquired an obsession with cleanliness in the small Zuccotti Park. This mayor—whose city handles garbage by piling it in bags on the street that forever break and scatter their contents across the streets—wants us to believe he is concerned about public safety.

Will the failures that renamed New York's mayor spread to yield a Mubarak Obama too? Or will the Arab Spring—so blithely praised by Secretary of State Hillary Clinton as "freedom struggles"—resurface here to confront the Clintons with their hypocritical complicity in repression policies at home?

The deepening economic inequality, the moneyed corruption of politics, and the collapsing fortunes and prospects of the mass of Americans: none of those basic conditions and causes of Occupy Wall Street have been addressed by Bloomberg or President Obama. Instead, they seek to repress those who expose and oppose those conditions.

Meanwhile, the system that keeps reproducing those conditions—a capitalism becoming increasingly intolerable—loses more bases of support. In times like these, the criticism of weapons risks losing to the weapon of criticism. Will the Arab Spring be reborn as the American Winter?

Occupy Production: A Vision for Democracy at Work

December 2, 2011

As the Occupy movement keeps developing, it seeks solutions for the economic and political dysfunctions it exposes and opposes. For many, the capitalist economic system itself is the basic problem. They want change to another system, but not to the traditional socialist alternative (e.g., the former Soviet Union or China). That system, too, seems to require basic change.

The common solution these activists propose is to change both systems' production arrangements from the ground up. Every enterprise should be democratized. Workers should occupy their enterprise by collectively functioning as its board of directors. That would abolish the capitalist exploitative system (employer vs. employee) much as our historical predecessors abolished the parallel exploitative systems of slavery (master vs. slave) and feudalism (lord vs. serf).

In workers' self-directed enterprises, those who do the work also design and direct it and dispose of its profits: no exploitation of workers by others. Workers participate equally in making all enterprise decisions. The old capitalist elite—the major corporate shareholders and the boards of directors they choose—would no longer decide what, how, and where to produce and how to use enterprise profits. Instead, workers—in partnership with residential communities interdependent with their enterprises—would make all those decisions democratically.

Only then could we avoid repeating yet again the capitalist cycle: (1) economic boom bursting into crisis; followed by (2) mass movements for social welfare reforms and economic regulations; followed by (3) capitalists using their profits to undo achieved reforms and regulations; followed by (1) the next capitalist boom, bust, and crisis. US capitalism since the crash of 1929 displays this three-step cycle.

In democratized enterprises, the workers who most need and benefit from reforms would dispose of the profits of enterprise. No separate class of employers would exist and use enterprise profits to undo the reforms and regulations workers achieved. Quite the contrary, self-directing workers would pay taxes only if the state secures those reforms and regulations. Democratized enterprises would not permit the inequalities of income and wealth (and, therefore, of power and cultural access) now typical across the capitalist world.

Actually existing socialist systems, past and present, also need enterprise democratization. Those systems' socialization of productive property plus central planning (vs. capitalism's private property and markets) left far too much unbalanced power centralized in the state. In addition, reforms (guaranteed employment and basic welfare, far less inequality of income and wealth, etc.) won by socialist revolutions proved insecure. Private enterprises and markets eventually returned and erased many of those reforms.

Traditional socialism's problems flow also from its undemocratic organization of production. Workers in socialized state enterprises were not self-directed; they did not collectively decide what, how, and where to produce nor what to do with the profits. Instead, state officials decided what, how, and where to produce and how to dispose of profits. If socialist enterprises were democratized, the state would then depend for its revenue on collectively self-directed workers. That would institutionalize real, concrete control from below to balance state power from above.

Workers' self-directed enterprises are a solution grounded in the histories of both capitalism and socialism. Establishing workers' self-directed enterprises completes what past democratic revolutions began in moving societies beyond monarchies and autocracies. Democratizing production can finally take democracy beyond being merely an electoral ritual that facilitates rule by the 1 percent over the 99 percent.

Occupy the Corporation
December 22, 2011

Imagine a democratic alternative to police evictions of Occupy encampments across America's cities and towns. What if the decision to evict or not had been made by referendum? Voters could have determined whether to continue the long overdue public debates over inequality, injustice, and capitalism that were launched and sustained above all by the Occupy encampments.

But that never happened in a society where private corporations own parks, lots, and other possible Occupy sites. The corporate shareholders and boards of directors of those sites—a tiny minority of the population—could shut down Occupy encampments by invoking property rights. That tiny minority never wanted a national debate that questioned its disproportionate wealth and power. Private property enabled a minority with 1 percent of the wealth and income to make decisions affecting everyone regardless of what a 99 percent majority might want.

In the "public" sites chosen by occupiers, much the same happens. There, tiny numbers of politicians decide to evict, and usually for the same reasons. In New York City, for example, the billionaire mayor who bought his way into politics and power boasted publicly about "his" authority to evict occupiers from Zuccotti Park. In most cases, local politicians, dependent on donations from corporations and the 1 percent and on mass media owned by them, make the same decisions. No surprise there.

Public opinion polls consistently showed majorities of Americans in sympathy with the Occupy Wall Street movement and its basic goals of correcting the inequalities of wealth, income, and power in our society. Yet capitalism's distribution of wealth empowered the 1 percent to overrule those majorities.

The solution for this denial of democracy is to Occupy the Corporation. In one important sense, the workers inside every corporation already occupy it. They are the majority inside every corporation, while the board of directors makes up one small minority and the major shareholders another. If the workers occupied the corporation in the different sense of democratizing it, they would transform corporate capitalist enterprises into democratic, workers' self-directed enterprises. Then the workers as a whole—a workplace community—would democratically make all the decisions now reserved for corporate boards of directors and their major shareholders. The self-directed workers would then decide what, how, and where to produce and what to do with the profits. And they would collaborate with the residential communities that interact with them to build a society far more genuinely democratic than anything that now exists. Such worker self-directed enterprises would have considered, and likely arranged, a democratic decision about Occupy movement encampments.

If corporations became worker self-directed enterprises, many other decisions would likewise be made very differently from how they are made today. For example, workers would not likely overpay a few of their fellow self-directors at the expense of all the others. That would sharply reduce today's personal wealth inequalities, which corrupt our politics. Likewise, worker self-directors would not have stopped raising real wages in the United States after the 1970s while productivity kept rising. That made sense for capitalist boards of directors to enrich themselves and their shareholders, but it would not have made sense for worker self-directors. Had real wages risen steadily after the 1970s (as they had for the previous century), there would have been no need for the vast growth in workers' debts since the 1970s. That would not have been good news for private megabanks issuing credit cards and mortgages, but it would have better served the interests of a working class now mired in unsustainable debt. Occupy the Corporation is also a solution for the economic crisis now devastating this country and the globe, making "middle-class disappearance" a common term and generating mounting political and social conflict.

Capitalism's current crisis needs to be treated differently from the last one, the Great Depression of the 1930s. Then, reforms and regulations (including heavy taxation of corporations and the rich) were the preferred cure. Millions of Americans took to the streets and union halls in successful campaigns to change President Roosevelt's policies and win a New Deal of reforms and regulations, overcoming corporate resistance. But in the last half-century, corporations' boards of directors and major shareholders used the profits gathered into their hands—and the power those profits buy—to undo the New Deal. The liberals and left wing of the Democratic Party proved unable or unwilling to prevent corporations from achieving that goal.

If we had occupied the corporations decades ago—reorganizing them as cooperatives directed democratically by their workers—they would not have undone the reforms and regulations that so many people worked so hard to put into place in the 1930s. The lesson of the undoing of the New Deal is this: We cannot respond to this latest capitalist crash with another set of reforms and regulations that leave the organization of enterprises unchanged. If we do, we will have ourselves to blame as we watch corporate boards of directors and major shareholders undo them yet again. Only this time, it will happen faster, because they have had so much practice since the 1930s. The lesson of America's painful struggles with capitalism's instability is this: Occupy the corporations and democratize them.

Class, Change, and Revolution

February 16, 2015

The winds of change are blowing harder. The crisis since 2007 has renewed criticism of capitalism, but pressure for change has built for far longer than that. So it is time to draw some lessons from the major social changes of the past and apply them now. One of the most important lessons concerns class. How activists see and act on today's class system can make social movements more effective now than in the past—as a brief historical review can show.

The overcoming of slavery, in the US Civil War but also at other times and places across the globe, was a revolutionary change always accompanied by passionate promises. Most emancipation supporters spoke of human freedom, liberation, progress, and social harmony if slavery were abolished. Opponents claimed that ex-slaves would be less protected and worse off than if they continued as slaves. Masters and slaves saw the world, their class structure, and the future differently.

Overcoming feudalism, at the end of medieval Europe and in other times and places across the globe, was likewise celebrated and condemned. For one side, freeing serfs from their feudal ties to the land would bring a new dawn of human freedom. "Liberty, equality and fraternity" were core goals, not merely slogans, of Paris's 1789 revolutionaries. On the other side, skeptics warned that feudalism's end would plunge society into brutish chaos that the world would regret. Landlords and serfs viewed their class structure and a postfeudal world differently.

In the twentieth century, most socialists before and after the revolutions in Russia, China, and beyond passionately affirmed their project as aimed at nothing less than emancipating capitalism's working-class majorities. Critics countered that workers were or would be worse off economically and politically once socialism displaced capitalism. Socialism's advocates and those who preferred capitalism viewed class and the world in fundamentally different ways.

Notwithstanding their actual achievements, the revolutions against slavery, feudalism, and capitalism have never yet reached the freedoms, equalities, and social harmonies that so many had enthusiastically promised and sought. Critics and skeptics then and to this day point to that failure to insist that those revolutions' greatest goals were unattainable utopias. Others have blamed the revolutions' failures and distortions on leaders (Napoleon, US politicians after 1865, Stalin, Mao, others) or abstractions such as "insufficient democracy." Such lessons drawn from past revolutions contribute to hesitation and ambivalence now about revolutionary change. Meanwhile, capitalism's social and ecological costs grow more intolerable. People increasingly appreciate that capitalism is a key systemic problem of and for our time, but they see no revolutionary solution that can overcome the limits and avoid the failures of past revolutions.

Yet another and very different lesson can be drawn. That is the point to be made here.

Overcoming slavery ended that system's injustices on many levels. It increased human freedom in significant ways. Yet it also enabled the reorganization of ex-slaves and ex-masters into other relations of continuing un-freedom. In some places and times, slavery gave way to feudalism; serfs and lords replaced slaves and masters. In other places and times, slavery gave way to capitalism; employers and employees took the places of masters and slaves.

Abolishing feudalism likewise ended many of its systemic injustices to move society forward in terms of human freedoms. However, when capitalism emerged from feudalism's dissolution, as in post-seventeenth-century Europe, the landlord–serf structure transformed into the employer–employee structure. The novels of Honoré de Balzac, Émile Zola, Maxim Gorky, and Charles Dickens, among others, much like the social criticism of Karl Marx, express deep disappointment about the gap between what they hoped for from the end of feudalism and what early capitalism actually delivered.

When "actually existing socialisms" replaced the systems in pre-1917 Russia, pre-1949 China, and so on, outcomes were again mixed. Workers did acquire far greater job security and unprecedented levels of educational, medical, housing, and other social services. Yet they remained un-free in subordinated positions within and alienated from socialist institutions—workplaces, schools, politics, and the state. Those

conditions facilitated the eventual implosions of Eastern European socialist societies in the 1980s and the remarkable changes since then inside the People's Republic of China.

The key question: Why did social movements against slavery, feudalism, and capitalism that eventually toppled those systems prove unable to achieve their most revolutionary goals? One answer concerns a
certain blindness that gripped the revolutionaries. In each case, they
saw parts of the problem and devised successful strategies to solve them.
They overcame those parts of slavery, feudalism, and capitalism that
they identified as intolerable affronts to their notions of human progress
and freedom. Yet they missed and left intact another part of all of those
systems. Thereby they inadvertently blocked their revolutions' progress,
frustrated their deepest aspirations, and provided support for the persistent criticisms by revolutions' enemies.

If we recognize and examine the revolutionaries' shared blindness—
their neither seeing nor using a particular class perspective—then contemporary social movements need not repeat that blindness nor suffer
its consequences once again. If they equip themselves with the missing
class perspective and its insights, movements for basic social change can
go further than their predecessors in realizing the project for genuine
human liberation.

Those predecessors were mostly blind to one particular notion of
class that defined it as the economic process of producing a social surplus. The concepts used by past revolutionaries instead defined class
otherwise in terms of the unequal social distributions of wealth (rich
vs. poor) and/or power (rulers vs. ruled). Their revolutionary effort to
equalize wealth and democratize power left in place another kind of inequality located in the core structure of production. That was and is the
inequality separating those who produce a surplus in society from those
who take and live on a surplus they did not help produce.

For this different surplus concept of class, the definition focuses
precisely on production, on who produces and who gets the surplus.
That surplus is defined as the excess of total output over that portion of
it that sustains the output's direct producers (at whatever level of consumption social history has yielded them).

The production of a surplus is a class process because it immediately defines two positions within a relationship: the direct producers and the first receivers of that surplus. When the direct producers are different persons from the first recipients, that differentiation entails a set of social consequences (political and cultural as well as economic) that includes contradictions, tensions, and conflicts. Marx, who first articulated this particular surplus-focused concept of class, used the term "exploitation" to identify all those class processes in which direct producers are different persons from the first recipients of surpluses. Those recipients of the surplus exploit its direct producers: They obtain a portion of the total product, which they did not directly participate in producing. Moreover, the exploiters use and distribute that surplus to maintain their privileged economic, political, and cultural positions in society.

In slave systems of production, masters exploit slaves. In feudalism, lords exploit serfs. In capitalism, employers exploit workers. In actually existing socialism, state officials displace private individuals (boards of directors elected by shareholders) as corporate employers. Yet by occupying precisely that position, state officials likewise exploit workers—hence the term, "state capitalism."

Ending slavery—the ownership of one person by another—and a slave system of production does not end exploitation. Indeed, slave exploitation could give way (and often did through revolution) to feudal or capitalist exploitation. Similarly, the demise of feudalism and capitalism could give way to alternate forms of exploitation. Indeed, as many in Eastern Europe are now discovering, ending state capitalisms there reintroduced private capitalist exploitation with its attendant social ills. In all these cases, revolutions failed to achieve many of the desired freedoms and liberations.

A class-*qua*-surplus perspective was absent or marginal in all those revolutions. The prevailing revolutionary mentality thus lacked the following particular understanding: Liberty, equality, fraternity, democracy, and revolutionaries' other basic social goals require the end of exploitation in all its forms. That end is a necessary (although not sufficient) condition.

Ending exploitation means transforming workplaces such that direct producers of surpluses become likewise the first recipients of those surpluses. Democratically run cooperatives replace the hierarchical systems that had previously sustained exploitation in workplaces. In other words, workers' self-directed enterprises take the places of slave, feudal, or capitalist (private or state) enterprises.

Conditions of production that exclude exploitation will thereby undermine the parallel oppressions and inequalities in politics and culture. Understanding class in surplus terms, and that exploitation has multiple forms, future revolutions against slave, feudal, and capitalist (private and state) systems will be more likely to realize their deepest goals. That is because they will no longer accept being deflected into constructions of merely different forms of exploitation rather than refusing exploitation in all its forms.

For 2015, having this class perspective would mean that social movements for liberty, equality, fraternity, and democracy would necessarily include commitments to end all exploitative organizations of work. That would make struggles in 2015 for those goals different from earlier struggles. We will have learned the lessons of those struggles. Those include respect for what previous revolutionaries did achieve in ending deeply entrenched and powerfully defended social institutions like slavery, feudalism, and private and state capitalisms. But they also include recognition of their failures (a) to identify all these as forms of exploitative class processes and (b) to admit that the resulting revolutions ended one form but erected another.

What is possible now is a new class perspective that defines revolution in 2015 as clearly and explicitly targeted to end exploitation in any form. Central to such a revolution then is the demand to transform workplaces into genuine cooperatives where the workers (direct producers) function also and collectively as their own directors (first surplus recipients). In that way, the workers would make the basic workplace decisions: what, how, and where to produce and what to do with the surpluses. Workers who become their own bosses in this collective, democratic, and cooperative way will enjoy the personal growth and social power it conveys. They will not easily (or ever) accept again the subordinations of exploitation in production and oppression in hierarchical, undemocratic political and cultural structures.

DEBATES ON THE LEFT

What's Left of the American Left?

March 13, 2011

"In contradiction" best describes the American left today. On the one hand, it is fragmented and dispirited, feeling itself distant from the tumble of daily US politics and acutely disgusted by its many-layered corruptions. It hardly knows itself as a part of society, so deep runs its alienation. After all, leftists, too, are affected by the mass media's wishful pretense that the American left has simply disappeared and the extreme right's paranoid caricatures that recycle 1950s McCarthyism.

Yet the US left is actually quite strong and getting stronger by the minute. Very many young people find far more meaning in the left social criticisms of Jon Stewart, Bill Maher, and Stephen Colbert than they do in the stale Republican or Democratic activities that those popular comedians mock. The devotees of much current popular music want and respond to lyrics rich with social criticism. The assaults of the right in the United States on access to abortion, on civil rights and civil liberties, on the separation of church and state, and on immigrants are less and less suffered in silent resentment and increasingly opposed by a revived left criticism and activism. From the mass mobilizations of immigrants to the outpouring of support for the embattled public employees in Wisconsin to the gatherings of support for Planned Parenthood, the US left's size, depth, and diversity are evident.

The proportion of respondents polled about their religious affiliation who answer "none" is growing faster than any other group of respondents. As one famous philosopher wrote, "the criticism of society begins with the critique of religion." The million who marched in 2003 against the invasion of Iraq quietly persuaded a majority to make recent national polls repeated referenda against all three US wars (Iraq, Afghanistan, and Pakistan).

The young are perhaps outraged most by the vulnerability and erosion of many social conditions they had taken for granted as permanent. Anger and activism are rising against the incapacity or unwillingness of the political establishment to restore those conditions. The radical generation of the 1960s, after middle years devoted to careers and families, is now returning to political engagement likewise to restore those conditions. That combination of rising youthful passion and political experience with mass radical action represents a potent mass base for a new US left political formation to emerge.

Organization is what the US left lacks. Not issues, not members, not a wide public audience: the US left now has all of them in abundance. Indeed, the economic crisis that exploded in 2008—now becoming a social crisis because the "recovery" bypassed the majority that needed it most—has only enhanced that abundance. Yet a deeply rooted and continuously nurtured aversion to unified organization undermines the US left's social influence and collective action at every turn. The decline of past left organizations—the socialist and communist parties, student groups such as Students for a Democratic Society and Student Nonviolent Coordinating Committee, major segments of organized labor—has fostered a sense of the futility of organization. The demonization of those and other left organizations, by liberal as well as conservative voices, renders individual left thought and action sometimes acceptable but collective criticism and activity always deeply suspect.

The US left will become a political force with immense potential if it can generate and ally unified organizations able to mobilize and express their constituents' views and aspirations. Such allied organizations can enable the US left to reach and enlist the mass of the citizenry in left responses to the current economic/social crisis rather than the right responses of further social subservience to private business interests, further cutbacks of state services and employment, union-busting, and so on. Only organization can yield the financial resources needed to defeat the current program of corporations and the rich that aims to return the United States to the unequal income and wealth distributions of the late nineteenth century (with its concomitant politics and culture).

Solidarity—the theme of the 2011 Left Forum—was well chosen to suggest and inspire the US left's attention to this new imperative of organization.

A New Dawn for the US Left

June 3, 2011

Prospects for the left in the United States are far better than they seem to most observers across the political spectrum (excepting those who fantasize imminent revolutionary uprisings spearheaded by seventy-nine-year-old sociology professors).[29] The economic crisis has bitten hard and deep. Millions of people have been impacted by high unemployment and home foreclosures, by decreased job benefits and job security, and by the realization that none of these afflictions will end soon. A sense of betrayal is settling into the popular consciousness. People are coming to believe that despite their hard work and "playing by the rules," a long-term decline is placing the American Dream increasingly out of their reach.

The economic crisis activated, intensely and very publicly, the hegemonic alliance among big business, the richest 5 percent of citizens, and the state. Business and the rich insisted on (and the federal government complied with) corporate bailouts costing huge sums of public money. The state borrowed that money rather than taxing big business and the richest 5 percent of citizens. This three-way hegemonic alliance is now proceeding to utilize the suddenly and vastly increased state debt to shift the cost of the crisis onto the mass of people. First, its members depict enlarged state debt as costing too much in state outlays for interest and repayment—threatening what the state can do for people in the future. Second, they insist that therefore "there is no choice but to" cut public payrolls and services and raise taxes (in combinations depending on what voter constituencies will allow). A crucial part of the hegemonic alliance among big business, the richest 5 percent, and the state is the role of the

---

29. Frances Fox Piven, "Occupy's Protest Is not Over. It Has Barely Begun," *Guardian*, September 17, 2012.

state as the socially acceptable object of anger, protest, and rage deflected from the economic power and privileges of its hegemonic partners.

As a result, the Tea Party movement is, so far, the only systematically organized expression in the United States of mass opposition to the crisis and its social effects. But they do not see the state's policies as reflecting complicity with its hegemonic partners' determination to emerge from the crisis unchecked in their activities and richer than before. Tea Party activists are, after all, specialists in demonizing the state as the root of all social problems.

As often happens, though, the usefulness of the Tea Party movement to the hegemonic alliance is partial and temporary. Once the deflection of people's upset seems secure and likewise the shifting of the crisis's costs onto mass austerity, the ruling class will have no further use for the Tea Partiers. The Tea Party movement's demonization of the state risks disrupting the hegemonic partnership, which does not want or need to cut the defense budget or cripple the many other (and likewise, costly) ways the state subsidizes business and favors the richest citizens. It does not want to provoke a mass backlash against reduced state services, because that might rediscover the most obvious alternative to austerity—namely, taxing business and the rich to avoid deficits and thereby obviate austerity.

When the Tea Party movement pursues what the hegemons see as an excessive government-cutting agenda, the temporary allies will find themselves on a collision course. Since the hegemonic alliance is more powerful than the Tea Party movement, the latter's prospects in the United States now looks decidedly poor. As its significant corporate financiers shift their strategy, Tea Party activists may well disassemble and shrink back into its more socially marginalized feeder organizations.

For different reasons and from a different history, the American left also leans toward anti-government sentiment, but the crucial point is that unlike the Tea Party, the left has no taboo against focusing its activism also against big business and the richest 5 percent. The crisis has revived and renewed those voices on the US left that stress its nature as systemic—a crisis of the economic system that does not originate in or reduce to government policies. The ideological grounds for a left resurgence are developing in the consciousness of American citizens.

The left's solutions are not restricted to re-regulation or punishment of corrupt speculators. They affirm, but also go beyond, massive public employment programs and other economic stimulants paid for not by borrowing (and socially burdensome deficits), but rather by taxing corporations and the richest citizens. Their solutions increasingly include transformation of enterprises such that workers collectively, cooperatively, and democratically owning and operating enterprises would become a growing business sector.

In short, the US left is working its way to a comprehensive alternative program to exit the crisis, one taxing the corporations and the richest 5 percent—those who contributed most to the crisis, who are the most able to pay for resolving it, and who have received the most state aid so far and therefore "recovered" the most. Those sympathetic to the left have their work to do, but the prospects for success suggest excitement and energy and no longer the demoralization that afflicted them for so long.

In contrast, the Tea Partiers' proposals for shrinking government offer immediate pain and suffering to the mass of Americans, while also fraying their connections to the hegemonic alliance in the United States. Tea Party prospects are not good. A resurgent US left can take from the Tea Party movement those of its supporters who can identify business and the rich as adversaries, who harbor anticapitalist impulses. The political terrain in the United States has shifted and the US left now has major opportunities.

A Socialism for the Twenty-First Century

June 7, 2013

Capitalism has stopped "delivering the goods" for quite a while now, especially in its older bases (Europe, North America, and Japan). Real wage stagnation, deepening wealth and income inequalities, unsustainable debt levels, and export of jobs have been prevailing trends in those areas. The global crisis since 2007 only accelerated those trends. In response, more has happened than Keynesianism returning to challenge neoliberalism and critiques returning to challenge uncritical celebrations of capitalism. Capitalism's development has raised a basic question again: What alternative economic system might be necessary and preferable for societies determined to do better than capitalism? That old mole, socialism, has thus returned for interrogation about its past to draw the lessons about its present and future.

The Historical Background of Socialism

Since the mid-nineteenth century, socialism has mostly been differentiated from capitalism in two basic ways. Instead of capitalism's private ownership of means of production (land, factories, offices, stores, machinery, etc.), socialism would transfer that ownership to the state as the administrator for public, social, or collective ownership. Instead of capitalism's distribution of resources and products by means of market exchange, socialism would substitute state central planning to accomplish that distribution. Marxism was generally viewed as the basic theoretical criticism of capitalism that went on to define and justify a social transition from capitalism to socialism. Communism was generally viewed as a distant, rather utopian stage of social development beyond socialism wherein class differences would disappear, the state would wither away as a social institution, work activity would be transformed, and distribution would be based purely on need.

Before 1917, socialism comprised both the critical analysis of capitalism and the anticapitalist programs promoted by various social movements, labor unions, writers, and political parties. They advocated transitions from private toward state ownership of means of production and from market toward state-planned distribution. Socialism was stunningly successful at winning hearts and minds; it spread quickly across the globe. By 1917, a revolution in Russia enabled a new government to replace the capitalism it had inherited with what it understood as socialism. Bolshevik leaders thus moved to nationalize productive property in industry and institute planning as hallmarks of the new economy of the Soviet Union.

Yet Soviet socialism also changed and complicated the meaning of socialism in the world. Beyond being a general theory and program of anticapitalism, socialism came to be the label applied to what was said and done in and by the Soviet Union. This change had profound consequences. Socialists around the world split into two wings or segments. (Of course, some individuals and some parties articulated combinations, variations, and even departures from these two basic wings of socialism, but they were quite secondary in terms of their historical importance and social impacts.) For one wing, the evolving Soviet revolution was the realization of what socialism had always sought. It therefore had to be defended at all costs from capitalism's assaults. That wing increasingly defined socialism as what the Soviet Union did after 1917; Soviet socialism became the model to be replicated everywhere.

The other wing disagreed. Socialism's traditional theory and program did not need—and ought not—to be adjusted to replicate what happened in the Soviet Union. Some in this wing criticized what the Bolsheviks did in the Soviet Union (particularly in terms of political freedoms and civil liberties). Others believed that peaceful, nonrevolutionary, and electoral strategies were surer roads to socialism than Bolshevik revolutionary politics. For them, "evolutionary" socialism was a better road to take than revolutionary socialism. Classical socialism, for this wing, was very different from what happened and evolved in the Soviet Union.

As debates between the two wings intensified (especially in relation to World War I), the admirers of the Soviet Union changed their names from socialists to communists. Where before these names had differentiated shorter-term from longer-range goals of all socialists, after 1917 they distinguished the more pro- from the more anti-Soviet socialists. The Soviet Union's survival and growing strength after 1917 (especially in contrast to the Depression-wracked capitalist world of the 1930s); its victory over Hitler in World War II; and then the successful Chinese, Vietnamese, and Cuban revolutions after 1945 brought the communist wing ever greater prominence in defining what socialism meant.

Peculiar ambiguities emerged. Sometimes, communism and socialism were treated synonymously as the alternative to capitalism. Yet leaders and spokespersons of countries where self-described communists achieved government power described their societies as "socialist" and definitely not yet "communist." Socialists who were critical of the Soviet Union increasingly insisted on the importance of differences between socialism and communism in theory and practice. On the one hand, communists and socialists advocated the same basic transitions from private to public ownership of means of production and from markets to planning. On the other, they differed—often sharply—over the speed, forms, and social conditions appropriate for the transition from capitalism and over the role of civil liberties and democratic freedoms once socialism was achieved.

The noncommunist wing of the socialist movement also grew in strength and influence after 1917. Large, mass-based socialist parties became regular, major players in the electoral politics of many countries. Communist parties played such roles less often. Sometimes communist and socialist parties collaborated on shared objectives, and sometimes differences created great enmity between them. Socialist parties focused on electoral politics, increasingly rejecting revolutionary strategies, tactics, and language. The socialist wing largely accommodated itself to the view that capitalism seemed securely in place. The role for socialists was then to expose its flaws (injustices, wastes, and inefficiencies) and struggle politically to impose governmental rules, constraints, and interventions that would impose "a human face" on capitalism. Socialists thus focused on obtaining redistributive tax structures, government-provided social safety nets, and state-regulated markets. In many countries, the socialists became the more or less accepted mass-based left that favored a state-regulated, social-welfare capitalism. Opposing the socialists was a basic right that favored less state regulation, a capitalism in which the private capitalist sector was dominant.

Toward the end of the twentieth century, the relationship between the socialist and communist wings altered drastically. With the collapse of the Soviet Union and its Eastern European allies in 1989, and following strategic shifts inside the People's Republic of China, the growth of the communist wing of the socialist movement reversed into sharp decline. The communists had established socialisms—based on state ownership of industrial enterprises and central planning—that had shown spectacular rates of economic growth and exemplary advances in the standards of living for the mass of their citizens. However, they had not been able to create the broader social conditions needed to sustain that growth, to simultaneously protect themselves from a hostile capitalist world, and all the while to retain the ideological and political support of their countries' populations. When serious crises hit them in the late 1980s, few social forces proved able or willing to save or rebuild the systems the communists had constructed. Worse still, those systems' speedy conversions into varying forms of monopoly capitalism and corrupted politics raised further disquieting questions about what the systems of "actually existing socialisms" really had been.

At first, the socialist wing largely replaced a declining communism to become the dominant contemporary form and definition of socialism. However, the global resurgence of neoliberal capitalism after 1970 eventually weakened support for the socialist wing, although not as effectively as had happened earlier to the communist wing. Neoliberal ideologues portrayed the collapse of the Soviet Union and Eastern Europe as proof positive that the long battle between capitalism, on the one hand, and socialism or communism, on the other, had been definitively "won" by the former. To remain a communist or even a socialist, in their traditional senses, was portrayed as a sign of atavistic, antiquarian self-delusion. History had rendered its verdict; it was final; and there was no appeal. Not only had the Soviet Union and its Eastern European allies collapsed, but their subsequent gangster capitalism, crony capitalism, and other unattractive capitalisms further undermined socialists' confidence in their earlier views of "actually existing socialisms."

In the wake of these post-1970s developments, many socialists around the world devolved and merged into "progressive forces" within capitalism. For them, socialism had stopped being an alternative to capitalism. There simply was no such left alternative anymore. Frustrated and deeply disappointed, not a few of the former activists, militants, and supporters of both wings of traditional socialism disengaged from politics altogether. For those ex-communists and ex-socialists who did remain politically active, they were mostly "progressives who recognized history's verdict" and devoted themselves to making capitalism as equitable, democratic, and generally humane as possible. For some (e.g., the Italian left) that meant renouncing the names "socialist" and "communist" in favor of others ("democrat" was especially popular).

Then history suddenly mocked and undid the so-called verdict that had allegedly condemned socialism and communism to the status of passé fashions. In the global economic meltdown that began in 2007, capitalism "hit the fan." Its extreme instability was exposed. Capitalism's utter dependence on the state (to rescue it from crisis) was all the more ironic and telling given the previous decades during which neoliberal ideologues had endlessly vilified the state and called for its drastic reduction. Capitalism's gross injustices were underscored as its crisis victimized the many (the jobless, the homeless) while bailing out the few. Capitalists' control of the state was likewise highlighted as it provided "recovery" for the few while imposing austerity on the many.

History suddenly reminded people that capitalism's contradictions, flaws, and injustices were what had generated socialism and communism in the past. Those same qualities had never been overcome. When they exploded into view again in 2007, similar critical movements and upsurges were regenerated. Names and nuances would be different (such as the "indignados" of Spain or the "occupiers" of Wall Street, and much else). New parties would arise (e.g., "anticapitalist" or "left"). New alternatives to capitalism would emerge and show significant theoretical and strategic importance. In all cases, however, their resemblances and debts to the classical traditions of socialism and communism would be no more difficult to see than their differences.

Traditional socialism, in both of its major wings, was remarkably successful up to the 1970s. Its theoretical formulations (Marxist and non-Marxist, critical and programmatic) and its institutional embodiments in social movements, labor unions, and parties (ruling as well as oppositional) were powerful agents of that success. However, socialism's global spread was checked after the 1970s. Former communist parties disappeared or lost influence in most countries. Many socialist parties enhanced their accommodations to capitalism by tolerating or even supporting first neoliberalism and then, since 2009, government austerity policies. The last thirty years also witnessed the sharply reduced presence of explicitly socialist and Marxist perspectives within many cultural domains. Adherence to those perspectives fell correspondingly.

In short, some agents of socialism's extraordinary global expansion across the century before the 1970s morphed into obstacles and barriers to further success. Likewise, socialism's enemies often found the resources and the ways to slow, stop, or reverse its progress. In any case, socialism's history provides key raw materials for making the changes needed now to fashion a socialism for the twenty-first century. Its past achievements and failures, when faced honestly, are informing a new socialism capable of moving beyond a capitalism riddled with environmental as well as economic crises as it deepens profoundly divisive and unsustainable inequalities.

What to Do Now

A new socialism for the twenty-first century begins by assessing the limits of classical socialism. That assessment's priority focus is not external (how others hindered socialism's progress)—but rather internal. Where socialists were responsible for their own difficulties, there they can make significant changes. Serious self-criticism might begin by questioning classical socialism's definition of its chief tasks as changing the ownership of productive property from private to public and the distribution of productive inputs and outputs from market to planning. These were changes at the macro level of society, far removed from most people's daily, micro-level lives. Many socialists believed that macro-level transitions would determine similar micro-level transitions. Shifting from capitalist (private) to socialist (collective) productive property ownership and from market to planning systems of distribution would cause parallel transitions from capitalist to socialist individuals in their personalities and in their daily work, home, and community lives.

Where communists achieved government power, they made many of traditional socialism's prescribed macro changes. As a result, genuine benefits accrued at the micro level in the forms of much improved job security and wages and much improved access to education, housing, and medical care. Where socialists gained governmental power, they made parallel (albeit slower and more modest) macro changes in the same direction, with corresponding benefits for the micro level. The changes and resulting benefits won for communists and socialists the considerable supports they enjoyed across most of the twentieth century. At the same time, the political power concentrated at the macro level (and institutionalized in the party and the state) and narrow ideological conformity provoked considerable criticism and opposition over much the same period.

But neither the macro-level changes nor the micro-level benefits ended the exploitative employer–employee relationship that defines the capitalist workplace. At that micro level, employed workers still used their brains and muscles to produce outputs whose values exceeded the values of what they obtained in return as real wages. In some communist countries, that value relationship was denominated in the administered prices set by central planners. In most countries, the value relationship was denominated in market prices. In either case, what matters is the difference between what workers added in production to the value to the raw materials, tools, and equipment used up in production and the value of their wages. That difference (the "surplus" in Marx's theory or "net revenue" or "profit" in other theories) continued to be appropriated and distributed by persons other than those workers nearly everywhere that socialists or communists shaped economies. True, the surplus-appropriators could be state officials (e.g., commissars) rather than privately elected boards of directors, or perhaps they were heavily state-regulated private boards, but in any case, they exploited the surplus producers precisely as Marx specified in his *Capital*. In simplest terms, in actually existing socialism and communism, the workers who produced the surplus continued to be excluded from appropriating and distributing it.

A parallel from slavery may prove instructive here. Critics of slavery often defined their objectives as improving slave conditions: achieving better diets, clothing, housing, integrity of slave families, and so on. Other critics took a very different approach: they demanded abolition of slavery. Socialists and communists, who often began as abolitionists in their relation to capitalist exploitation, evolved over the last century into advocates of the improvement of workers' conditions while leaving intact the workplace relationship of employer and employee. Communists, in effect, substituted state for private capitalism, whereas the socialists stressed state-regulated versus private (relatively less regulated) capitalism. Workers got better working conditions where communists and socialists were powerful, but they did not get an end to exploitation and all its social effects.[30]

A socialism for the twenty-first century must include and stress the importance of micro-level social transformation at the base of society in the workplace. Ending exploitation in workplaces is that transformation. Instead of workers producing surpluses for others to appropriate and distribute, they must now do that for themselves collectively. They must become their own board of directors. Ending workplace exploitation means that nonworkers, whether private individuals or state officials, can no longer appropriate or distribute workers' surpluses. As "producer cooperatives" or "democratized enterprises" (among other names), such transformed workplaces represent a priority goal of a new socialism. That socialism stresses the micro-level transformation of society—the end of exploitation wherever people work—as the necessary companion or counterpart to the traditional macro focus on property ownership and distribution mechanisms. The macro and micro components of socialism would both become equally necessary, conditions of each other's existence, mutually reinforcing as well as mutually dependent. Neither will be viewed or treated by policy as determinant of the other. Both will shape one another much as they both shape and are shaped by the larger social and natural contexts.

Such a socialism for the twenty-first century situates the workers—the majority—as key micro-level agents of its project and of the new society being established. Workers will transform their factories, offices, and stores into producers' cooperatives or what are increasingly called worker self-directed enterprises (WSDEs, described in detail in my 2012 book, *Democracy at Work: A Cure for Capitalism*). They will likewise defend them both from regression back to capitalist enterprises and from subordination to any state or party apparatus. Workers will operate their enterprises as the continuing core of the transition from capitalism to socialism. As their own boards of directors, workers will collectively appropriate and distrib-

---

30. For a full presentation and documentation of this argument, with special reference to Soviet socialism, see Stephen A. Resnick and Richard D. Wolff, *Class Theory and History: Capitalism and Communism in the USSR* (New York: Routledge, 2002).

ute the surpluses they produce. They will thereby have replaced capitalists. Workers' democratic self-government in the workplace will then have superseded capitalism's undemocratic organization of the workplace.

Other social institutions formerly dependent on receiving distributions of capitalist surpluses from the appropriators will then be dependent instead on workers directing their own enterprises and thus distributing their own surpluses. Government revenue, for example, to the extent it depends on taxes on enterprise surpluses, would then flow from (and hence be responsive to) workers in their capacity as enterprise self-directors. The state would then become directly and financially dependent on the organized (in and by their enterprises) workers in a way and to a degree unequaled in human history. Correspondingly, the risks of power passing from the mass of people in their residences and workplaces to a state bureaucracy—a serious problem for traditional socialism—would be reduced.

When the workers collectively and democratically distribute the surpluses they produce, they will have a powerful influence on how the society's surpluses are distributed. That influence will likely work against the sorts of extreme inequality in the distribution of personal income typical of capitalist societies. For example, workers in WSDEs will not likely distribute wildly disproportionate shares of the surplus in the forms of huge salaries for top executives while the mass of employees barely get by. There will be little need for redistributive tax systems because enterprises' initial distributions of income—both as individual wages and as distributed shares of the surplus—from WSDEs will be far more egalitarian. The long history of capitalism's failed efforts to avoid highly unequal distributions of wealth, income, political power, and cultural access can finally be overcome by a transition to a nonexploitation-based economic system.

The socialism for the twenty-first century sketched above combines the traditional macro focus on socialized productive property and planning with the micro focus on a democratization of workplaces. Removing workplace exploitation represents a major step toward achievement of the French Revolution's goals: liberté, égalité, and fraternité. Capitalism took some steps but prevented others. Its spokespersons and defenders forever celebrated (and still do) a democracy that is rigidly excluded from the system's enterprises (where most adults spend most of their active lives). Capitalism's history repeatedly demonstrates that the absence of democracy inside enterprises undermines it elsewhere in society (or else yields caricatures, as in "democratic" elections corrupted by the system's economic inequalities).

By including the democratization of enterprises—as embodied in WSDEs—a twenty-first-century socialism can also recapture, renew, and refocus the hope, commitment, and passions inaugurated in the French Revolution. Revolutionary upsurges have punctuated capitalism ever since despite all the efforts of modern societies finally to extinguish them. A socialism for the twenty-first century can build on the centuries-long interest in communal and cooperative work organizations among both religious and secular communities. It can partner with present-day cooperative institutions whose multiplicity and potential have been celebrated by Gar Alperovitz, author of *America Beyond Capitalism: Reclaiming Our Wealth, Our Liberty, and Our Democracy* (2011) and *What Then Must We Do?* (2013).

Imagine democratic enterprises interacting with democratic residential communities—economic and political democracies reinforcing one another and making one another real, not merely formal. Jointly they would codetermine how society functions and changes. That vision and goal animates a socialism for the twenty-first century. It builds upon, while also critically departing from, traditional socialism's contradictory history. It embodies the aspirations of all those who contemplate the present in the spirit of knowing that we can do better than capitalism.

Debating Capitalism—Redefining Outdated Terms
September 21, 2013

Reasonable conversation about capitalism is possible again. Debates about its strengths and weaknesses resume. The United States's post-1950 taboo against honestly evaluating capitalism finally is fading. The public increasingly ignores over-the-top celebrations of capitalism as humanity's peak achievement, God's choice, perpetual prosperity generator, or guarantor of individual freedom. Politicians, journalists, and academics could stop their uncritical cheerleading for capitalism, although most still pay their bills that way.

The reasons are many. Capitalism no longer "delivers the goods" to most Americans. With consumer debt already high, more borrowing can no longer postpone hard times. The American Dream slips farther out of reach. As Cold War memories recede, labels like socialism or communism no longer stifle debate. Destroyed cities like Detroit; students with unsustainable debts; declining wages, benefits, and job security; and millions unemployed or foreclosed—to them, the usual rationalizations of capitalism seem hollow and ridiculous.

A July 2013 national survey found 26 percent of Americans believing that capitalism is "not working too well" and another 16 percent that capitalism is "not working at all well." Imagine the consequences if a new political party arose to represent those 42 percent by demanding basic changes in the economic system.

However, that survey and resumed debates about capitalism have not yet faced or solved a shared problem. Widespread confusion and disagreement surround what capitalism means and thus what exactly "is not working." This situation weakens the clarity and appeal of solutions offered by capitalism's critics.

A two-dimensional definition of capitalism—as private property plus markets—prevailed for the past 150 years. It neatly contrasted socialism or communism as public property and planning. Privately owned enterprises producing goods and services and free market exchanges of resources and products defined capitalism. State-owned and -operated enterprises and government-planned resource and product distributions defined socialism or communism. Those definitions' inadequacies should have been obvious. They persisted likely because they served leaders in both systems well.

Private capitalists and their supporters demonize government regulations, taxes, and public services they oppose as socialism or communism and equate them with atheism, revolution, violence, and dictatorship. The old definitions work for them. Keynesians and social democrats advocate government intervention to preserve capitalism by offsetting its excesses and flaws. Because they fear being called communists, they use the old definition (that of communism being total state ownership and planning) to reject communism emphatically. Leaders in countries such as the Soviet Union and China—products and custodians of "revolutions against capitalism"—defined their economies as opposites, negations of capitalism. Polarized definitions—capitalism as private property and markets and socialism or communism as public property and planning—usefully emphasize their difference and distance from capitalism.

Those polarized definitions are now being challenged and displaced. This is partly because of their close associations with socialist and communist economies that imploded and capitalist economies languishing in deep crises. Searches for alternatives to both systems uncovered the old definitions' flaws. New agendas for effective economic change begin with different definitions.

Definitions focused on private versus public property distinguish capitalist from socialist economies poorly. For example, the 1917 Soviet revolution guaranteed private property in land—the agricultural economy's key resource—to millions of peasants. De facto private property comprised the "family plots" alongside collectivized agriculture after 1930. Soviet-style socialisms often did not "abolish" private property. Likewise, capitalist economies often did not abolish public property: postal systems, utilities, schools, transport systems, credit agencies, and many other sectors remained public enterprises.

Markets-versus-planning definitions are likewise problematic. Socialist economies always used markets among other mechanisms for distributing resources and products. That included wage-labor markets. Of course, socialist governments planned, controlled, and intervened in most markets. Yet government planning and intervention also exist in capitalism and shape all sorts of market supplies and demands (including labor markets). Keynesian economists mostly favor capitalism while advocating greater government intervention in it. Planning and markets, like public and private property, usually have coexisted over recent centuries. Nor did they tend toward the opposites favored in the old definitions.

How should we now differentiate capitalism from other economic systems? Marx's work helps by defining capitalism in terms of its organization of production, the internal structure of enterprises (factories, offices, and stores). Capitalist enterprises exclude most workers from key decisions: what, how, and where to produce and how to use net revenues (in Marx's terms, the enterprise's "surplus value"). Capitalist enterprise decision makers include only enterprise owners (e.g., major shareholders) and the boards of directors they select.

For this definition, capitalism can exist whether the enterprise is owned privately or publicly and whether it distributes its outputs by market exchanges or a state plan. In short, capitalism defined as a particular organization of production exhibits different forms: private and state and market and planned.

For this definition, a new socialist alternative to capitalism entails democratically transformed enterprises. All the workers have become the board of directors. They collectively employ themselves. They democratically decide what, how, and where to produce and how to use net revenues. They do that together with the similarly organized residential communities they interact with. In this new definition, socialism too would exhibit different forms: workers' self-directed enterprises publicly or privately owned and with planning or markets. Socialist societies would debate and decide among possible forms.

This new definition enables today's critics of capitalism to focus on what earlier critics missed when they advocated changes from private to public property and from markets to planning. It clarifies what is to be done now, namely, a transition that includes turning capitalist into workers' self-directed enterprises and workers cooperatives.

Without such a definition, those increasingly dissatisfied with capitalism now risk repeating the failed transitions of the past. Previous socialist and communist critics of capitalism proved unable, in those transitions, to go beyond state and planned forms of capitalism. We could do better this time by insisting that genuinely democratized enterprises be part of any transition beyond the capitalisms and socialisms of the past. Democratized enterprises give working people the means to hold any state apparatus accountable (because they provide its resources). Democratized enterprises could attract mass support. They embody that "vision thing" social critics need.

LESSONS FROM LABOR

Lost Elections, Strategic Lessons for Workers' Movements Everywhere

June 12, 2012

Last week's elections in Wisconsin and in San Diego and San Jose, California, brought victories for capitalists' over workers' priorities. Majorities of voters endorsed politicians' plans to ease state and city budget difficulties by cutting public employees' jobs, wages, pensions, and rights to bargain collectively with employers over those crucial dimensions of their lives. Private-sector workers reacted to five years of economic crisis with little help from their government by voting against benefits won in collective bargaining by public-sector workers. Conservative and pro-business ads had persuaded them that their taxes paid for public workers' better benefits and salaries. Majorities of private-sector workers believed voting to cut those benefits and break public employee unions would relieve their present and future tax burdens.

Why did this happen, and what strategic lessons can we learn from answering that question? To understand last week's election results, we need to consider the 1930s Great Depression when the opposite happened. Then, unions grew faster than at any time before or since. Instead of losing legal protections, workers gained them more than ever before or since. When unemployment during the Depression reached 25 percent, workers gained all sorts of benefits, more than at any time before or since. Establishing Social Security helped those over sixty-five. Creating the federal unemployment compensation system helped tens of millions of unemployed. And federal jobs provided income and dignity to over 12 million Americans between 1934 and 1941. Huge majorities of voters reelected Franklin D. Roosevelt, the president who delivered these huge gains for workers, four consecutive times.

Why did capitalism's collapse in the 1930s affect workers so differently from what is happening in the current crisis? Back then, workers' interests were advanced by a powerful alliance coordinating two sets of organizations active in two different segments of society. One ally, the Congress of Industrial Organizations (CIO), built strong industrial unions to confront employers on the job about work, power, and income there. The CIO achieved the greatest union organizing drive in US history; there had been nothing like that before, nor has there been anything like it since then. The other ally, the socialist and communist parties, worked largely in residential communities and social and cultural movements, as well as in politics—throughout the public spaces of society. The CIO demanded a better deal for people at work within capitalism. The socialists and communists demanded and fought for basic social change to an alternative system that would do better than capitalism for most people.

The alliance was close. CIO unions got their allies' help in many organizing drives and struggles with employers. The socialists and communists got an audience and base in the unions. The labor–socialist–communist alliance informed, mobilized, and organized Americans so successfully that Roosevelt had to provide massive, expensive help to average Americans despite the economic crunch of the Great Depression. What is more, Roosevelt had to pay for that help in large part by taxing corporations and the rich far more than they were taxed before.

The lesson that American history teaches is thus not the need for just any alliances or cooperation between unions and the community. We have had them in various forms for many decades, and while some gains were made, those alliances could not prevent unions and the left from declining steadily and severely. The key lesson is this: What makes all the difference is a very particular alliance, one between unions and an explicitly anticapitalist social and political movement.

Here's why that particular alliance was so successful then and why its absence is so costly now. Unions succeed more in workplace bargaining when employers must worry that refusing to compromise might strengthen anticapitalist movements. Unions are less vulnerable to criticism as narrowly caring only for their own members when they are continuously and clearly allied with organizations struggling for a better society for everyone. Socialists and communists built the community contacts and consciousness that undermined and defeated pro-business arguments against the CIO union drives and against the programs Roosevelt developed. Working together, the two allies strengthened and legitimated each other. The absence of that alliance now enables the results of the June 5 elections, just as its absence in recent decades facilitated right-wing shifts. In contrast, the presence of such an alliance in Europe (although weaker now than it once was) explains why so many countries there have shifted far less to the right.

Skeptics might argue that however successful the union-socialist-communist alliance was in the 1930s, it proved vulnerable to destruction thereafter. Yet the explanation for the long, post-1930s decline of unions and the left reinforces our basic argument here. That is because the 1930s marked not only the peak of the union/anticapitalist alliance. As we can briefly show, it also marked the breakup of that alliance.

As Roosevelt confronted a fast-deteriorating capitalist collapse and the fast-rising power of the CIO-socialist-communist alliance, he fashioned a political New Deal. He would take from corporations and the rich the tax increases and loans to pay for Social Security, unemployment compensation, and the federal jobs program. In return, he would get the CIO-socialist-communist alliance to celebrate him as the savior of the country and the Democrats as the people's party. Most important, he would get the alliance to drop, or at least downplay, the critique of capitalism and the activities for a change of system.

In winning the needed support for his deal, Roosevelt split the capitalists and the rich (half agreed, while the other half hated the deal and him), thereby weakening the Republican Party that represented them best. That party took the next fifty years to recover its pre-Depression power. The deal also split the union-socialist-communist alliance. Most of its members agreed to celebrate the state interventionist social welfare capitalism Roosevelt installed in the 1930s. Some approvingly called it socialism (as did enraged right-wingers, too). Except for a few radicals, the union-socialist-communist alliance downplayed serious anticapitalist activity in favor of enthusiastic support for the New Deal as a "progressive" development of US capitalism.

In the loss of a vibrant socialist and communist movement devoted to system change, the capitalists, the rich, and the Republicans who had never accepted Roosevelt's deal saw a weakness they could exploit. They proceeded to undermine support for the New Deal by demonizing the socialists and communists with McCarthy-type attacks on them as disloyal, attacking unions as guilty by association with the socialists and communists, and further splitting the alliance to weaken its political power. For unions and progressives to reduce government persecution (for violating the 1947 Taft-Hartley Act, which restricted the power and activities of labor unions) and avoid public vilification, they had to end any links to their former socialist and communist allies.

The capitalists-rich-Republicans alliance succeeded as the union-socialist-communist alliance split and both factions commenced a half-century decline. Unions were increasingly isolated from the kind of mass radical support that served workers' interests so well in the depths of the Depression. The June 5, 2012, elections are only the latest signs and results of that isolation.

American history teaches how to achieve the best results for workers' interests on the job, in the community, and socially. It requires building a robust alliance between labor unions and movements or political parties (or both) seriously committed to an anticapitalist agenda for social change. The historic significance of the Occupy Wall Street movement lies in its taking a big first step toward rebuilding such an alliance.

Detroit's Decline Is a Distinctively Capitalist Failure
July 23, 2013

Capitalism as a system ought to be judged by its failures as well as its successes.

The automobile-driven economic growth of the 1950s and 1960s made Detroit a globally recognized symbol of successful capitalist renewal after the Great Depression and the war (1929–1945). High-wage auto industry jobs with real security and exemplary benefits were said to prove capitalism's ability to generate and sustain a large "middle class," one that could include African Americans, too. Auto-industry jobs became inspirations and models for what workers across America might seek and acquire—those middle-class components of a modern "American Dream."

True, quality jobs in Detroit were forced from the automobile capitalists by long and hard union struggles, especially across the 1930s. Once defeated in those struggles, auto capitalists quickly arranged to rewrite the history so that good wages and working conditions became something they "gave" to their workers. In any case, Detroit became a vibrant, world-class city in the 1950s and 1960s; its distinctive culture and sound shaped the world's music much as its cars shaped the world's industries.

Over the past forty years, capitalism turned that success into the abject failure culminating now in the largest municipal bankruptcy in US history. The key decision makers—major shareholders in General Motors, Ford, and Chrysler and the boards of directors they selected—made many disastrous decisions. They failed in competition with European and Japanese automobile capitalists and so lost market share to them. They responded too slowly and inadequately to the need to develop new fuel-saving technologies. Perhaps most tellingly, they responded to their own failures by deciding to move production out of Detroit so they could pay other workers lower wages.

The automobile companies' competitive failures, and then their moves, had two key economic consequences. First, they effectively undermined the economic foundation of Detroit's economy. Second, they thereby dealt a major blow to any chances for an enduring US middle class. The past forty years have displayed those consequences and the capitalist system's inability or unwillingness to stop, let alone reverse, them.

Real wages in the United States stopped growing in the 1970s and have not grown since, even as workers' rising productivity generated even more profits for employers. Rising consumer debt and overwork postponed for a few years the impacts of stagnant real wages on consumption. But by 2007, with wages stagnant and further consumer borrowing capacity exhausted, a long and deep crisis arrived. Employers used the resulting unemployment to attack job security and benefits and the public sector built up in the 1950s and 1960s to support the middle class (e.g., by low-cost public higher education).

Auto industry capitalists took the lead and Detroit exemplified the economic decline that resulted. In the deep crisis since 2007, General Motors and Chrysler got federal bailouts, but Detroit did not. The auto companies got wage reductions (via the tiered wage system) that assured Detroit's wage-based economy could not recover, even as auto company production and profits did. The failures of private capitalism thus drew in the complicity of the federal government.

Despite what the heroic sit-down strikes and other actions of the United Auto Workers had earlier won for their members, the auto companies' decision-making powers remained in the hands of major shareholders and their boards of directors. They used that power to evade, weaken, and eventually undo what union struggles had won. The unions proved incapable of stopping that process. Detroit's capitalists thus undermined the middle-class conditions workers had extracted from them—and thus destroyed the "capitalist success" city built on those conditions.

Detroit's decline, like the parallel decline of the United Auto Workers, teaches an inescapable lesson. The very contracts that militant unions win with employers give those employers great incentives to find ways around those contracts. They usually do.

The top-down structure of capitalist enterprises provides major shareholders and boards of directors with the resources (corporate profits) to cut or remove the good conditions unions can sometimes win. That's how this system works. Detroit has "been there and done that." The solution is not more contracts.

If the autoworkers had transformed the auto companies into worker cooperatives, Detroit would have evolved very differently. Worker cooperatives would not have moved production, thereby undermining their jobs, families, and communities, including especially Detroit. Workers would not have destroyed themselves and their communities that way. Moving production, a distinctly capitalist strategy, was key to Detroit's population dropping from 1.8 million in 1950 to 700,000 today.

Workers cooperatives would also have searched and likely found alternatives to moving that might have saved Detroit. Workers cooperatives, for example, would likely have paid less in dividends to owners and salaries to managers than was typical at Ford, General Motors, and

Chrysler. Those savings, if passed on in lower automobile prices, would have enabled better completion with European and Japanese car makers than Detroit's Big Three managed.

We cannot know how much more Detroit's auto industry might have benefited from technical progress had it been organized as a workers' cooperative. We can guess that workers have greater incentives to improve technology in cooperatives they own and operate than as employees in capitalist enterprises. Finally, worker cooperatives would likely have switched to producing (and helped promote) mass-transit vehicles or other alternatives to the automobile to retain jobs and well-being once they saw that continued automobile production could not secure those priorities for worker cooperatives.

What kind of a society gives a relatively tiny number of people the position and power to make corporate decisions impacting millions in and around Detroit while it excludes those millions from participating in those decisions? When those capitalists' decisions condemn Detroit to forty years of disastrous decline, what kind of society relieves those capitalists of any responsibility to help rebuild that city?

The simple answer to these questions: no genuinely democratic economy could or would work that way.

What Drove Organized Labor's Decline in the United States?

September 2, 2013

Organized labor's decline in the United States over the past half century is well known; what drove that decline, less so. The New Deal's enemies—big business, Republicans, conservatives—had developed a coordinated strategy by the late 1940s. They would break up the coalition of organized labor and socialist and communist parties: the mass base that had forced through the 1930s New Deal. Then each coalition member could be individually destroyed.

One line of attack used anticommunist witch-hunts (McCarthyism) to frighten socialists and labor unions into dissociating themselves from former communist allies. Another attack targeted socialists by equating them with communists and applying the same demonization. Still another attack, the 1947 Taft-Hartley Act, directly weakened labor unions, their organizing capability, and their alliance with the left.

Business and political leaders, mass media, and academics cultivated a paranoid anxiety among Americans: suspect anything even vaguely leftist, see risks of "subversion" everywhere, and avoid organizations unless religious or loudly patriotic. Legal, ideological, and police pressures rendered communist and socialist parties tiny and ineffective. Destroying unions took longer. The unionized portion of private sector workers fell from a third to less than 7 percent now. Since 2007, conservatives used crisis-driven drops in state and city tax revenues to intensify attacks on public employee benefits and unions. Both were denounced as "excessive and unaffordable for taxpayers." That, plus public worker layoffs, reduced public sector unionization.

Nor did labor unions or the left find or implement any successful strategy to counter the fifty-year program aimed to destroy them.

To reverse organized labor's decline and rebuild the left requires either reviving the old New Deal coalition or forming a new comparably powerful alliance. That means confronting and outwitting the long demonization of unions and the left. It requires a strategy that engages and wins struggles with employers. More important, it requires a strategy to reposition labor unions and their allies as champions of broad social gains for the 99 percent. To escape the label of "special interest" unions must work for far more than their own members.

The needed strategy is available. It proposes a new alliance among willing labor unions, community organizations, and social movements. The alliance's basic goal is a social transition in which worker cooperatives become an increasing proportion of business enterprises. The increasingly used term worker self-directed enterprises (WSDEs) stresses democratic decision making. In WSDEs, all workers democratically decide what, how, and where to produce and how to use the net revenues their work generates. In WSDEs, whether or not workers are owners or self-manage, they function, collectively and democratically, as their own board of directors, their own bosses.

This goal and strategy could solidify this alliance. Democratizing enterprises realizes inside them the same goals that inspire many community organizations and social movements. WSDEs established and nurtured by community organizations and social movements could, in turn, provide important financial and other resources for their allies.

Labor unions could regain strength from such an alliance. For example, consider employers who demand concessions (lower wages and benefits) and threaten otherwise to relocate enterprises, often abroad. Unions have mostly compromised on concessions to retain employers. The proposed new alliance offers a new bargaining tool for these situations. If an employer relocated, the alliance would assist workers to try to continue the enterprise as a WSDE. The relocated employer risks competition from a WSDE asking customers to favor it over an employer who had abandoned workers and communities for higher profits.

To establish new WSDEs in such ways, unions would draw upon their allied community organizations and social movements to mobilize local political support as well as funding. Local politicians could not easily refuse job-saving demands from that alliance (proven daily in Europe).

Another way for the proposed alliance to help form WSDEs would be a bold new federal or state program to combat unemployment. This would follow the example of Italy's 1985 Marcora Law. That law offers a new, second alternative to the usual unemployment dole. An unemployed worker can instead choose to take all unemployment benefits as an immediate lump-sum payment and pool that with lump sums similarly chosen by at least nine other unemployed workers. The total must then be used as start-up capital for a workers' coop. Marcora's success is one reason Italy has many more worker coops than the United States.

These and still other actions by the proposed new alliance could build a significant WSDE sector while helping solve major US social problems. That sector would enable many Americans to see and evaluate WSDEs. A WSDE sector gives Americans two new freedoms of choice: (a) between working in a top-down, hierarchical capitalist firm or a democratized worker coop, and (b) between buying the products of capitalist or cooperative enterprises. A significant WSDE sector would add its demands for government technical, financial, and other supports to those from other economic sectors.

As the Republican and Democratic parties increasingly cannot or will not serve average Americans' economic needs, the proposed alliance, strategy, and actions would do exactly that. Here lie opportunities for resurgence in the labor movement and the left.

While reminiscent of the old New Deal coalition, the proposed new alliance would differ in one crucial dimension. The old coalition believed that it could not win more than progressive taxation, new regulations, and new institutions (such as Social Security). It could not transform enterprises themselves. The old coalition left in their corporate positions the major shareholders and the boards of directors they selected. Those shareholders and boards then used corporate power and profits to systematically evade, weaken, and, when possible, dismantle the New Deal across the past forty years.

Building a WSDE sector in the economy applies the lesson of those years. To secure gains for working people requires a social transition that puts them in charge of producing society's goods and services. A democratic society requires a democratic economy and that, the new alliance would insist, means a transition to democratically organized enterprises. When this September's AFL-CIO convention considers building an alliance with community groups and social movements, the strategic focus on WSDEs ought to be included.

Lessons from Chattanooga

February 17, 2014

> "We're outraged by politicians and outside special interest groups interfering..."
> —UAW secretary-treasurer Dennis Williams

Many factors led to the United Auto Workers' (UAW) loss in the recent union election at the Volkswagen (VW) factory in Tennessee. Likewise many lessons can be learned. One especially important lesson concerns how one factor—"outside influence"—works so one-sidedly in the United States.

Several UAW spokespersons and supporters bemoaned "outside interference" in this election. It was chiefly Republican politicians and activists and business groups that tried actively to persuade VW workers to vote against unionizing the factory, while the VW management remained neutral. Yet outside interference always influences union elections. Outcomes are never results merely of what employers and employees say and do in election campaigns.

Just as important is the way workers see the larger world and their places within it. That emerges from the workers' families and households, the education they received, the mass media they engage, and from political parties and government. All their life experiences shape how they think about everything, including voting in union elections.

Organizations of business, the wealthy, and the conservatives (think tanks, foundations, hired public relations firms, advertising enterprises, major newspapers, mass radio and TV stations, Internet outlets, and social media) work constantly to shape workers' life experiences and thus how they see the world. Because of their dependence on financing from businesses and the wealthy, most Republicans and Democrats avoid conflicts with their campaigns to shape public opinion. Conservatives pander to them.

No alternative, different way to see the world similarly surrounds workers in their daily lives. Workers' organizations (unions, think tanks, independent media) are many fewer, poorer, and much weaker. "Outside influences" shape workers' consciousness one-sidedly because of the gross disparity of resources available to those exerting that influence. What made local Republicans and conservatives' billboards persuasive was public opinion; the shape of that opinion defeated unionization in Tennessee. How differently "outside influences" work in other countries is suggested by this simple fact: virtually all of VW's 105 factories elsewhere are unionized.

During the middle 1930s, millions joined unions for the first time—the greatest unionization drive in history. The history of unionization in the United States reinforces the point. We had never seen anything like it before, nor have we since. Unionization then was achieved by a remarkable alliance: unions (allied in the Congress of Industrial Organizations) plus large, active socialist and communist parties. Those parties widely and effectively contested the "outside influences" stemming from business, the wealthy, and conservatives. Socialists and communists mobilized their own media, writers, artists, and academics into play. Their demonstrations on many social issues made news and their organizations disseminated a distinctive interpretation of that news. They contradicted what business, the wealthy, and conservatives asserted and not only around particular issues. Many among them also contested the economic system, arguing that the United States could and should do better than capitalism. Interested teachers, clergy, students, immigrant and racial minorities, and the general public thus continuously encountered perspectives other than those of business, the wealthy, and conservatives.

How workers thought about and responded to union activists in the 1930s reflected the "outside influences" stemming from their socialist and communist allies. Those influences helped make unionization so stunningly successful then.

Consider the claim—evidently somewhat effective in Chattanooga—that high wages won by the UAW caused Detroit's economic collapse. That the UAW's enemies would make that claim is not remarkable; that some workers took it seriously is. Every significant decision at Ford, General Motors, and Chrysler since their beginnings was made exclusively by their major shareholders and boards of directors, all small handfuls of individuals. They alone decided what vehicles and fuel efficiencies to produce, what technologies to use, how many workers to hire, and where to locate or relocate factories (north, south, at home, or abroad). They always excluded workers from participation in those decisions (and opposed the UAW's participation in wage decisions). They insisted on management prerogatives and expertise and corporate responsibilities.

While Detroit's auto industry was booming, those decision makers took full credit; it was all about their entrepreneurial geniuses. Then, their many bad corporate decisions (on auto design, technical composition, fuel efficiency, marketing, and much else) badly weakened the industry. That plus far better decisions among European, Japanese, and Korean auto producers reduced US firms' profits and market shares. US firms' major shareholders and boards of directors then decided to leave Detroit, ignoring their decision's disastrous effects. In contrast, while German manufacturers pay their unionized workers much more than their US counterparts, they have not abandoned their workers or their cities. Germany has no equivalent of Detroit.

As Detroit declined, auto company decision makers conveniently reversed themselves and asserted their nonresponsibility. They were suddenly not the powerful "captains of industry" they once called themselves. Instead, they want folks to believe that the UAW forced high wages on them and that they left Detroit because the UAW victimized them. Some Tennessee workers found such assertions plausible and voted accordingly. By contrast, the profound impact of German unions and their socialist and communist allies on public opinion there helps explain why this year VW's unionized German workers are enjoying a 5.6 percent wage increase at a time of 1.2 percent inflation.

Only a sustained counterprogram of mass education could at least partly shift "public opinion" so that it functions less as an anti-union "outside interference." The construction today of an alliance parallel to the one that proved successful in the 1930s might accomplish that counterprogram. Labor needs to rebuild collaborations with academics—students as well as teachers—and political activists who understand past and present contrary to the claims promoted by business, the wealthy, and conservatives. In short, a besieged labor movement needs again to become part of a much broader social movement. This time the urgency is less to grow (as in the 1930s) and more a matter of organized labor's survival.

ALTERNATIVES

The Threats of Business and the Business of Threats

May 10, 2011

More and more, we hear that nothing can be done to tax major corporations because of the threat of how they would respond. Likewise, we cannot stop their price gouging or even the government subsidies and tax loopholes they enjoy. For example, as the oil majors reap stunning profits from high oil and gas prices, we are told it is impossible to tax their windfall profits or stop the billions they get in government subsidies and tax loopholes. There appears to be no way for the government to secure lower energy prices or seriously impose and enforce environmental protection laws. Likewise, despite high and fast rising drug and medicine prices, we are told that it is impossible to raise taxes on pharmaceutical companies or have the government secure lower pharmaceutical prices. And so on.

Such steps by "our" government are said to be impossible or inadvisable. The reason: corporations would then relocate production abroad or reduce their activities in the United States or both. And that would deprive the United States of taxes and lose more jobs. In plain English, major corporations are threatening us. We are to knuckle under and cut social programs that benefit millions of people (college loan programs, Medicaid, Medicare, Social Security, nutrition programs, and so on). We are not to demand higher taxes or reduced subsidies and tax loopholes for corporations. We are not to demand government action to lower their soaring prices. And if we do, corporations will punish us.

Three groups deliver these business threats to us. First, corporate spokespersons, their paid public relations flunkies, hand down the word from on high (corporate board rooms). Second, politicians afraid to offend their corporate sponsors repeat publicly what corporate spokespersons have emailed to them. Finally, various commentators explain the threats to us. These include the journalists lost in that ideological fog that always translates what corporations want into "common sense." Commentators also include the professors who translate what corporations want into "economic science."

Of course, there are always two possible responses to any and all threats. One is to cave in, to be intimidated. That has often been the dominant "policy choice" of the US government. That's why so many corporate tax loopholes exist, why the government does so little to limit price increases, and why government does not constrain corporate relocation decisions. No surprise there, since corporations have spent lavishly to support the political careers of so many current leaders. They expect those politicians to do what their corporate sponsors want. Just as important, they also expect those politicians to persuade people that it's "best for us all" to cave in when corporations threaten us.

What about the other possible response to threats? Government could make a different policy choice, define differently what is "best for us all." In plain English, it could persevere in the face of business threats and to do so, it could counterthreaten the corporations. When major corporations threaten to cut or relocate production abroad in response to changes in their taxes and subsidies or demands to cut their prices or serious enforcement of environmental protection rules, the US government could promise retaliation. Here's a brief and partial list of how it might do that (with illustrative examples for the energy and pharmaceutical industries):

Inform such threatening businesses that the US government will shift its purchases to other enterprises.

Inform them that top officials will tour the United States to urge citizens to follow the government's example and shift their purchases as well.

Inform them that the government will proceed to finance and organize state-operated companies to compete directly with threatening businesses.

Immediately and strictly enforce all applicable rules governing health and safety conditions for workers, environmental protection laws, equal employment and advancement opportunity, and so on.

Present and promote passage of new laws governing enterprise relocation (giving local, regional, and national authorities veto power over corporate relocation decisions).

Purchase energy and pharmaceutical outputs in bulk for mass resale to the US public, passing on all the savings from bulk purchases.

Seize assets of enterprises that seek to evade or frustrate increased taxes or reduced subsidies.

Laws enabling such actions either already exist in the United States or could be enacted. In other countries today, existing models of such laws have performed well, often for many years. These could be used and adjusted for US conditions.

A much better basis than threat and counterthreat is available for sharing the costs of government between individuals and businesses. That basis would be achieved by a transition to an economic system where workers in each enterprise functioned collectively and democratically as their own board of directors. Such worker-directed enterprises eliminate the basic split and conflict inside capitalist corporations between those who make the key business decisions (what, how, and where to produce, for example) and those who must live with and most immediately depend on those decisions' results (the mass of employees).

One concrete example can illustrate the benefits of this alternative to the threat-counterthreat scenario. Corporations have used repeated threats (to cut or move production) as a means to prevent tax increases and to secure tax reductions. Likewise they have made the same threats to secure desired spending from the federal government (military expenditures, federal road and port building projects, subsidies, financial supports, and so on). In effect, corporate boards of directors and major shareholders seek to shift tax burdens onto employees. Their success over the last half-century is clear. Tax receipts of the US government have increasingly come (1) from individual rather than corporate income taxes and (2) from middle and lower individual income groups rather than from the rich. In worker-directed enterprises, the incentive for such shifts would vanish because the people who would be paying enterprise taxes are the same people who would be paying individual income taxes. Taxation would finally become genuinely democratic. The people would collectively decide how to distribute taxes on what would genuinely be their own businesses and their own individual incomes.

Manifesto for Economic Democracy and Ecological Sanity

February 2, 2012

A new historical vista is opening before us in this time of change. Capitalism as a system has spawned deepening economic crisis alongside its bought-and-paid-for political establishment. Neither serves the needs of our society. Whether it is secure, well-paid, and meaningful jobs or a sustainable relationship with the natural environment we depend on, our society is not delivering the results people need and deserve. We do not have the lives we want, and our children's future is threatened because of social conditions that can and should be changed. One key cause for this intolerable state of affairs is the lack of genuine democracy in our economy as well as in our politics. One key solution is thus the institution of genuine economic democracy as the basis for a genuine political democracy as well. That means transforming the workplace in our society as we propose in what follows.

We are encouraged by the Occupy Wall Street (OWS) movement spreading across the United States and beyond. Not only does OWS express a widespread popular rejection of our system's social injustice and lack of democracy. OWS is also a movement for goals that include economic democracy. We welcome, support, and seek to build OWS as the urgently needed, broad movement to reorganize our society, to make our institutions accountable to the public will, and to establish both economic democracy and ecological sanity.

Capitalism and "Delivering the Goods"

Capitalism today abuses the people, environment, politics, and culture in equal measures. It has fostered new extremes of wealth and poverty inside most countries, and such extremes always undermine or prevent democratic politics. Capitalist production for profit likewise endangers us by its global warming, widening pollution, and looming energy crisis. And now capitalism's recurrent instability (what others call the "business cycle") has plunged the world into the second massive global economic crisis in the last seventy-five years.

Yet both Republican and Democratic governments have failed to bring a recovery to the great mass of the American people. We continue to face high unemployment and home foreclosures alongside shrinking real wages, benefits, and job security. Thus, increasing personal debt is required to secure basic needs. The government uses our taxes to bring recovery from the economic crisis to banks, stock markets, and major corporations. We have waited for bailouts of the corporate rich to trickle down to the rest of us; it never happened. To pay for their recovery we are told now to submit to cuts in public services, public employment, and even our Social Security and Medicare benefits. The budget deficits and national debts incurred to save capitalism from its own fundamental flaws are now used to justify shifting the cost of their recovery onto everyone else. We should not pay for capitalism's crisis and for the government's unjust and failed response to that crisis. It is time to take a different path, to make long-overdue economic, social, and political changes.

We begin by drawing lessons from previous efforts to go beyond capitalism. Traditional socialism—as in the Soviet Union—emphasized public instead of private ownership of means of production and government economic planning instead of markets. But that concentrated too much power in the government and thereby corrupted the socialist project. Yet the recent reversions back to capitalism neither overcame nor rectified the failures of Soviet-style socialism.

We have also learned from the last great capitalist crisis in the United States during the 1930s. Then an unprecedented upsurge of union organizing by the Congress of Industrial Organizations (CIO) and political mobilizations by socialist and communist parties won major reforms: establishing Social Security and unemployment insurance, creating and filling 11 million federal jobs. Very expensive reforms in the middle of a depression were paid for in part by heavily taxing corporations and the rich (who were also then heavily regulated). However, New Deal reforms were evaded, weakened, or abolished in the decades after 1945. To increase their profits, major corporate shareholders and their boards of directors had every incentive to dismantle reforms. They used their profits to undo the New Deal. Reforms won will always remain insecure until workers who benefit from the reforms are in the position of receiving the profits of their enterprises and using them to extend, not undermine, those reforms.

The task facing us, therefore, goes well beyond choosing between private and public ownership and between markets and planning. Nor can we be content to re-enact reforms that capitalist enterprises can and will undermine. These are not our only alternatives. The strategy we propose is to establish a genuinely democratic basis—by means of reorganizing our productive enterprises—to support those reforms and that combination of property ownership and distribution of resources and products that best serve our social, cultural, and ecological needs.

Economic Democracy at the Workplace and in Society

The change we propose—as a new and major addition to the agenda for social change—is to occur inside production: inside the enterprises and other institutions (households, the state, schools, and so on) that produce and distribute the goods and services upon which society depends. Wherever production occurs, the workers must become collectively their own bosses, their own board of directors. Everyone's job description would change: in addition to your specific task, you would be required to participate fully in designing and running the enterprise. Decisions once made by private corporate boards of directors or state officials—what, how, and where to produce and how to use the revenues received—would instead be made collectively and democratically by the workers themselves. Education would be redesigned to train all persons in the leadership and control functions now reserved for elites.

Such a reorganization of production would finally and genuinely subordinate the state to the people. The state's revenues (e.g., taxes) would depend on what the workers gave the state out of the revenues of the workers' enterprises. Instead of capitalists (a small minority) funding and thereby controlling the state, the majority—workers—would finally gain that crucial social position.

Of course, workplace democracy must intertwine with community democracy in the residential locations that are mutually interactive and interdependent with work locations. Economic and political democracy need and would reinforce one another. Self-directed workers and self-directed community residents must democratically share decision making at both locations. Local, regional, and national state institutions will henceforth incorporate shared democratic decision making between workplace and residence-based communities. Such institutions would draw upon the lessons of past capitalist and socialist experiences.

Benefits of Workplace Democracy

When workforce and residential communities decide together how the economy evolves, the results will differ sharply from the results of capitalism. Workplace democracy would not, for example, move production to other countries as capitalist corporations have done. Workers' self-directed enterprises would not pay a few top managers huge salaries and bonuses while most workers' paychecks and benefits stagnate. Worker-run enterprises sharing democratic decision making with surrounding communities would not install toxic and dangerous technologies as capitalist enterprises often do to earn more profits. They would, however, be far more likely to provide daycare, elder care, and other supportive services. For the first time in human history, societies could democratically rethink and reorganize the time they devote to work, play, relationships, and cultural activities. Instead of complaining that we lack time for the most meaningful parts of our lives, we could together decide to reduce labor time, to concentrate on the consumer goods we really need, and thereby to allow more time for the important relationships in our lives. We might thereby overcome the divisions and tensions (often defined in racial, gender, ethnic, religious, and other terms) that capitalism imposes on populations by splitting them into fully employed, partly employed, and contingent laborers, and those excluded from the labor market.

A new society can be built on the basis of democratically reorganizing our workplaces, where adults spend most of their lifetimes. Over recent centuries, the human community dispensed with kings, emperors, and czars in favor of representative (and partly democratic) parliaments and congresses. The fears and warnings of disaster by those opposed to that social change were proved wrong by history. The change we advocate today takes democracy another necessary and logical step: into the workplace. Those who fear (and threaten) that it will not work will likewise be proven wrong.

An Immediate and Realistic Project

There are practical and popular steps we can take now toward realizing economic democracy. Against massive, wasteful, and cruel unemployment and poverty, we propose a new kind of public works program. It would differ from the federal employment programs of the New Deal (when FDR hired millions of the unemployed) in two ways. First, it would focus on a "green" and support service agenda. By "green" we mean massively improving the sustainability of workplace and residential communities by, for example, building energy-saving mass transportation systems, restoring waterways and forests, weatherizing residential and workplace structures, and establishing systematic antipollution programs. By "support service" we mean new programs of children's daycare and elder care to help all families coping with the conditions of work and demographics in the United States today.

However, the new kind of public works program we propose would differ even more dramatically from all past public works projects. Instead of paying a weekly dole to the unemployed, our public works program would emphasize providing the unemployed with the funds to begin and build their own cooperative, self-directed democratic enterprises.

The gains from this project are many. The ecological benefits alone would make this the most massive environmental program in US history. Economic benefits would be huge as millions of citizens restore self-esteem damaged by unemployment and earn incomes enabling them to keep their homes and, by their purchases, provide jobs to others. Public employment at decent pay for all would go a long way toward lessening the gender, racial, and other job discriminations now dividing our people.

A special benefit would be a new freedom of choice for Americans. As a people, we could see, examine, and evaluate the benefits of working inside enterprises where every worker is both employee and employer, where decisions are debated and decided democratically. For the first time in US history, we will begin to enjoy this freedom of choice: working in a top-down, hierarchically organized capitalist corporation or working in a cooperative, democratic workplace. The future of our society will then depend on how Americans make that choice, and that is how the future of a democratic society should be determined.

The Rich Roots Sustaining this Project

Americans have been interested in and built various kinds of cooperative enterprises—more or less noncapitalist enterprises—throughout our history. The idea of building a "cooperative commonwealth" has repeatedly attracted many. Today, an estimated 13.7 million Americans work in 11,400 Employee Stock Ownership Plan companies (ESOPs), in which employees own part or all of those companies. So-called not-for-profit enterprises abound across the United States in many different fields. Some alternative, noncapitalist enterprises are inspired by the example of Mondragon, a federation of over 250 democratically run worker cooperatives employing 100,000 based in Spain's Basque region. Since their wages are determined by the worker-owners themselves, the ratio between the wages of those with mostly executive functions and others average 5:1 as compared to the 475:1 in contemporary capitalist multinational corporations.

The US cooperative movement stretches today from the Arizmendi Association (San Francisco Bay) to the Vida Verde Cleaning Cooperative (Massachusetts) to Black Star Collective Pub and Brewery (Austin, Texas), to name just a few. The largest conglomerate of worker-owned cooperatives in the United States is the "Evergreen Cooperative Model" (or "Cleveland Model"), consisting of the Evergreen Cooperative Laundry

(ECL), the Ohio Cooperative Solar (OCS), and the Green City Growers. These cooperatives share (a) common ownership and democracy at the workplace, (b) ecological commitments to produce sustainable goods and services and create "green jobs," and (c) new kinds of communal economic planning, mediated by "anchor institutions" (e.g., universities, nonprofit hospitals), community foundations, development funds, state-owned banks or employee ownership banks, and so on. Such cooperatives are generating new concepts and kinds of economic development.

These examples' varying kinds and degrees of democracy in the workplace all attest to an immense social basis of interest in and commitment to noncapitalist forms of work. Contrary to much popular mythology, there is a solid popular base for a movement to expand and diversify the options for organizing production. Workplace democracy responds to deep needs and desires.

Economic Democracy, Not Austerity or Keynesian Growth

May 10, 2012

Recent defeats of Dutch, Greek, and French governing parties show rising opposition to their austerity policies. Across Europe and North America, similar oppositions mount. Bailing out large financial and other corporations with borrowed money has been the almost universal government plan for coping with global capitalist crisis. The result—rising government deficits and debts—was followed by "austerity policies" to reduce those deficits and debts. After suffering a crisis and then bailouts that bypassed them to favor major corporations, people now face austerity cutbacks of government jobs and services to offset the bailouts' costs. As opposition mounts, will it seek Keynesian "growth" or go beyond capitalism to economic democracy?

Keynesianism (expansionary state economic intervention) never was capitalists' preferred policy for capitalism's recurring recessions and depressions. Their Plan A was government borrowing to bail out major financial and other corporations followed by "austerity policies." Austerity repays the costs of bailouts by siphoning money away from (cutting) government jobs and services. Only when anticapitalist movements threaten from below, as in the 1930s, do anxious capitalists abandon Plan A and shift to Plan B—eventually formalized as Keynesianism. Through government spending, Keynesian policies claim credit for jobs and income "growth" and aim to keep political control away from anticapitalist forces. Keynesianism's dependence on radicals' pressure from below explains its strength in the 1930s versus its weakness today.

Capitalists prefer austerity for many reasons. Because universal suffrage allows politics to undo capitalism's consequences such as unequal wealth, income, and power distributions, capitalists worry about how far universal suffrage will go. Majorities may, during crises, reject bailouts and austerity. The Greek and French just did. They may then demand Keynesian "growth" through government jobs and income and wealth redistribution. Or they may demand transition beyond capitalism to democratize their economies by socializing means of production, planning the economy, and transforming enterprises into self-directed worker collectives. No wonder that conservative mainstream economics (so-called neoclassical economics) celebrates capitalism as a self-healing system requiring no government intervention.

Keynesianism also frustrates crisis mechanisms that discipline workers to capitalists' advantage. Rising unemployment makes worried jobholders accept reduced wages, benefits, and job security: good news for employers. As falling wages reduce costs for surviving capitalists, they anticipate rising profit opportunities. They will then invest, renewing growth and prosperity. That's how most capitalists prefer to "let the market work through" economic crises.

In contrast, Keynesian government spending lessens unemployment and thus slows or prevents falling wages and benefits. It also usually requires increased state borrowing, money supply, and/or taxes on capitalists and the rich. They oppose such tax increases, balk at lending to ever-more-indebted governments and worry about inflationary risks posed by money supply increases.

"Austerity policies" (capitalists' Plan A) aim to pay for bailouts while reducing government deficits. They may also include some state charity for the worst victims of crisis. Republicans and Democrats (or, in Europe, conservatives and social democrats) squabble over how much charity to provide alongside the austerity they impose.

Keynesianism is capitalists' Plan B when radicalized and organized workers demand systematic entitlement, not charity, and threaten capitalism itself. In the United States during the 1930s, successful mass unionization by the Congress of Industrial Organizations and mass radicalization by socialist and communist parties built social movements with strong anticapitalist components. In response, President Franklin Delano Roosevelt offered a deal. Instead of austerity, he provided unprecedented government services to people (today perhaps called a "growth" plan). He established the Social Security and unemployment compensation systems and created and filled over 12 million federal jobs for the unemployed. Despite three times today's level of unemployment and a worse federal budget crisis, FDR funded greatly expanded government public services. President Obama plans to reduce Social Security and never mentions a federal hiring program. Capitalism then faced a powerful threat from below; today it does not (yet).

FDR funded his deal by taxing corporations and the rich and partly by borrowing from them (the lesser evil for them). Many of them agreed because they, too, feared the anticapitalist opposition. FDR persuaded most of the left, in exchange for expanded state services and jobs, to downplay anticapitalism. Many abandoned "socialism" as a goal; some redefined it to be what FDR proposed. FDR's deal built an alliance that won four consecutive presidential elections.

Keynesianism—the formalized theory and policies drawn from John Maynard Keynes's work in 1930s Britain—developed after FDR's deal. It prompted a revised understanding of the Great Depression. Attention shifted away from how anticapitalist and working-class pressure from below reoriented FDR's policies. Instead, smart economists and astute politicians were depicted using Keynes's "brilliant new economics" to moderate, manage, and exit capitalist crises.

After 1945, corporations and the rich still supported Keynesian government spending (they feared depression's return), but they got reduced taxes for themselves. They also got some shift in government expenditures from social services to more capitalist-friendly defense and infrastructural improvements. Keynesians also mostly joined neoclassical economists in dismissing Marx's anticapitalist economics. Capitalism's crises, they insisted, were well understood and managed (by Keynesianism). They were mere temporary blips punctuating capitalism's prosperous growth. Anticapitalism was theoretically outmoded and politically suspect in Cold War times.

Keynesian economics was, for enthusiasts, superior to the mainstream orthodoxy that had always endorsed austerity policies for crises. Keynesianism became the new orthodoxy from the 1930s to the 1970s. Then, a capitalist boom returned dominance to neoclassical economics (renamed neoliberalism). Even after the 2007 crisis hit, Keynesians (e.g., Paul Krugman) have so far failed to regain policy-making dominance.

The "great" debate between neoclassical and Keynesian economists is neither great nor much of a debate. Both sides endorse, celebrate, and defend capitalism. Their "debate"—between Plans B and A, more or less government intervention to sustain capitalism—periodically revives as a substitute for seriously engaging with critical economic theories, anticapitalist social movements, and their demands for economic democracy. The debate between austerity and growth policies is a sideshow for the main event: capitalism's weakening battles with its own contradictions and with looming demands for transition beyond capitalism to economic democracy.

Yes, There Is an Alternative to Capitalism: Mondragon Shows the Way

June 24, 2012

There is no alternative ("Tina") to capitalism?

Really? We are to believe, with former British prime minister Margaret Thatcher, that an economic system with endlessly repeated cycles, costly bailouts for financiers, and now austerity for most people is the best human beings can do? Capitalism's recurring tendencies toward extreme and deepening inequalities of income, wealth, and political and cultural power require resignation and acceptance—because there is no alternative?

I understand why such a system's leaders would like us to believe in Tina. But why would others?

Of course, alternatives exist; they always do. Every society chooses—consciously or not, democratically or not—among alternative ways to organize the production and distribution of the goods and services that make individual and social life possible.

Modern societies have mostly chosen a capitalist organization of production. In capitalism, private owners establish enterprises and select their directors who decide what, how, and where to produce and what to do with the net revenues from selling the output. This small handful of people makes all those economic decisions for the majority of people—who do most of the actual productive work. The majority must accept and live with the results of all the directorial decisions made by the major shareholders and the boards of directors they select. This latter also select their own replacements.

Capitalism thus entails and reproduces a highly undemocratic organization of production inside enterprises. Tina believers insist that no alternatives to such capitalist organizations of production exist or could work nearly so well, in terms of outputs, efficiency, and labor processes. The falsity of that claim is easily shown. Indeed, I was shown it a few weeks ago and would like to sketch it for you here.

In May 2012, I had occasion to visit the city of Arrasate-Mondragon, in the Basque region of Spain. It is the headquarters of the Mondragon Corporation (MC), a stunningly successful alternative to the capitalist organization of production.

MC is composed of many cooperative enterprises grouped into four areas: industry, finance, retail, and knowledge. In each enterprise, the co-op members (averaging 80–85 percent of all workers per enterprise) collectively own and direct the enterprise. Through an annual general assembly the workers choose and employ a managing director and retain the power to make all the basic decisions of the enterprise (what, how, and where to produce and what to do with the profits).

As each enterprise is a constituent of the MC as a whole, its members must confer and decide with all other enterprise members what general rules will govern MC and all its constituent enterprises. In short, MC worker-members collectively choose, hire, and fire the directors, whereas in capitalist enterprises the reverse occurs. One of the cooperatively and democratically adopted rules governing the MC limits top-paid worker/members to earning 6.5 times the lowest-paid workers. Nothing more dramatically demonstrates the differences distinguishing this from the capitalist alternative organization of enterprises. (In US corporations, chief executive officers can expect to be paid 400 times an average worker's salary—a rate that has increased twentyfold since 1965.)

Given that MC has 85,000 members (from its 2010 annual report), its pay equity rules can and do contribute to a larger society with far greater income and wealth equality than is typical in societies that have chosen capitalist organizations of enterprises. Over 43 percent of MC members are women, whose equal powers with male members likewise influence gender relations in society different from capitalist enterprises.

MC displays a commitment to job security I have rarely encountered in capitalist enterprises: it operates across, as well as within, particular cooperative enterprises. MC members created a system to move workers from enterprises needing fewer to those needing more workers—in a remarkably open, transparent, rule-governed way and with associated travel and other subsidies to minimize hardship. This security-focused system has transformed the lives of workers, their families, and their communities, also in unique ways.

The MC rule that all enterprises are to source their inputs from the best and least costly producers—whether or not those are also MC enterprises—has kept MC at the cutting edge of new technologies. Likewise, the decision to use a portion of each member enterprise's net revenue as a fund for research and development has funded impressive new product development. Research and development within MC now employs 800 people with a budget over $75 million. In 2010, 21.4 percent of sales of MC industries were new products and services that did not exist five years earlier. In addition, MC established and has expanded Mondragon University; it enrolled over 3,400 students in its 2009–2010 academic year, and its degree programs conform to the requirements of the European framework of higher education. Total student enrollment in all its educational centers in 2010 was 9,282.

The largest corporation in the Basque region, MC is also one of Spain's biggest corporations (in terms of sales or employment). Far better than merely surviving since its founding in 1956, MC has grown dramatically. Along the way, it added a cooperative bank, Caja Laboral (holding almost $25 billion in deposits in 2010). And MC has expanded internationally, now operating over seventy-seven businesses outside Spain. MC has proven itself able to grow and prosper as an alternative to—and competitor of—capitalist organizations of enterprise.

During my visit, in random encounters with workers who answered my questions about their jobs, powers, and benefits as cooperative members, I found a familiarity with and sense of responsibility for the enterprise as a whole that I associate only with top managers and directors in capitalist enterprises. The easy conversation (including disagreement)—for instance, between assembly-line workers and top managers inside the Fagor washing-machine factory we inspected—was similarly remarkable.

Our MC host on the visit reminded us twice that theirs is a cooperative business with all sorts of problems: "We are not some paradise, but rather a family of cooperative enterprises struggling to build a different kind of life around a different way of working."

Nonetheless, given the performance of Spanish capitalism these days—25 percent unemployment, a broken banking system, and government-imposed austerity (as if there were no alternative to that either)—MC seems a welcome oasis in a capitalist desert.

System Change, or There and Back Again: Capitalism, Socialism, Fascism

November 17, 2014

Societies where capitalist economic systems prevail today confront government gridlock. Facing serious and deepening economic problems, even when their leaders can sometimes agree on particular policies, the policies are frequently inadequate to solve the problems. Therefore, questions challenging capitalism occur now more often and more influentially than they have for many decades. Renewed interest in systemic changes, both socialist and fascist, agitates many societies.

Historically, capitalism's problems often led its leaders (economic and political) to make adjustments and changes in income and wealth distributions, government regulations affecting enterprises and markets, international relations, and so on. For example, progressive income taxes and minimum wages were legislated, antimonopoly rules were enacted, and tariffs and foreign wars were imposed. Sometimes, capitalism's leaders lacked the capacity to execute such solutions or the solutions proved insufficient. Then, more systemic changes arrived on social agendas. The two most important of such systemic changes were traditional socialism and fascism. These were achieved by peaceful or violent means, by parliamentary reforms or by revolutions, depending on the circumstances of time and place.

By traditional socialism, we mean here the sorts of systemic changes associated with the Soviet Union and China, but also with European social democracy. By fascism, we mean the sorts of systems exemplified by Mussolini's Italy and Hitler's Germany.

Capitalism's deepest problems sooner or later drove political and economic groups within its national boundaries to pursue what they saw as systemic solutions. By that, they meant first and foremost changing the state and integrating it much more closely with enterprises (factories, offices, and stores). Transitions to traditional socialism and fascism have historically been the major different, alternative forms of such systemic solutions. Neither has yet proved a durable solution. Modern societies have returned from fascist or traditional socialist periods to forms of capitalism that reestablished a greater distance between enterprises and the state. Yet those forms of capitalism keep generating business cycles and inequalities that eventually become the serious problems that bring yet another turn toward traditional socialism or fascism. The deepening problems of the early twenty-first century raise the distinct possibility of another cycle of fascist and traditional socialist experiments or, as we shall show, perhaps a genuinely new solution.

In fascist solutions, problems of unemployed labor and insufficient profitable outlets for capital (with the attendant economic stagnation and social conflicts) prompt massive state intervention. The state destroys or displaces the traditional leftist political parties and labor unions (often with violence, imprisonment, and exile). It then substitutes various combinations of its own agencies (usually in the leading roles) supported by and integrated with nationalist and socially conservative parties and movements. Government leaders then organize close relationships with leading private capitalist groups to coordinate an "organic" direction to the nation's economic and social development. Those close, collaborative relationships organize full employment at wage levels that effectively guarantee capitalists' profits and government revenues. Fascistic government-capitalist relationships also manage the necessary tax structures, prices and currency values to support those objectives. Last, government revenues are coordinated with corporate production and investment decisions to serve fascism's noneconomic goals (often military, diplomatic, nationalist, or expansionary).

In the traditional socialist solution, problems of unemployment, economic stagnation, and mounting social conflict also prompt massive state intervention. However, socialist state intervention has very different goals and modalities especially in relation to private capitalist enterprises. In the cases of socialist governments in Soviet Russia and the People's Republic of China (PRC), the forces that brought them into power drove them to dispossess most private owners of capitalist enterprises, thereby socializing them. They removed most private capitalists from their positions within those enterprises. In their place, traditional socialist governments placed one set of state officials as enterprise operators. Those state officials were to operate the socialized means of production for the benefit of the whole people and as their agent. Traditional socialists understood that change of ownership of the means of production as a central definition and component of socialism. Socialist state officials thus replaced the capitalist enterprises' boards of directors formerly elected by private owners of the means of production. In the case of noncapitalist means of production (owned and operated by individual peasants, craft-persons, etc.), individual private property was often preserved or even expanded (as when the post-1917 Soviet government distributed land as private property to peasants).

Once in power, traditional socialists also assigned another set of government officials the tasks of planning and administering the distribution of productive resources and outputs. Centralized plans sometimes replaced market exchanges as the economy's mechanism of distribution. More typically, those plans usually included major segments of the economy where market exchanges continued to serve as distribution mechanisms. Prices in markets were sometimes set by central planners and sometimes allowed to be determined by demand and supply conditions. Traditional socialist government revenues (from state enterprise profits, taxes, etc.) were spent on priorities such as economic growth, military security and public services (education, health care, and so on).

German fascism lasted twelve years, while Italian fascism endured twice as long. The Soviet Union lasted seventy years until its traditional socialism collapsed in 1989, while the PRC continues in its sixty-fifth year. Recently, the PRC permitted and enabled a vastly enlarged private capitalist sector. In that way, the PRC moves toward Western European–style socialism. The latter entails a largely private capitalist economic system: private ownership of the means of production prevails with markets as the chief means of distributing resources and products. The government owns and operates some industrial groups (perhaps the "commanding heights" of the economy), usually imposes fairly high taxes to fund considerable government services, regulates markets significantly, and manipulates fiscal and monetary policies to manage capitalist cycles through an active Keynesian interventionism.

Both fascism and traditional socialism have their left and right forms. Left forms will usually be the more willing to lessen inequalities of wealth and income, limit nationalism and war, and tolerate secularism. Right forms will usually be less interested in and more tolerant of unequal wealth and income distributions and more likely to celebrate nationalism, allow or pursue military engagements, and embrace conservative religion.

In various forms, growing masses of people in Western Europe, North America, and Japan now confront a capitalism whose long-term, historic changes present deepening problems while diminishing the resources needed for solutions. The capitalism born and developed first in those areas concentrated its production and distribution facilities there from the 1750s to the 1970s. That capitalism condemned the "Third World" to struggle for centuries to escape the awful effects of its global division of labor and consumption.

Over the same years, in protracted struggles, workers in capitalism's centers forced capitalists to raise real wages as partial compensation for rising levels of exploitation on the job and growing wealth and income inequalities. But by the 1970s, jet travel and modern telecommunications enabled the profitable relocation of capitalist enterprises from Western Europe, North America, and Japan to much lower wage nations in Asia, Latin America, and Africa. The jobs, benefits, security of employment, and wage incomes in the former regions are falling, while they are rising in the latter regions. The combined result is a global decline in labor's share of total income, record corporate profits, and stock market booms alongside deepening economic inequality and problems for Western Europe, North America, and Japan. Exemplifying this historic process in the starkest terms, Detroit, once the showplace of Western capitalism, is now a largely abandoned economic wasteland. It lost well over half the population it had in the 1960s and is undergoing the largest urban bankruptcy in US history.

Such a capitalist history provokes questions and challenges to capitalism. Piecemeal reforms, marginal electoral shifts, and reformulated monetary and fiscal policies seem too little and too late for problems that go to the heart of capitalism as a system. Fascism and traditional socialism are returning to popular agendas, at first in fits, starts—and many disguises. Both have deep antipathies to overcome or maneuver around. In Greece, mass support for conventional, center-right, and center-left political parties evaporates in favor especially of a new leftist party, Syriza, wavering between traditional socialism and new socialist directions. In part to counter this leftward political surge, a fascistic alternative (Golden Dawn) arises in Greek politics. The development is sharpest and clearest in Greece likely because the crisis has been worse there for the mass of people than elsewhere. But similar evolutions are under way in other European countries (e.g., the French socialist party's surge provokes both action to its left as the party's anti-austerity commitments fade, and action on its right with rising votes for the fascistic National Front). In the United States, too, the Tea Party and Occupy movements illustrate comparable developments, albeit much less developed and less self-conscious.

Yet capitalism's second major crisis in the last seventy-five years will not invite the same fascistic and traditional socialistic responses provoked by its first. What differs now are the conclusions widely drawn from the histories of both fascism and traditional socialism since the 1930s. Too many aspects of fascism function as object lessons of what must not be done again. Some of the aspects of traditional socialism function similarly. Where states took over ownership and operation of industrial (and eventually also much agricultural) production, the statism and then implosions of Soviet and Eastern European socialisms and their parallels within the PRC weaken the appeal of traditional socialism. Those qualities also reinforced the last half-century's critiques and demonization of those socialisms.

In the more moderate traditional socialisms of Western Europe, the crisis since 2007 exposed their capitulation to dominant neoliberal capitalism. In Greece and now again in France, traditional socialist parties rode into power as enemies of austerity. European governments had mostly responded to the capitalist crisis with bailouts of banks, large corporations, and stock markets, and temporary, debt-financed stimuli. These were to be paid for by austerity (higher taxes and lower social spending) imposed on the mass of people. Once in power, traditional socialist parties proved unable or unwilling to stop austerity, let alone reverse that policy and make the capitalists who produced the crisis pay to overcome it. Such failures destroyed the Greek Socialist Party and now threaten the French, among others. Traditional European socialism thus joins the Soviet model in declining as an option for those disaffected by capitalism.

So perhaps the key question becomes whether genuinely new and different sorts of fascism and socialism are or could be emerging. Will they be means for people in Western Europe, North America, and Japan to escape the fate of a capitalism leaving for new, more profitable fields for investment? Will new fascisms and socialisms shape those regions' struggles against the new global division of labor organized by capitalism as it moves production to the East and the South?

In the United States, larger capitalists increasingly buy the two major political parties, their apparatuses and candidates, and make office holders dependent on armies of their lobbyists and their immense public relations budgets. A gradual merger of capitalists and government is thereby coming into being, one that may formalize new leading institutions to overcome capitalism's current problems. The biggest problem for such a new fascistic formation would be the mass base it would need to cultivate, organize, and sustain. Fundamentalist religions might play such a role. Yet the nagging question remains: Would not the global imperatives of the capitalist partners in such a fascism continue the relocation of production that lies at the root of such societies' deepening economic problems?

In the United States, a new kind of socialism may also be emerging. It is based on an insistence that the macro dimensions of traditional socialism—an emphasis on ownership of the means of production and economic planning—be grounded on and interdependent with a micro-level reorganization of enterprises. Enterprises are to be democratized, ending the typical top-down hierarchical capitalist organization (major shareholders select the board of directors that hires the managers and mass of laborers and makes all the key enterprise decisions). Worker self-directed enterprises (WSDEs) would become the mass social and economic base where wealth is generated and revenues are provided to the state. Conjointly with democratically organized residential communities that are interdependent with the WSDEs, local decisions would be codetermined and all state actions held accountable. The state would facilitate economic, political, and cultural coordination among WSDEs and residential communities, but the state power arising from that facilitation function would be ultimately determined by, accountable to, and balanced by the economic and political power organized horizontally at the base of society.

The mass inclusion at the base would emerge from the structure of WSDEs and their interdependent democratic residential communities. In both the WSDEs and those communities, all individuals—as workers in WSDEs and as citizens in residential communities—participate democratically in making the key decisions. These include deciding what, how, and where to produce and what to do with the surpluses and profits generated in and by the WSDEs.

The location of production would be decided democratically, altering the geographic division of labor. The technologies would be decided democratically, altering the ecological and environmental dimensions of production. The objects of investment would be decided democratically, altering the society's development path. Capitalism's abandonment of Western Europe, North America, and Japan would come to an end because capitalism itself would be displaced as the prevailing economic system governing both enterprise organization and its relation to the state.

Silence Is Louder Than Their Words: Effective Economic Policies Neither Candidate Advocates

October 31, 2012

The 2012 presidential election arrives five years into a severe economic crisis that both Republican and Democratic policies failed to end. The latest unemployment rate (7.8 percent) is not even halfway back to the 2007 level of 5 percent, from the crisis high of 10 percent. Jobs have not recovered, but corporate profits and the stock market did, thanks to huge government bailouts. Average real weekly earnings of most workers fell 2.4 percent from October 2010 to the present—during what business, media, and political leaders enjoyed calling a "modest recovery." That 2.4 percent real wage drop means that workers lost the equivalent of six days' wages (one week and one day) per year between late 2010 and now. Income and wealth inequalities thus deepened further across the crisis. No end of these developments is in sight.

Do Barack Obama and Mitt Romney debate alternative policies to overcome this enduring economic crisis, given the failed policies to date? No. First, they exclude smaller party candidates who do advocate some alternative policies. Second, they exclude key alternatives from their statements and arguments.

Here are a few of those alternative policy options that Obama and Romney agree to ignore.

In the last comparably severe economic crisis, a key policy was federal employment. Franklin D. Roosevelt created and filled over 12 million government jobs from 1934 to 1941 (not counting military employment that exploded thereafter). Obama and Romney act as if Roosevelt's policy never happened.

Under Italy's Marcora Law (successfully functioning since 1985), unemployed Italians can choose either to take weekly unemployment checks or to receive all of them in an up-front lump sum payment. To qualify for the lump sum, they must combine with at least nine other unemployed persons' similarly chosen lump sums to form the start-up capital of a new cooperative enterprise run entirely by those workers. Such workers' self-directed enterprises (WSDEs) have been durable job creators that inspire exemplary levels of work, commitment, and productivity. Neither Obama nor Romney has said one word about this employment policy alternative.

Mondragon Corporation—a collective of over 100 cooperatives and WSDEs—began in 1956 and is now among Spain's ten largest corporations. Most of its more than 100,000 workers are also members, and they make all the basic decisions governing the corporation. They prioritize job creation and job retention rather than profits. Spain's Basque region—where Mondragon cooperatives are concentrated—has an unemployment rate around 11 percent, while the rate for the mostly capitalist enterprises in the rest of Spain now exceeds 25 percent. A collaboration or alliance with the Mondragon Corporation to apply its lessons in the United States is another policy option that Obama and Romney never discuss.

The United States has long included many workers' or producers' cooperatives—rough equivalents of WSDEs. Their accumulated experience and know-how are invaluable resources for alternative policies. The model for this might be the Small Business Administration, long active in the United States. The Small Business Administration assists small capitalist businesses to form, grow, survive, and compete with big business, thereby preserving small business jobs. A parallel WSDE administration could do likewise for existing and new WSDEs. Besides reducing unemployment, Americans would acquire an important new freedom of choice. They could practically compare democratic self-governance inside WSDEs with traditional top-down hierarchically organized capitalist enterprises. Once again, Obama and Romney say nothing about any of this.

The alternative policies listed above would cost money to implement properly. Presidential candidates could and should debate alternative policies to raise the needed revenues. For example, government could return federal tax rates on business profits and on high personal incomes to their levels in the 1950s and 1960s. Rates were then much higher (and loopholes fewer) than today. Higher rates were justified then to provide the means needed to rebuild the US economy after the damages and dislocations of the Great Depression and World War II. Individuals and businesses were to contribute in proportion to their capabilities. The same justification applies now to rebuild from the damage done by the last thirty years of deepening economic inequality and the extreme economic crisis since 2007. Returning to the higher individual income tax rates of the 1950s and 1960s would tap the richest, most-able-to-pay Americans. Given the trillions now hoarded by businesses unwilling to invest in a crisis-ridden economy, no great fall in business investment would result from taxing them more. These revenue increases could pay for the four policies above and further stimulate the economy. Obama and Romney ignore this tax option even though it would lower federal budget deficits that both candidates claim are a major concern.

The last alternative policy example could raise significant new revenues for the government to use to stimulate economic growth. This alternative policy would simultaneously reduce gross injustice in our tax system. In the United States, cities and towns rely on property taxes. Land, housing structures, commercial and industrial buildings, and cars are major kinds of property subject to a tax on their values; property exempted from such a tax includes stocks, bonds, and all other securities. If you own a $100,000 house, an annual property tax is required, but if you sell it and buy $100,000 in stocks, no property tax is required. This property tax system favors the tiny minority of US citizens who own the majority of stocks and bonds. An alternative policy (long overdue) would extend property taxes in the United States to include stocks and bonds. A federal property tax on stocks and bonds would raise many billions from those most able to pay, beneficiaries of the property tax system's gross injustice. Such a federal property tax could also lower the government's deficit. Obama and Romney exclude any mention of this policy alternative.

The likely direction of the US economy is suggested more by the policy alternatives that Obama and Romney ignore than by their statements and debates—until a social movement for basic change challenges their silences from below.

The Fall of the Berlin Wall and the Failures of Actually Existing Economic Systems

November 12, 2014

Hype went wild coming into last week's twenty-fifth anniversary of the fall of the Berlin Wall. "Freedom" had been achieved. The German Democratic Republic (GDR), or what Western media preferred to call communist East Germany, had been rejected. Its hated official spying on its people—the massive Stasi apparatus—could not continue. Liberty and prosperity would and did arrive as the country rejoined the "free world." The people had peacefully overthrown actually existing socialism and returned to capitalism. No one could miss that (officially hyped) interpretation of the fall of the Wall. Yet it is hardly the only one, although that was rarely admitted.

True enough, a repressive regime collapsed amid promises of liberty and prosperity. That happened across much of Eastern Europe. Yet liberty and prosperity mostly proved elusive to achieve or keep. Where freedom ushered capitalism back in, capitalism quickly took over and imposed its heavy burdens. Euphoria, like springtime, never lasted.

Reintegrating into European capitalism through German reunification has not been the blessing so many Germans imagined back in 1989. They gave up secure jobs, incomes, and generous social services. Retrieving freedom cost them heavily. The capitalism they rejoined has serious economic problems that keep constricting job opportunities and security, social services, and future prospects. Gains in some freedoms keep costing losses of others.

Official and other procapitalist enthusiasts marked the twenty-fifth anniversary with rather suspicious exaggerations. Perhaps they celebrated so loudly to drown out—like drunks with alcohol—their rising anxiety about what capitalist freedom keeps delivering.

A better way to celebrate would be to honestly assess and extract useful lessons from the GDR's experiment (1949–1990) in going beyond capitalism. Why did it collapse? What will future experiments in moving beyond capitalism need to do differently to survive and prosper? What does the Wall's fall—and parallel implosions of other socialisms—really mean?

Some, like former United Kingdom prime minister Margaret Thatcher, want socialist experiments to fail to "prove" that no workable alternative to capitalism exists. Yet that interpretation has faded with capitalism's post-1990 evolution. The global capitalism that surged then depended on unsustainable debt bubbles and sharply deepened wealth and income inequalities. The 2008 global collapse and subsequent austerity is shredding social safety nets everywhere. Ever-harsher versions of capitalism provoke mass movements with powerful currents critical of capitalism. Interest in Marx and Marxism renews. As was always true, capitalism's own contradictions generate interest in and experiments with different forms of socialism.

The fall of the Wall and the GDR shows the limits of its particular experiment in postcapitalism. Nor should anyone be surprised that some experiments in transition from one economic system to another proved unsustainable. That same lesson is taught by history's previous transitions.

Capitalism emerged similarly from feudalism in Europe. For example, lords and serfs sometimes confronted towns experimenting with a nonfeudal production arrangement. Merchants or others were using accumulated wealth as means to hire workers. The latter, often refugees from feudal manors, survived in a new way: selling their capacity to work. The wealthy got wealthier by selling the outputs in emerging markets and taking the profits.

Such experiments in capitalism were sometimes short, destroyed by surrounding feudal lords displeased by the towns' independence, greedy for their wealth, or both. Other capitalist experiments lasted longer but then disappeared for lack of raw materials, sufficient workers, or adequate markets or by attacks from feudal lords or capitalist competitors and so on. Europe's transition from feudalism to capitalism took centuries and involved many experiments that dissolved ("revolutions" followed by "restorations"). Eventually, evolving conditions—and lessons drawn from earlier, failed capitalist experiments—enabled experiments that succeeded and grew into today's capitalism. The transition from capitalism to socialism might well display comparable fits and starts.

Here then is an interpretation of the Wall's fall that draws useful lessons from the GDR's forty-one years. The GDR defined socialism as (a) transferring ownership and operation of most industry from private persons to state officials, and (b) giving government economic planning dominance over markets and prices. The state took over production and distribution. It thereby gathered extraordinary power with too few limits and too little counterbalancing power from below. While economic growth was impressive, it failed badly to engage its people in a commitment to the socialist system. The GDR's lack of personal liberties, consumer goods, and political freedoms built indifference and hostility to its socialist experiment.

Is the lesson then that adding political democracy could have saved the GDR? Not necessarily: If political parties had proliferated, what would have prevented a GDR-type government from controlling and manipulating them? What would have prevented political democracy from being as merely formal in the GDR as it is in most capitalist countries today, where multiple parties have hardly prevented capitalists from effectively dominating parties and politicians?

One lesson to draw from the GDR's history is that if socialist societies are to be run by, of, and for the people, then the people have to be in charge and that includes within the economy. Democracies (both capitalist and socialist) will remain merely formal when the economy continues to be run by small self-selecting minorities (in capitalism, major shareholders and the boards of directors they select, and in socialism, state officials). Those minorities will dominate until they are overthrown.

What might have saved the GDR, then, would have required going well beyond nationalizing industrial means of production and raising plans over markets. It would have had to democratize the enterprises (factories, offices, and stores) that produce and distribute goods and services. But it never dared to do that. The GDR's workers did not democratically produce and distribute—and thereby control—the economy's surpluses at their points of origin in enterprises. They did not therefore control the funds that enabled the state to function. Had enterprises been democratized, they would have held the means to limit and balance the state's power.

The GDR's workers might then have fought to preserve a socialism that had made them the operators and decision makers in and of their enterprises. Excesses of state power might have been stopped had workers in democratized enterprises used their enterprises' wealth and power to such ends. In this alternative interpretation of the fall of the Berlin Wall, when the GDR's experiment in socialism stopped at nationalization of industry and planned economy—"Germany is not yet ready for more"—they got it backward. Only by going further—by democratically reorganizing enterprises—might their experiment in socialism have survived.

Economic Prosperity and Economic Democracy: The Worker Co-op Solution

January 12, 2014

Among factors impeding formation of an organized, politically effective new left in the United States are deep frustrations among activists interested in doing that. The decline since the 1970s (and since 2008 especially) of capitalism's ability to "deliver the goods" to most citizens has opened many minds to question, criticize, and challenge the capitalist system. The remarkable Pew Research Center poll of December 2011 showed large percentages of Americans favorably disposed toward socialism. Many more would agree today. Yet left activists are increasingly frustrated by their lack of a viable systemic alternative that could attract those disaffected from capitalism.

Leftists are further frustrated because the traditional socialist alternatives fail to inspire the public or even mobilize leftists themselves. The implosions of Soviet and Eastern European socialisms, coupled with major shifts in China and beyond, have fueled that frustration. So too, in different ways, did Western European socialist parties' embraces of neoliberalism since the 1970s and austerity policies since 2007–2008. The Greek socialist party's collapse and likewise serious declines in electoral support for the German and other socialist parties reflect frustrations with the traditional socialisms they advocate.

Traditional socialist programs of major government economic intervention (through varying mixtures of regulation of enterprises and markets, state ownership and operation of enterprises, central planning, etc.) no longer rally much support. When sometimes they seem to (e.g., France's last presidential and legislative elections), traditional socialism proves thinly rhetorical and symbolic. Because French socialists failed to define or pursue a genuine alternative to a deeply unpopular capitalism, their support melted quickly.

Audiences offered traditional socialist visions have increasingly responded with skeptical indifference translatable as "been there, done that." Many have formed the judgment that traditional socialisms, where achieved, exhibited too many shortcomings, were unsustainable, or both. Provoked by the capitalist crisis since 2008, rapidly rising public interest in alternatives to capitalism has confronted falling confidence in traditional socialism.

The frustration of the left, given this exhaustion of traditional socialisms' appeal, arose from having no other broadly agreed-on vision of an attractive alternative to capitalism. The left could not provide what mass audiences craved as they deepened their criticisms of capitalism's longer term decline and short-term crisis.

Enter the notion of worker cooperatives or, better, the awkward but more specific term: worker self-directed enterprises (WSDEs). This centuries-old idea has been revived, redesigned, and applied to go well beyond traditional socialism. The result is a new vision of an alternative to capitalism that could help mobilize a new left.

WSDEs replace hierarchical, top-down capitalist enterprises run by major shareholders and the boards of directors they select with a democratic enterprise directed by all its workers. The latter, collectively and democratically, make all the key decisions of what, how, and where to produce. Most important, they decide how to use the enterprise's net revenue.

Governments' dependence (at municipal, regional, and national levels) on enterprise tax payments thereby becomes dependence on the people as workers. No longer will a separate interest—capitalists within enterprises—use taxes or any other distributions of net revenues to shape government policies against workers or citizens. Enterprise decisions on what, how, and where to produce will likewise no longer be capitalists' decisions, but instead will reflect enterprise workers' democratic choices.

The importance of such micro-level transformations of enterprises into WSDEs cannot be overstated. Because it had located key economic powers in state hands (regulating or owning enterprises and imposing planning above or in place of market exchanges), traditional socialism usually accumulated too much power in the state alone or in the state together with the major capitalist businesses it "regulated." Far too little real, institutionalized countervailing power resided with the workers inside enterprises. As a result, accountability and transparency were absent from economic life, as was economic democracy. That in turn undermined real political democracy.

WSDEs could solve that problem. In economies where WSDEs prevail, key financial resources of the state—its taxes on and/or borrowings from enterprises—represent distributions of those enterprises' net revenues made by their workers. Likewise, the use of any enterprise's net revenues to fund political parties, politicians, lobbying efforts, and think tanks would reflect its workers' democratic decisions. A key structural feature of capitalism—capital's dictatorship inside enterprises—always generated the incentives and provided the resources for capitalists to bend government to the service of capital against labor. In contrast, a WSDE-based economy would abolish that dictatorship and thus its political effects.

By establishing democracy inside the enterprise, WSDEs make government responsible and accountable to the people as workers. Political democracy remains merely formal when governments' direct dependence on people as voting citizens is not matched by governments' direct dependence on people—in large part the same people—as workers. Real political democracy requires its integrated partnership with economic democracy as envisioned in economies where WSDEs prevail. Traditional socialisms' overemphasis on macro-level differences from capitalism (substituting state-regulated or state-owned for private property and state planning for market exchanges) would be radically corrected by the micro-level transformation of enterprise organization from capitalist to WSDE.

Democratized enterprises would need to share powers with democratic, residence-based political structures at all government levels (municipal, regional, and national). The political consequences of enterprise decisions, like the enterprise consequences of political decisions, would require that decision making at both social sites (enterprise and residential community) be co-respective and interdependent. Enterprise-based democracy would codetermine with residence-based democracy the full spectrum of social decisions, including any state apparatus's functions and policies.

Transforming capitalist enterprises into WSDEs in this context would radically change workplaces, residential communities, and hence the daily life of virtually everyone. It could realize the systemic change that traditional socialisms pointed toward but never achieved: a viable and attractive alternative preferable to capitalism. It offers leftists a means to overcome their frustrations and a focus around which to regroup existing as well as building new left movements and organizations.

Socialism and Worker Self-Directed Enterprises

September 14, 2014

Global capitalism has huge problems coping with the second worst collapse in its history. Its extreme and deepening inequalities have provoked millions to question and challenge capitalism. Yet socialists of all sorts now find it more difficult than ever to make effective criticisms and offer alternatives that inspire.

Part of the problem lies with classic socialism as it evolved over the last 150 years. Positions and strategies that once mobilized the victims and critics of capitalism are no longer, by themselves, effective. Not only has capitalism changed, but its celebrants also developed powerful critiques of socialist theory and especially of actually existing socialisms such as the Soviet Union. Socialism has not responded well to capitalism's changes nor to its critiques; it has not made the necessary strategic and tactical shifts. Nonetheless, socialism retains the means to overcome its problems with some long-overdue self-criticism and innovation.

By "classic socialism" I mean the tradition that differentiated itself from capitalism chiefly in terms of macroeconomic institutions. Classic socialists defined capitalism as (1) private ownership of means of production and (2) distribution of resources and products by means of market exchanges. The socialist alternative entailed (1) socialized or public ownership of means of production (operated by the state as agent of the people as a whole) and (2) distribution of resources and products via state planning. Socialists attacked capitalism for the injustices, cyclical instability, and gross productive inefficiencies (e.g., unemployment, stagnation) that they traced to private enterprises and markets. In the socialists' alternative, a workers' state would control or own enterprises and plan the distribution of resources and products—in the democratically determined interests of the majority.

Such criticisms of capitalism and that transitional program to an alternative system rewarded socialists in their political, economic, and cultural work. Socialist movements spread across the countries of the world during the nineteenth and to the last third of the twentieth century. Socialists effectively challenged capitalism; often took and held political power; and influenced many academics, intellectuals, popular organizations, artistic projects, and so on. But now socialism's growth in many places has stalled or reversed.

Socialism's growth in the nineteenth and twentieth centuries frightened capitalists and their allies everywhere. To stop the spreading socialism, capitalism's supporters eventually learned that violent repression was often a poor or counterproductive weapon. They adjusted and refined their strategies. Socialism's difficulties today emerge partly from its enemies' more developed counterattacks, especially in the half-century since 1945. Socialists now need likewise to redesign and refocus their project for the new conditions of struggle against capitalism.

Basically, criticism of private property and markets plus advocacy of socialized property and planning are insufficient as an analytical framework or a political strategy. They no longer mobilize the discontent capitalism generates. Especially after 1945, the examples of the Soviet Union, Eastern Europe, and the People's Republic of China (PRC) were successfully demonized as unattractive alternatives to capitalism. With powerful ideological conditioning that used newly developed mass communications, it mattered little that those examples had many worthwhile social achievements.

Then too, significant failures and disasters occurred in those first examples of trying concretely to build actual socialisms (hardly unusual in the history of previous systemic transitions). If socialists do not offer their explanations of those failures, then the only analyses circulating will be those fashioned by socialism's enemies. That will then be yet another obstacle in socialism's future. Like all social movements, socialism has been shaped by and is partially responsible for the history it helped make.

The focus of the Soviet Union, PRC, and other examples of socialisms (including the social democracies where states merely regulated private enterprises and markets) flowed logically from classic socialism's basic ideas. Those states moved more or less to socialize productive property and subordinate markets to state planning. These were macro-level changes; that is, they changed certain broad social frameworks of the economic system. They were much less interested in and attentive to micro-level institutions. The internal organization of enterprises and households thus changed relatively little in transitions from capitalism to socialism.

After socialists took power (through revolutions or elections) inside enterprises, a few people still functioned much as private capitalist boards of directors had before. Those few still made the key decisions about what the enterprise produced, how and where, and what was done with its profits. What changed was who these people were; socialism replaced private boards selected by private shareholders with boards of officials selected by the state. In the Soviet Union's highly centralized industrial sector, that board of directors was the set of state officials called the Council of Ministers.

Workers inside state enterprises in actually existing socialisms produced the surplus that was received and disposed of by others, as had been the case in capitalism. But those others were now state officials. Before, private capitalists had made "free" exchanges with one another and the public to distribute resources and products. In socialism, state planning mostly regulated and controlled markets. Workers took their wages to the stores and bought what they could afford from what state planners made available. State planners often set wages and prices. Sometimes state planners simply substituted their administrative allocations for markets.

Up to the 1970s, classic socialism, defined and concretized in these ways, made great headway. But already after World War II, the shocks to capitalism from the Soviet Union's survival and economic growth, the loss of Eastern Europe, and the Chinese revolution prompted shifts and adjustments by capitalism that undermined socialism's further growth. Two of these shifts were the growth spurts capitalism achieved after 1945.

World capitalism experienced a first resurgence rebuilding from World War II's devastations and as part of the new Cold War. A second resurgence happened after the 1970s when governments (led by US president Ronald Reagan and UK prime minister Margaret Thatcher) deregulated markets and changed policies to support income and wealth redistribution upward to the richest capitalists in general and to financial capitalists in particular. Those resurgences served to undermine socialist critiques and alternatives. Capitalism's defenders celebrated its resilience, fast growth, consumer focus, rising worker living standards, and relative political openness. They simultaneously demonized actually existing socialisms for inadequate consumer goods and insufficient individual freedoms.

The post-1975 period brought decline and difficulties to those socialisms and by 1989 brought dissolution in Eastern Europe and major changes toward capitalism elsewhere. Those circumstances emboldened claims that the great struggle between capitalism and socialism was over; capitalism had won. The growing problems and shifts inside actually existing socialisms seemed to point the same way. A broad decline in the fortunes of all sorts of socialist movements and organizations took hold.

By 2007, the capitalism that had gone far down the deregulation path since 1975 drove itself into another serious global collapse, socialism had reached a low point. Weakness and decline were by then decades old. "Moderate" socialists had sometimes even found rationales to support neoliberal policies and governments. "Left" socialists had often shifted from opposition to capitalism as a system to opposing neoliberal policies in favor of Keynesian social welfare programs. After 2007, as capitalism's crisis deepened, socialism and socialists seemed incapable of connecting organically with the growing masses eager for criticism and opposition.

Even socialists who then attacked "austerity policies" to win elections (revealing yet again their disinclination to oppose capitalism as a system) retreated merely to less harsh versions of austerity once in power. George Papandreou in Greece and François Hollande in France were notorious examples. Into the political vacuum opened by the socialists' declines stepped new "anticapitalist" groups. They chose that name (and other names such as indignados, occupiers, and anarchists) in part because of alienation from classic socialism.

Yet socialists still have the accumulated history, experience, and theoretical means to define a socialism for the twenty-first century that can rally, mobilize, and unify capitalism's diverse victims and critics.

First, socialists need to recognize and accept that the classic socialist focus on macro-level institutional change—from private to social ownership of productive assets and from markets to planning—is insufficient conceptually and strategically. It pays far too little attention to transformations at the micro level and especially inside enterprises. Second, socialists need to stand emphatically for the transformation of the enterprise—more precisely, for its radical democratization. They must reconceptualize the socialization of enterprises so that it means above all to change their internal organization.

Criticism would then focus on capitalist enterprise organization as a hierarchical, undemocratic system for producing the goods and services society depends upon. A tiny minority of persons (directors and major shareholders) makes all the key economic decisions in capitalist enterprises. The mass of workers who must live with those decisions and their effects are excluded from making them. Capitalist enterprise organization is thus the opposite and enemy of the democratic enterprise organization that socialism affirms.

In socialism redefined along these lines, all the workers in an enterprise collectively and democratically make all the key economic decisions: what, how, and where to produce and what to do with the enterprise's surplus or profits. Such a socialism would advocate social ownership, planning, and the democratization of enterprises, that is, their transition from capitalist to worker self-directed enterprises (WSDEs).

Socialism would no longer ignore, minimize, or denigrate transition to WSDEs as classic socialism did. In many parts of the world, workers' efforts across the centuries to establish what were variously called producers' or workers' cooperatives or communes should be critically appropriated. Then they must be integrated into a new formulation of socialism for the twenty-first century.

Such a redefined and refocused socialism opens a path beyond capitalism different from what happened in the Soviet Union and PRC. In WSDEs, where workers collectively determine the production and distribution of surpluses, they wield real economic power. They—not government operatives—control the economic base. As their own collective boards of directors, the workers would be the ultimate sources (producers and distributors) of surpluses flowing to fund the state. Power would then finally have shifted away from capitalists and from the state.

Such a socialism would henceforth advocate and support workers either transforming capitalist enterprises into WSDEs or starting new WSDEs. A growing sector of WSDEs would function within and interact with a still largely capitalist economy (much as a capitalist sector arose within and complexly interacted with a still largely feudal economy a few centuries earlier). Socialist politics would become the multidimensional project of criticizing capitalism while building the conditions for the expansion of the socialist sector. All manner of conflicts and compromises, contradictions and alliances would characterize the relation of socialism and capitalism, much as parallel moments comprised the earlier relation of capitalism and feudalism.

In such a transition to socialism, workers would transform themselves—from undereducated, underinformed, and often deskilled drones, controlled and directed by others, into members of self-directed cooperatives. Their tasks are equitably shared, everyone develops multiple skills, and rotation of function keeps jobs from hardening into status ranks. Everyone partakes in turn in giving and taking orders to get jobs done. In such democratizations of workplaces and work processes, new kinds of people will emerge.

For WSDEs, increasing enterprise surpluses or profits becomes merely one of many objectives. Local health conditions, workers' family relationships, friendships, community solidarities, and the enterprise's relation to the natural environment are also objectives. Unlike capitalist enterprises' drive to maximize one objective, profit, the bottom line, at the expense of such other objectives, WSDEs would proceed differently. Their decisions would be driven by democratic compromises weighing all the ways that enterprise activities interact with people.

A socialism that includes and emphasizes WSDEs entails workers transforming their lives. Such a socialism finally places the basic economic power (producing and distributing the surplus) in the workers' hands. It is a formidable barrier to the undemocratic minority power that has haunted capitalisms and socialisms over the last 150 years. It is necessary if merely formal political democracy is ever to mature beyond corrupt and ritualized elections into a reality.

Index

About the Author

Richard D. Wolff is professor of economics emeritus at the University of Massachusetts, Amherst, and a visiting professor at the New School University in New York. Wolff's recent work has concentrated on analyzing the causes and alternative solutions to the global economic crisis. His groundbreaking book *Democracy at Work: A Cure for Capitalism* inspired the creation of the nonprofit organization Democracy at Work (www.democracyatwork.info). Wolff is also the author of *Occupy the Economy: Challenging Capitalism* and *Capitalism Hits the Fan: The Global Economic Meltdown and What to Do About It*. He hosts the weekly hour-long radio program *Economic Update*, which is syndicated on public radio stations nationwide, and he writes regularly for the *Guardian* and *Truthout*. Wolff appears frequently on television and radio to discuss his work, with recent guest spots on *Real Time with Bill Maher*, *Moyers & Company*, *Charlie Rose*, *Up with Chris Hayes*, and *Democracy Now!* He is also a frequent lecturer at colleges and universities across the country.

About the Editors

Michael Palmieri earned a B.A. in political science from Bloomfield College and is currently a masters candidate at the New School Graduate Program in International Affairs, working toward a degree in cities and social justice. His monthly op-eds and other writings can be accessed at NorthJersey.com.

Dante Dallavalle is a researcher assistant at the Center for Heritage and Archeological Studies at Montclair State University. He is pursuing a B.A. in cultural anthropology at the same institution.

Democracy at Work (d@w) is a nonprofit (501C3) organization that conceives, creates, and distributes media aimed at demonstrating why, and how, democratizing the workplace is a viable solution for a new and better economic system. We advocate for workers' self-directed enterprises (WSDEs) and strive to show how WSDEs could solve many of today's major economic problems.

d@w advocates and promotes a social transition from capitalist to cooperative enterprises. We view that transition as a necessary remedy for a capitalist system increasingly generating unacceptable economic and social outcomes. We present our vision for a better economy through a variety of media focused on three themes:

analysis and criticism of the growing US economic crisis

analysis of long-term trends in US capitalism

advocacy of WSDEs as an alternative and ultimately corrective solution

Based on the work of Professor Richard D. Wolff, d@w strives to advocate for alternative solutions to the current model of capitalism. Beyond Professor Wolff's many published books and articles, our current activities include:

Economic Update—an hour-long, weekly radio program hosted by Professor Wolff. This show is currently broadcast on thirty-five stations nationwide, is also made available by *Truthout*, and reaches an estimated 750,000 homes.

Two websites (rdwolff.com and democracyatwork.info) that are updated daily along with the d@w Facebook page and Twitter feed. The websites are devoted to gathering and organizing the written, audio, and video materials that are essential to the WSDE project. Web traffic at these sites has reached over 50,000 visitors per month.

"Global Capitalism: A Monthly Economic Update" is currently held at the historic Judson Memorial Church in Washington Square, New York City. Cosponsored by the Left Forum, this monthly public appearance by Prof. Wolff is filmed and distributed globally.

A schedule of public speaking events and media appearances for Professor Wolff organized across North America and Europe throughout the year.

For more information on these and other exciting projects d@w is developing, visit us at www.democracyatwork.info. Together, we can create a true democracy at work.

About Haymarket Books

Haymarket Books is a nonprofit, progressive book distributor and publisher, a project of the Center for Economic Research and Social Change. We believe that activists need to take ideas, history, and politics into the many struggles for social justice today. Learning the lessons of past victories, as well as defeats, can arm a new generation of fighters for a better world. As Karl Marx said, "The philosophers have merely interpreted the world; the point, however, is to change it."

We take inspiration and courage from our namesakes, the Haymarket Martyrs, who gave their lives fighting for a better world. Their 1886 struggle for the eight-hour day, which gave us May Day, the international workers' holiday, reminds workers around the world that ordinary people can organize and struggle for their own liberation. These struggles continue today across the globe—struggles against oppression, exploitation, hunger, and poverty.

It was August Spies, one of the Martyrs targeted for being an immigrant and an anarchist, who predicted the battles being fought to this day. "If you think that by hanging us you can stamp out the labor movement," Spies told the judge, "then hang us. Here you will tread upon a spark, but here, and there, and behind you, and in front of you, and everywhere, the flames will blaze up. It is a subterranean fire. You cannot put it out. The ground is on fire upon which you stand."

We could not succeed in our publishing efforts without the generous financial support of our readers. Many people contribute to our project through the Haymarket Sustainers program, where donors receive free books in return for their monetary support. If you would like to be a part of this program, please contact us at info@haymarketbooks.org.

Shop our full catalog online at www.haymarketbooks.org or call 773-583-7884.

Also Available from Haymarket Books

BRICS: An Anticapitalist Critique
Edited by Ana Garcia and Patrick Bond

Democracy at Work: A Cure for Capitalism
Richard Wolff

Exploring Marx's *Capital*: Philosophical, Economic and Political Dimensions
Jacques Bidet

Financialization in Crisis
Edited by Costas Lapavitsas

Marx's *Capital* Illustrated
David N. Smith

Returns of Marxism: Marxist Theory in a Time of Crisis
Edited by Sara R. Farris

The Capitalist Cycle
Pavel Maksakovsky

The Long Depression: How It Happened, Why It Happened, and What Happens Next
Michael Roberts

Your Money or Your Life: The Tyranny of Global Finance
Eric Toussaint

Zombie Capitalism: Global Crisis and the Relevance of Marx
Chris Harman